ETERNITY

KINGSTONE
COMICS

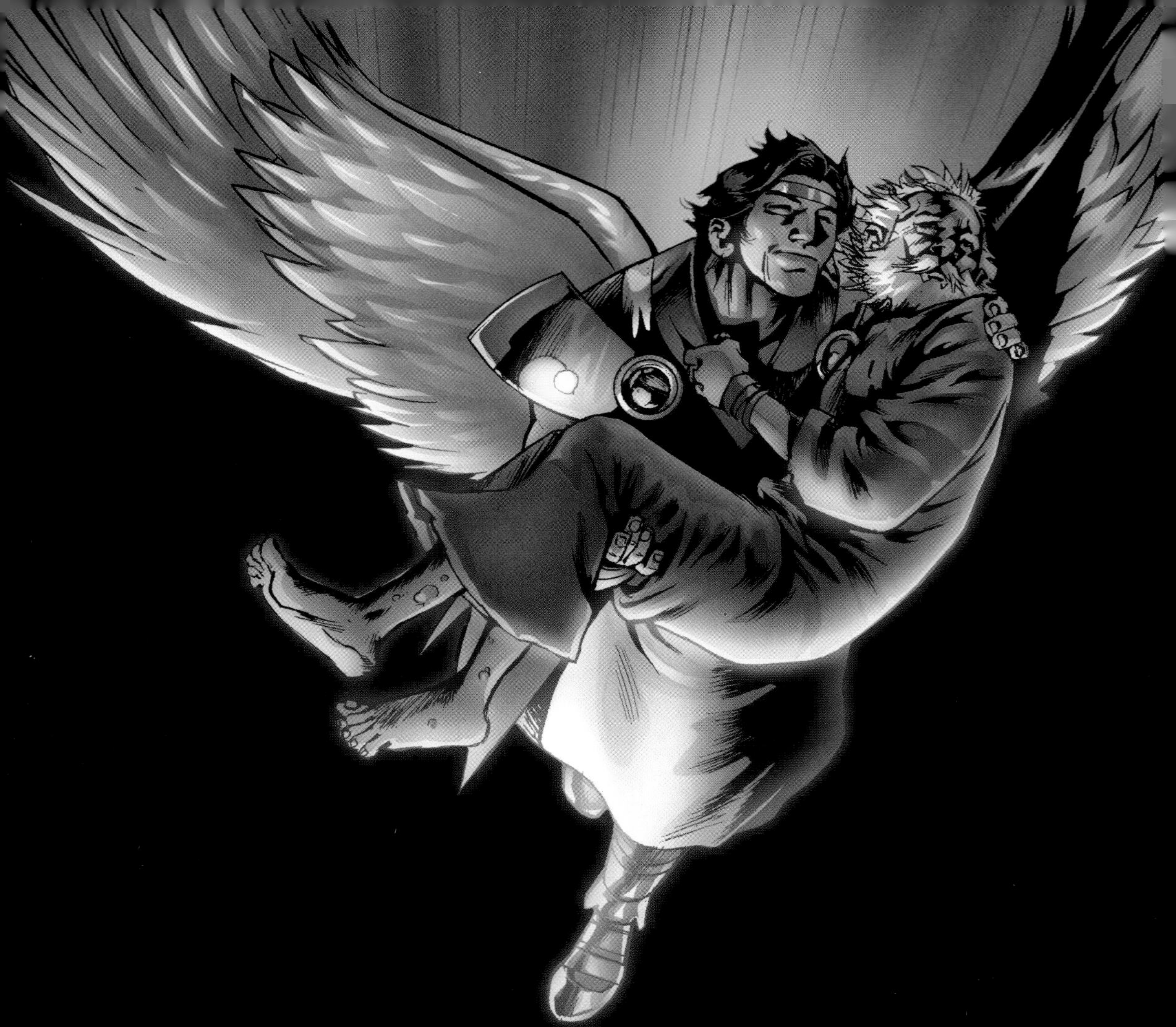

ETERNITY

WRITER: Randy Alcorn

EDITOR: Ben Avery

EDITORIAL: Kelly Ayris

HEBREW EDITOR: James A. Swanson

ARTIST: Javier Saltares

COLORIST: Ben Prenevost

LETTERS: Zach Matheny

PRODUCTION: Ken Raney

Published by Kingstone Comics
www.KingstoneMedia.com

Printed in Canada

KINGSTONE COMICS

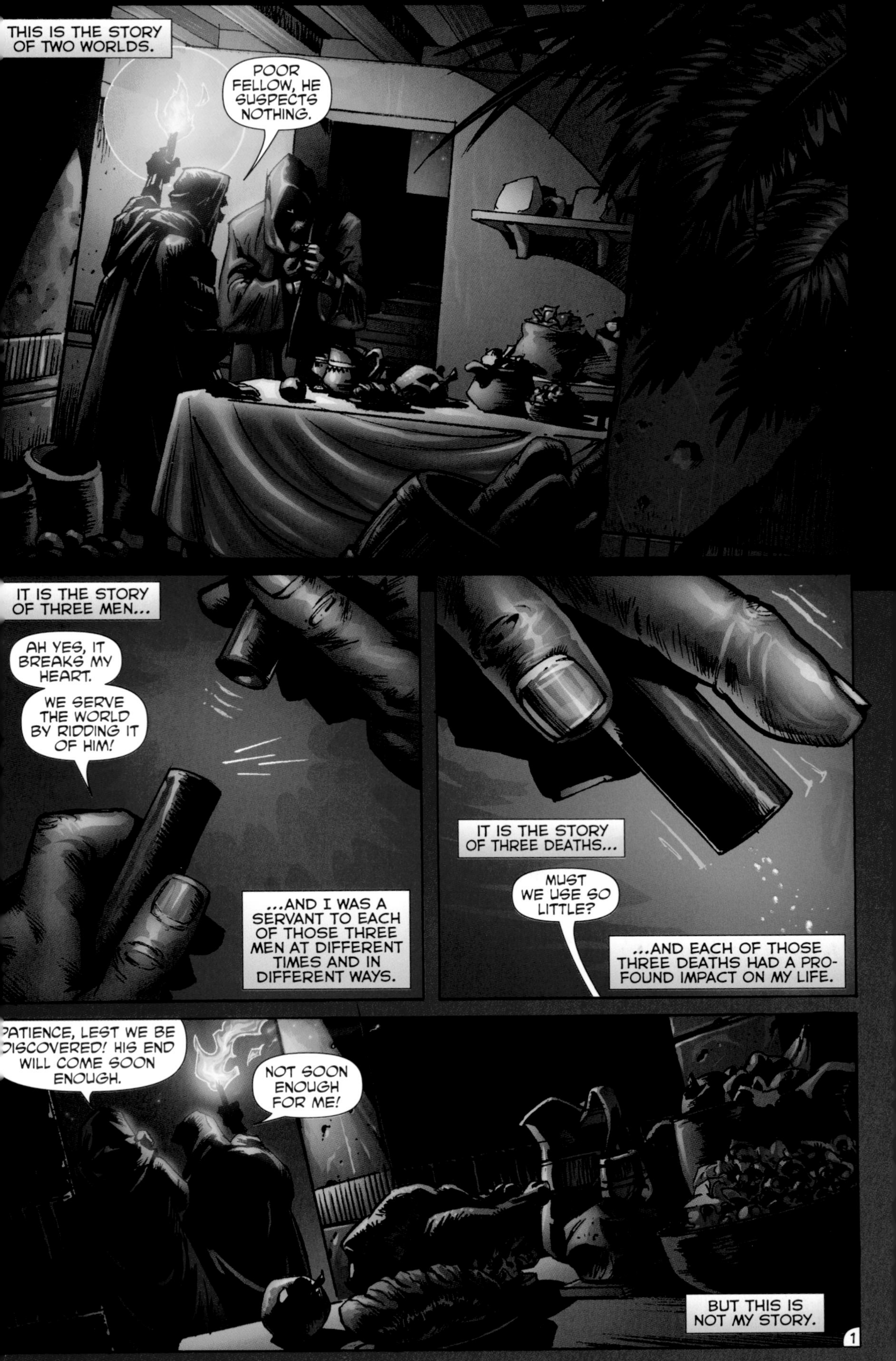
THIS IS THE STORY OF TWO WORLDS.
POOR FELLOW, HE SUSPECTS NOTHING.
IT IS THE STORY OF THREE MEN...
AH YES, IT BREAKS MY HEART.
WE SERVE THE WORLD BY RIDDING IT OF HIM!
...AND I WAS A SERVANT TO EACH OF THOSE THREE MEN AT DIFFERENT TIMES AND IN DIFFERENT WAYS.
IT IS THE STORY OF THREE DEATHS...
MUST WE USE SO LITTLE?
...AND EACH OF THOSE THREE DEATHS HAD A PROFOUND IMPACT ON MY LIFE.
PATIENCE, LEST WE BE DISCOVERED! HIS END WILL COME SOON ENOUGH.
NOT SOON ENOUGH FOR ME!
BUT THIS IS NOT MY STORY.
1

THIS STORY BEGINS IN JERUSALEM...

...ALTHOUGH IT STILL HAS NOT ENDED, AND REACHES FAR BEYOND THE BORDERS OF THAT CITY.

I AM THE STORYTELLER, TOBIAS THE SON OF MATTHIAS.

THOSE I PIECED TOGETHER FROM THE TEACHINGS OF ONE OF THE THREE MEN. YOU MAY KNOW OF HIM.

SOME SAY HE CAME TO EARTH FROM ANOTHER WORLD.

I SPEAK OF JESUS OF NAZARETH, WHOM THEY CALL THE GOD-MAN.

OF THE TWO OTHER MEN, ONE WAS A BEGGAR NAMED LAZARUS.

YOU MAY HAVE HEARD OF LAZARUS OF BETHANY, WHOM JESUS RAISED FROM THE DEAD.

BUT LAZARUS WAS A COMMON NAME. THIS LAZARUS WAS DESTITUTE. HIS HOME WAS THE STREET.

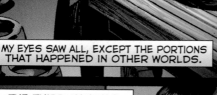

MY EYES SAW ALL, EXCEPT THE PORTIONS THAT HAPPENED IN OTHER WORLDS.

THE THIRD MAN WAS PHINEAS, MY MASTER. ALSO KNOWN AS DIVES, LATIN FOR "RICH MAN", A NICKNAME GIVEN TO HIM BY THE POOR WHO LIVED NEARBY.

A RICH MAN WHO HABITUALLY DRESSED IN FINE LINEN, LIVING IN SPLENDOR EVERY DAY.

IF YOU HAVE EARS TO HEAR, LISTEN NOW TO MY STORY.

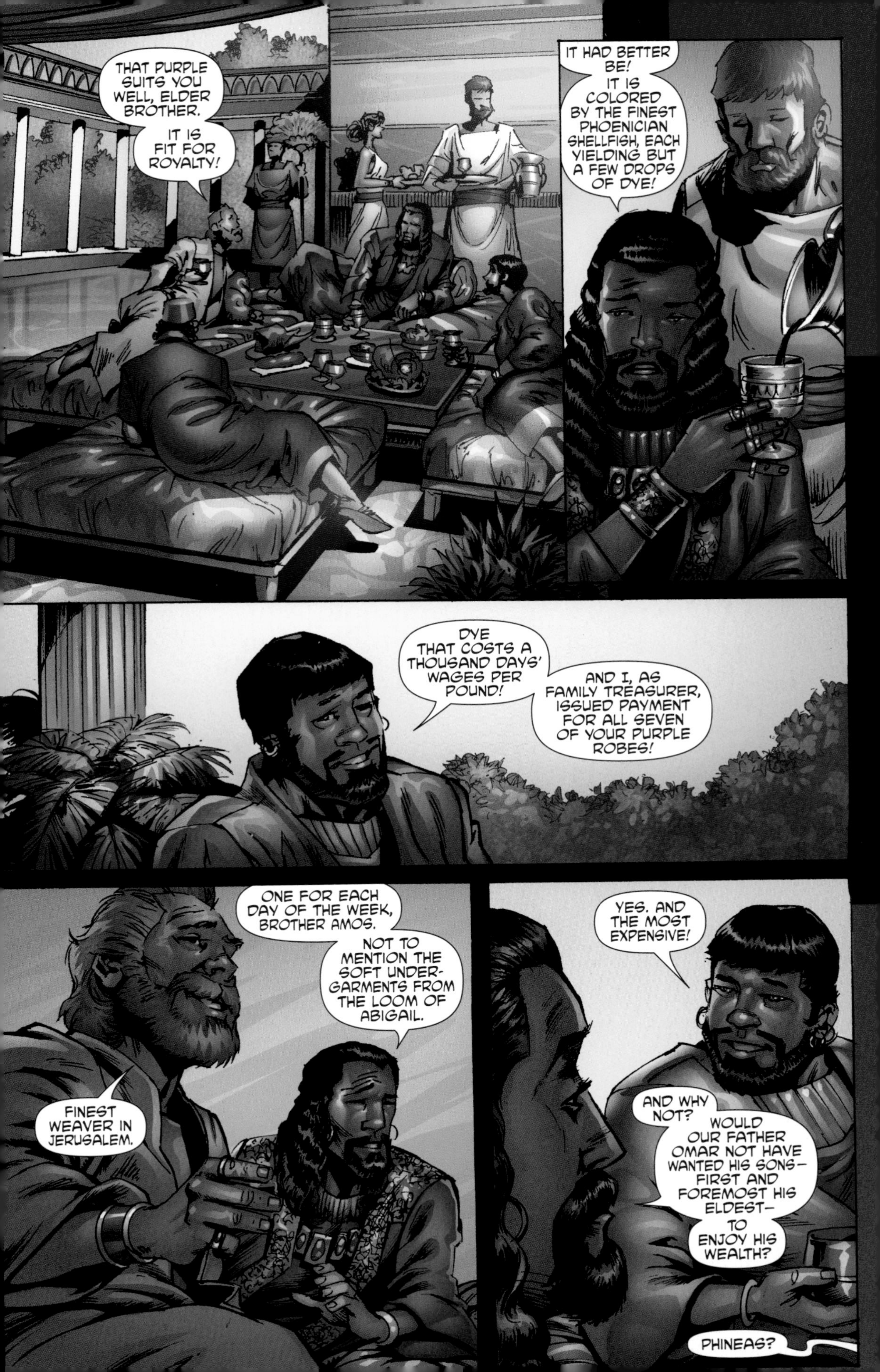
THAT PURPLE SUITS YOU WELL, ELDER BROTHER.
IT IS FIT FOR ROYALTY!
IT HAD BETTER BE!
IT IS COLORED BY THE FINEST PHOENICIAN SHELLFISH, EACH YIELDING BUT A FEW DROPS OF DYE!
DYE THAT COSTS A THOUSAND DAYS' WAGES PER POUND!
AND I, AS FAMILY TREASURER, ISSUED PAYMENT FOR ALL SEVEN OF YOUR PURPLE ROBES!
ONE FOR EACH DAY OF THE WEEK, BROTHER AMOS.
NOT TO MENTION THE SOFT UNDER-GARMENTS FROM THE LOOM OF ABIGAIL.
FINEST WEAVER IN JERUSALEM.
YES. AND THE MOST EXPENSIVE!
AND WHY NOT?
WOULD OUR FATHER OMAR NOT HAVE WANTED HIS SONS— FIRST AND FOREMOST HIS ELDEST— TO ENJOY HIS WEALTH?
PHINEAS?

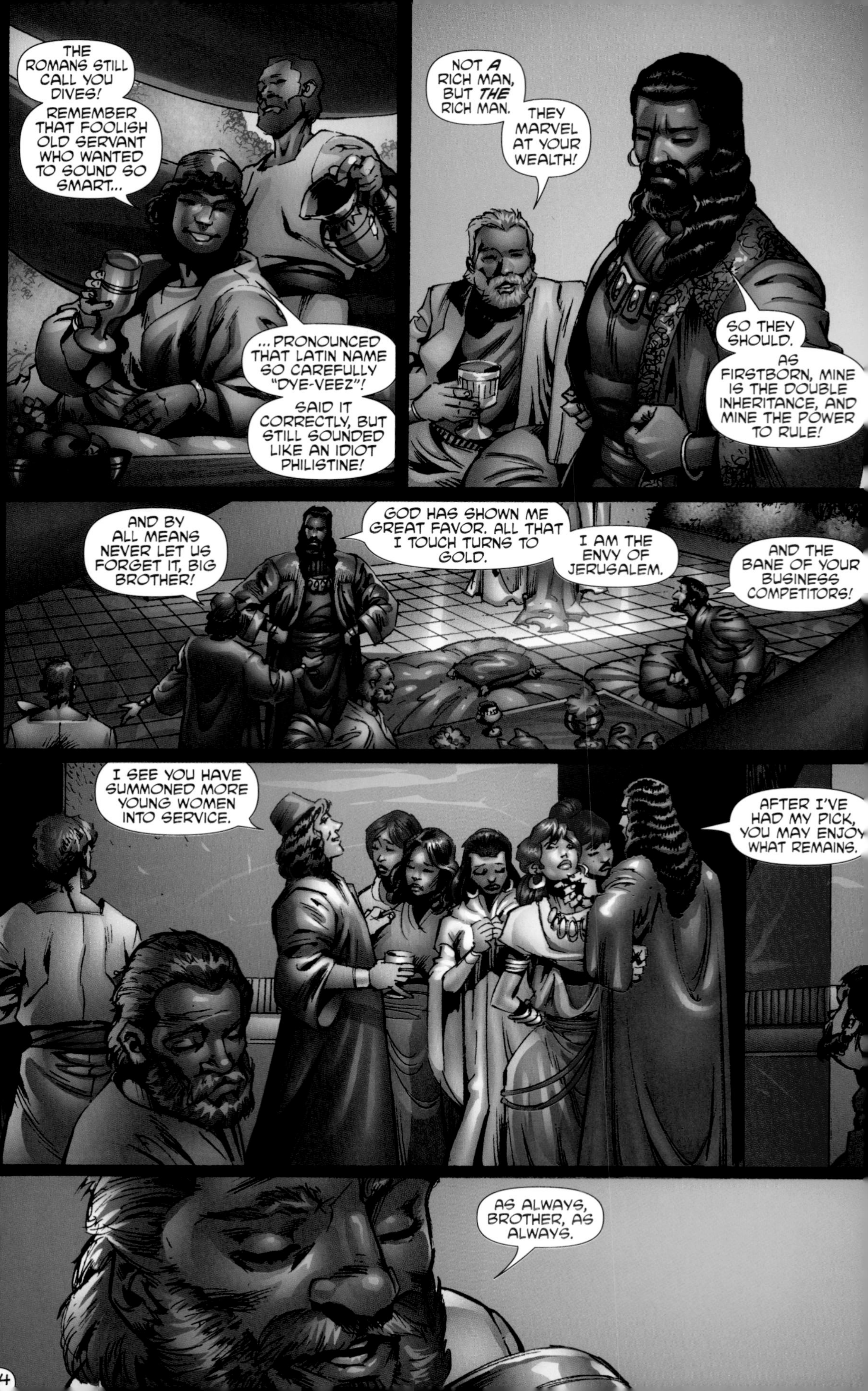
THE ROMANS STILL CALL YOU DIVES!
REMEMBER THAT FOOLISH OLD SERVANT WHO WANTED TO SOUND SO SMART...
...PRONOUNCED THAT LATIN NAME SO CAREFULLY "DYE-VEEZ"!
SAID IT CORRECTLY, BUT STILL SOUNDED LIKE AN IDIOT PHILISTINE!
NOT *A* RICH MAN, BUT *THE* RICH MAN.
THEY MARVEL AT YOUR WEALTH!
SO THEY SHOULD.
AS FIRSTBORN, MINE IS THE DOUBLE INHERITANCE, AND MINE THE POWER TO RULE!
AND BY ALL MEANS NEVER LET US FORGET IT, BIG BROTHER!
GOD HAS SHOWN ME GREAT FAVOR. ALL THAT I TOUCH TURNS TO GOLD.
I AM THE ENVY OF JERUSALEM.
AND THE BANE OF YOUR BUSINESS COMPETITORS!
I SEE YOU HAVE SUMMONED MORE YOUNG WOMEN INTO SERVICE.
AFTER I'VE HAD MY PICK, YOU MAY ENJOY WHAT REMAINS.
AS ALWAYS, BROTHER, AS ALWAYS.

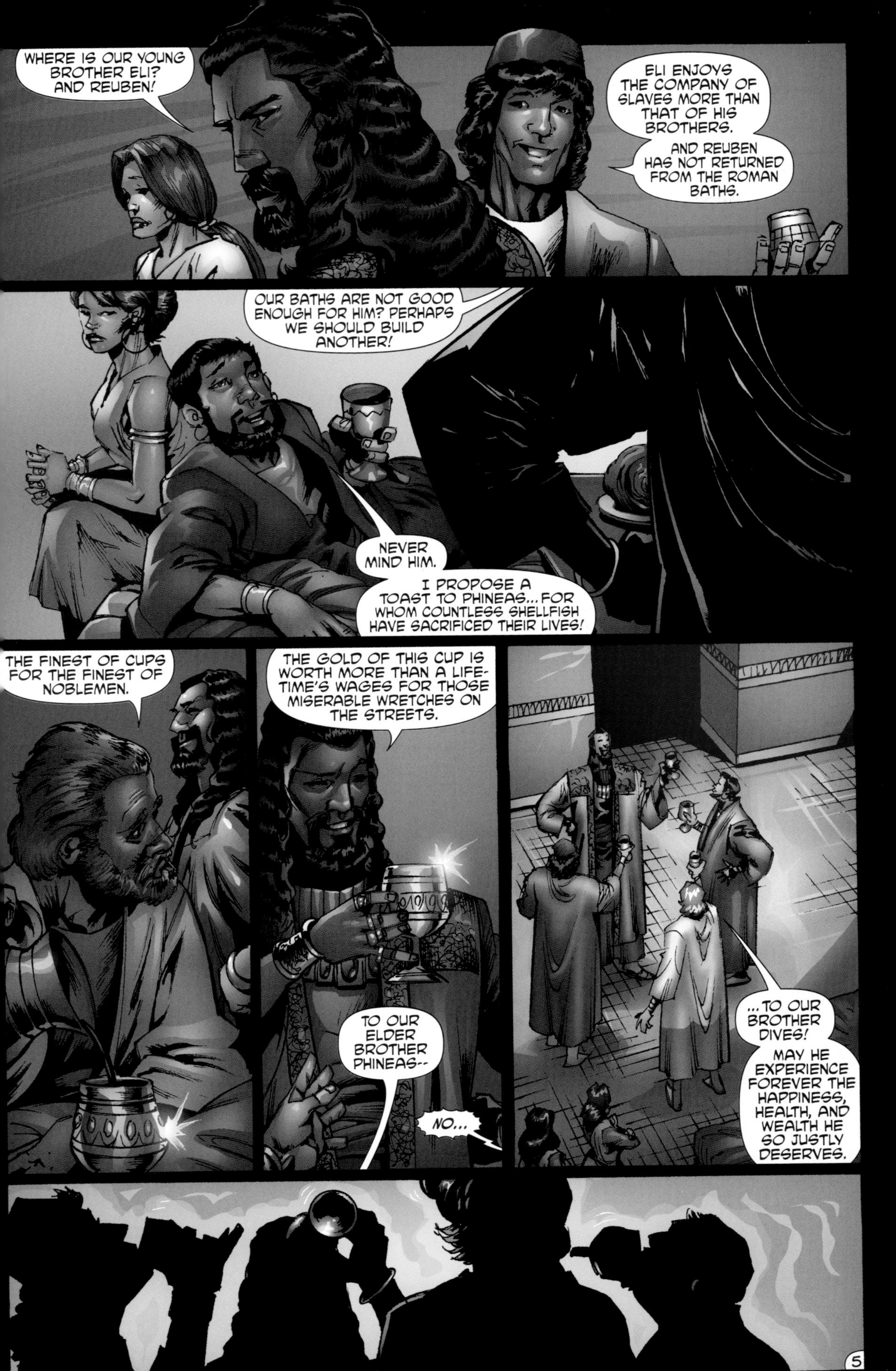
WHERE IS OUR YOUNG BROTHER ELI? AND REUBEN!
ELI ENJOYS THE COMPANY OF SLAVES MORE THAN THAT OF HIS BROTHERS.
AND REUBEN HAS NOT RETURNED FROM THE ROMAN BATHS.
OUR BATHS ARE NOT GOOD ENOUGH FOR HIM? PERHAPS WE SHOULD BUILD ANOTHER!
NEVER MIND HIM.
I PROPOSE A TOAST TO PHINEAS... FOR WHOM COUNTLESS SHELLFISH HAVE SACRIFICED THEIR LIVES!
THE FINEST OF CUPS FOR THE FINEST OF NOBLEMEN.
THE GOLD OF THIS CUP IS WORTH MORE THAN A LIFETIME'S WAGES FOR THOSE MISERABLE WRETCHES ON THE STREETS.
TO OUR ELDER BROTHER PHINEAS--
NO...
...TO OUR BROTHER DIVES!
MAY HE EXPERIENCE FOREVER THE HAPPINESS, HEALTH, AND WEALTH HE SO JUSTLY DESERVES.

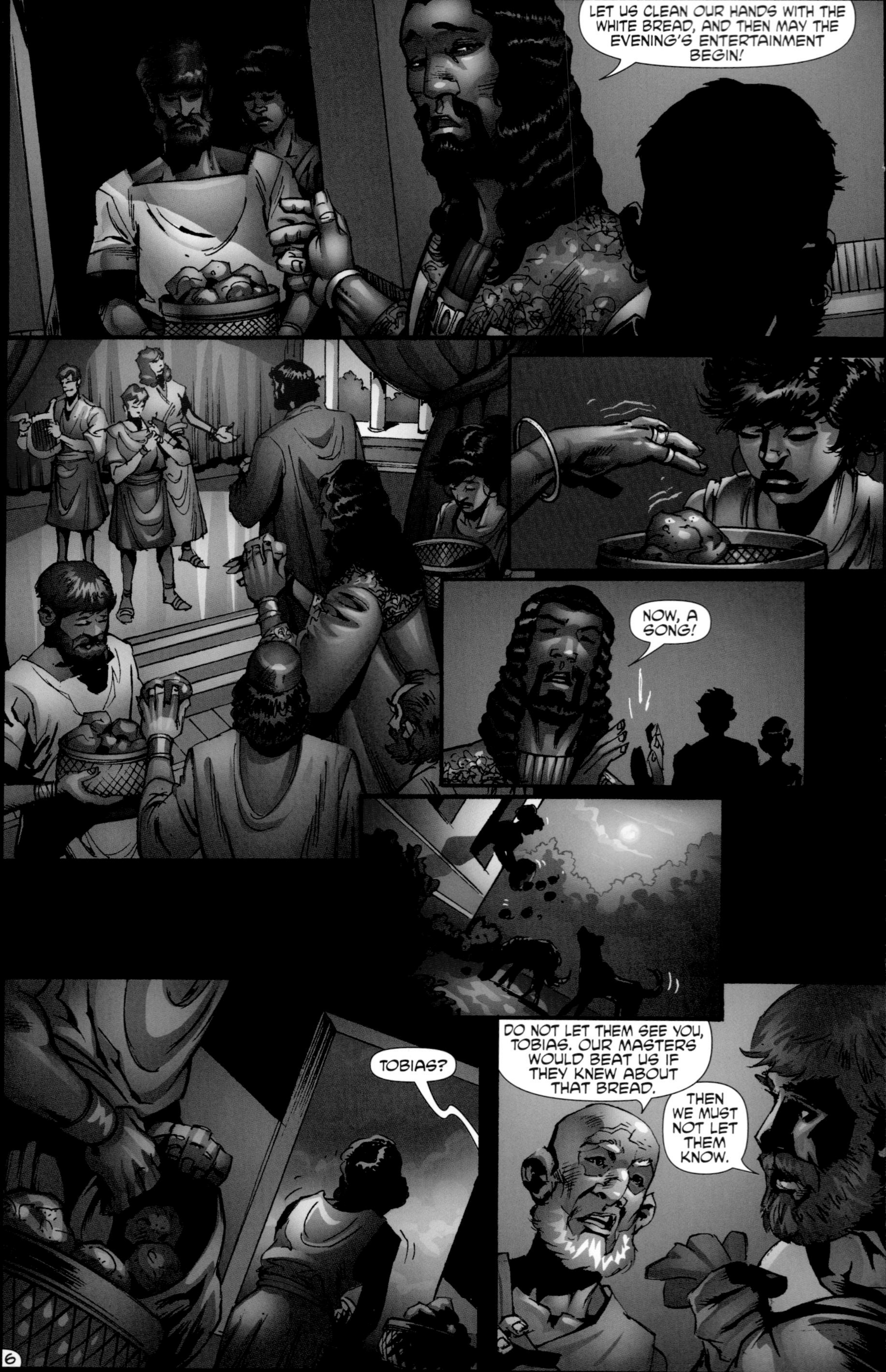
LET US CLEAN OUR HANDS WITH THE WHITE BREAD, AND THEN MAY THE EVENING'S ENTERTAINMENT BEGIN!
NOW, A SONG!
TOBIAS?
DO NOT LET THEM SEE YOU, TOBIAS. OUR MASTERS WOULD BEAT US IF THEY KNEW ABOUT THAT BREAD.
THEN WE MUST NOT LET THEM KNOW.

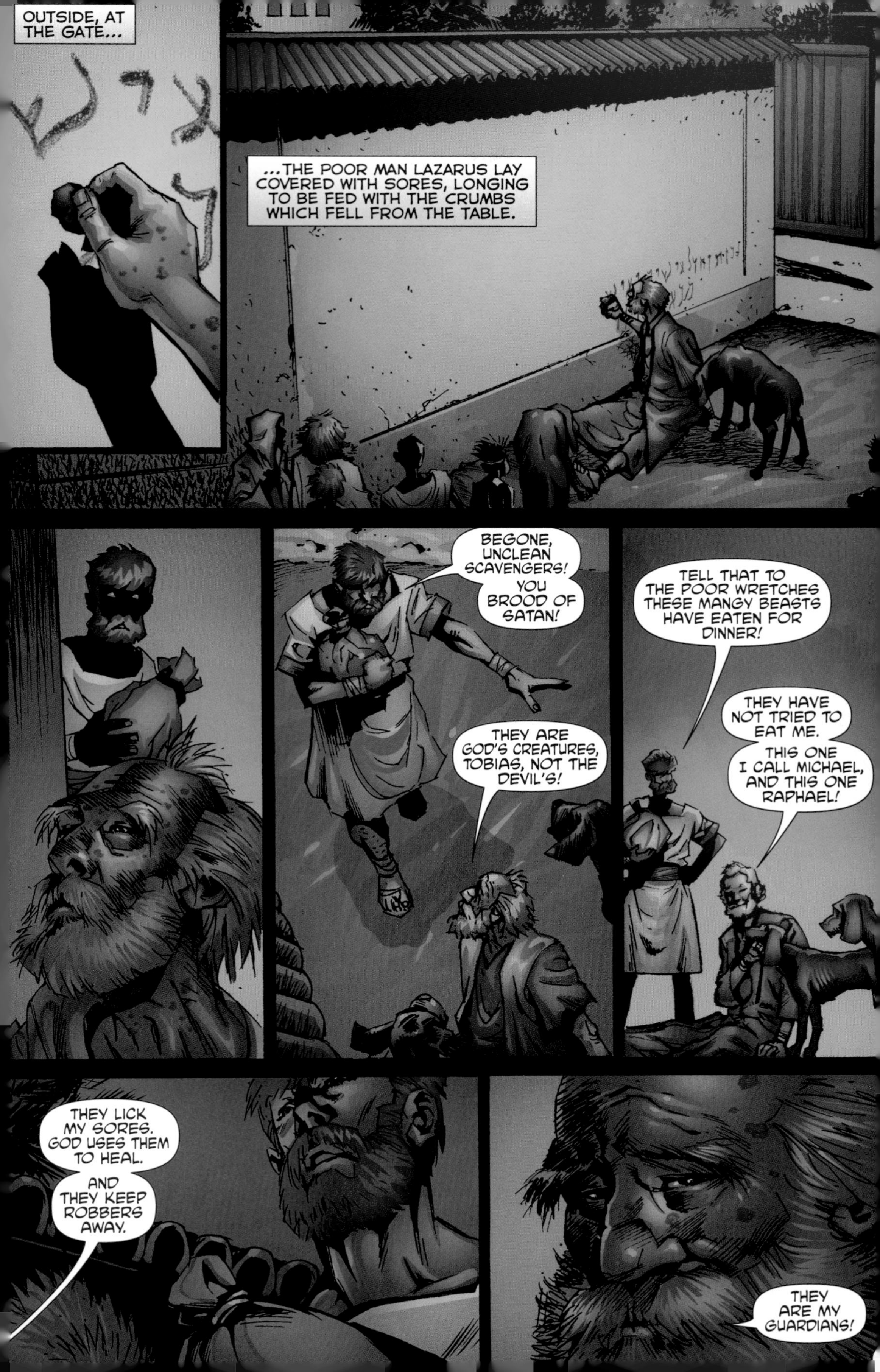
OUTSIDE, AT THE GATE...
...THE POOR MAN LAZARUS LAY COVERED WITH SORES, LONGING TO BE FED WITH THE CRUMBS WHICH FELL FROM THE TABLE.
BEGONE, UNCLEAN SCAVENGERS!
YOU BROOD OF SATAN!
THEY ARE GOD'S CREATURES, TOBIAS, NOT THE DEVIL'S!
TELL THAT TO THE POOR WRETCHES THESE MANGY BEASTS HAVE EATEN FOR DINNER!
THEY HAVE NOT TRIED TO EAT ME.
THIS ONE I CALL MICHAEL, AND THIS ONE RAPHAEL!
THEY LICK MY SORES. GOD USES THEM TO HEAL.
AND THEY KEEP ROBBERS AWAY.
THEY ARE MY GUARDIANS!

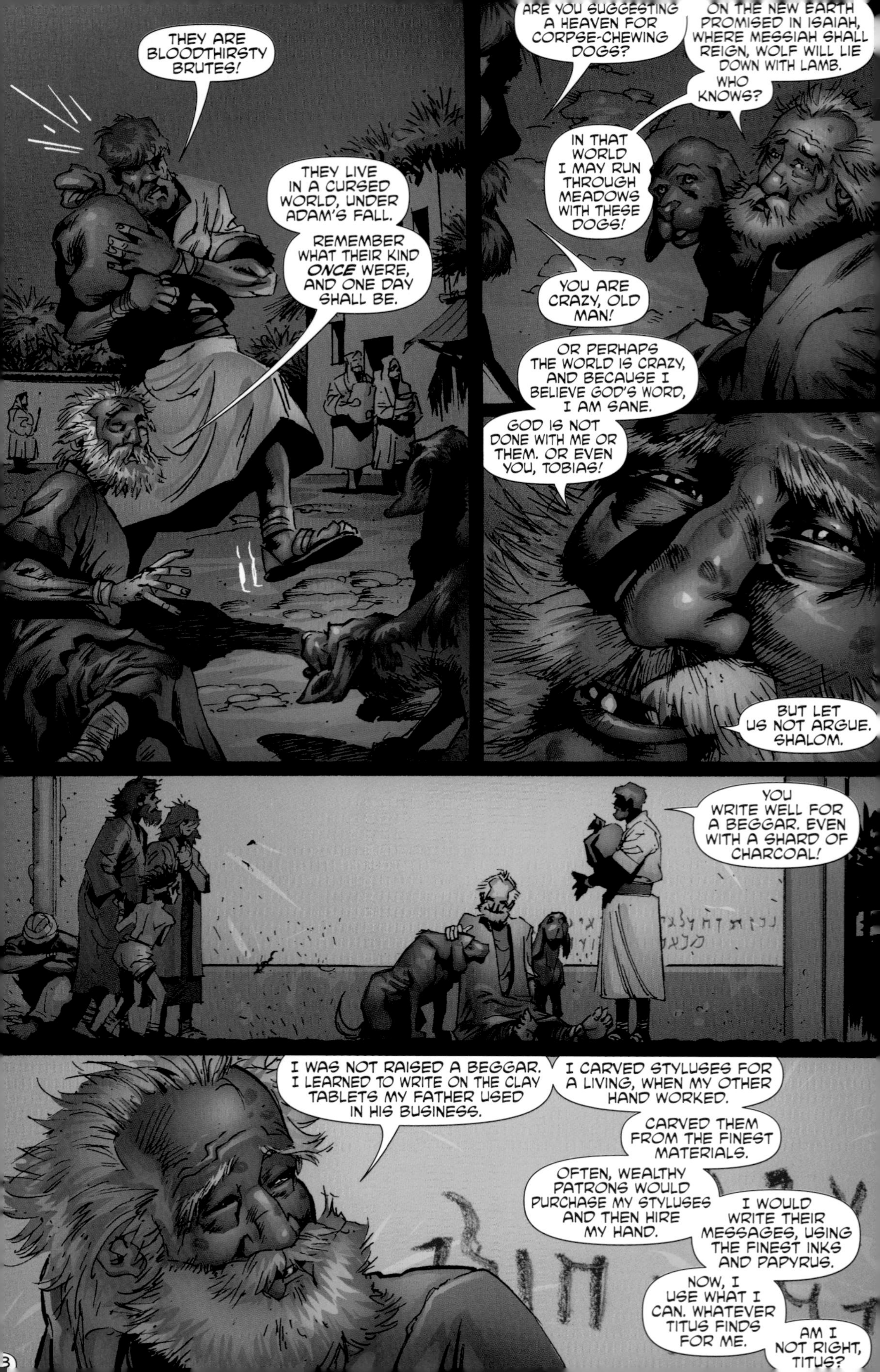
THEY ARE BLOODTHIRSTY BRUTES!
THEY LIVE IN A CURSED WORLD, UNDER ADAM'S FALL.
REMEMBER WHAT THEIR KIND *ONCE* WERE, AND ONE DAY SHALL BE.
ARE YOU SUGGESTING A HEAVEN FOR CORPSE-CHEWING DOGS?
ON THE NEW EARTH PROMISED IN ISAIAH, WHERE MESSIAH SHALL REIGN, WOLF WILL LIE DOWN WITH LAMB.
WHO KNOWS?
IN THAT WORLD I MAY RUN THROUGH MEADOWS WITH THESE DOGS!
YOU ARE CRAZY, OLD MAN!
OR PERHAPS THE WORLD IS CRAZY, AND BECAUSE I BELIEVE GOD'S WORD, I AM SANE.
GOD IS NOT DONE WITH ME OR THEM. OR EVEN YOU, TOBIAS!
BUT LET US NOT ARGUE. SHALOM.
YOU WRITE WELL FOR A BEGGAR. EVEN WITH A SHARD OF CHARCOAL!
I WAS NOT RAISED A BEGGAR. I LEARNED TO WRITE ON THE CLAY TABLETS MY FATHER USED IN HIS BUSINESS.
I CARVED STYLUSES FOR A LIVING, WHEN MY OTHER HAND WORKED.
CARVED THEM FROM THE FINEST MATERIALS.
OFTEN, WEALTHY PATRONS WOULD PURCHASE MY STYLUSES AND THEN HIRE MY HAND.
I WOULD WRITE THEIR MESSAGES, USING THE FINEST INKS AND PAPYRUS.
NOW, I USE WHAT I CAN. WHATEVER TITUS FINDS FOR ME.
AM I NOT RIGHT, TITUS?

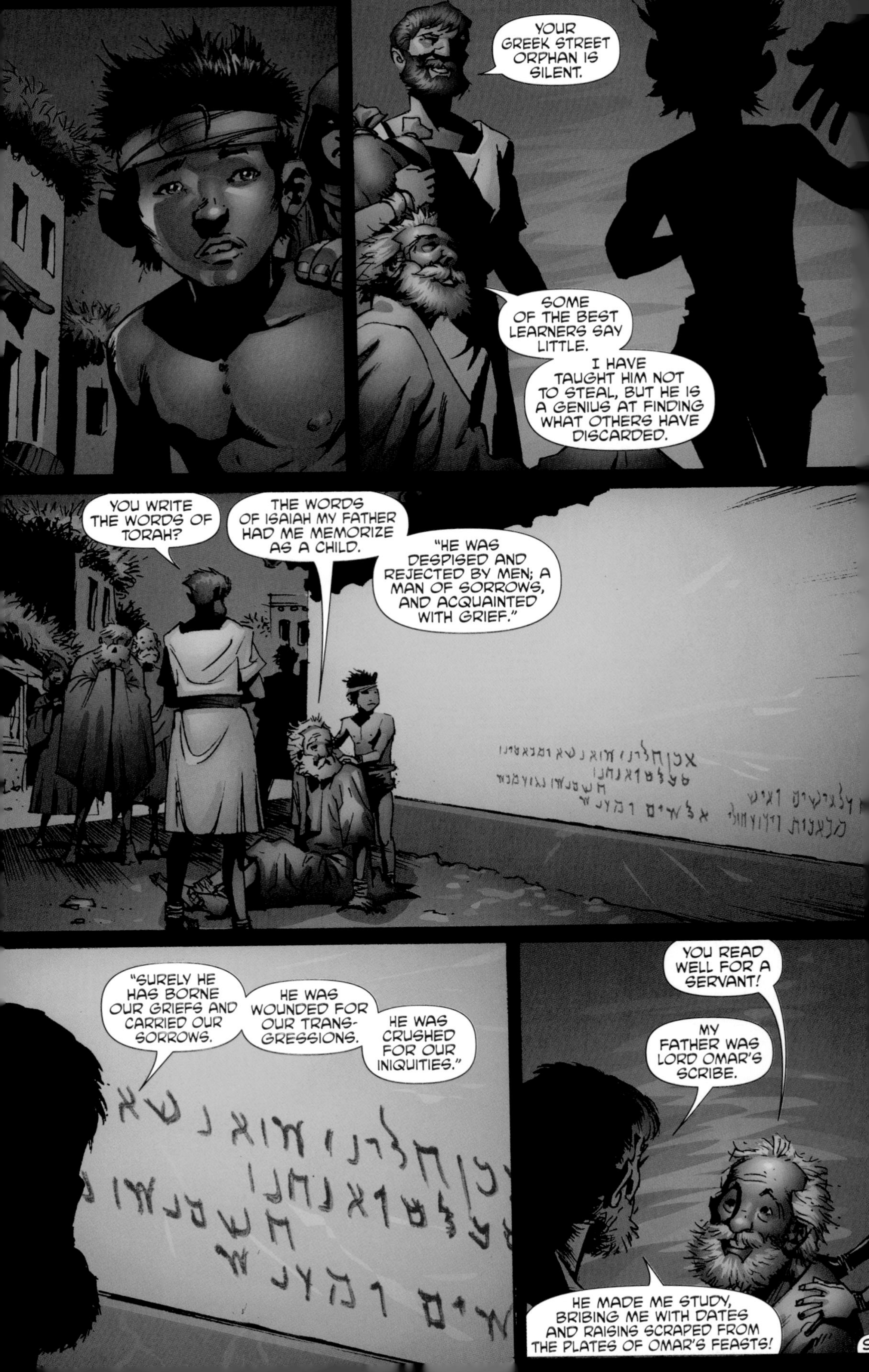
YOUR GREEK STREET ORPHAN IS SILENT.
SOME OF THE BEST LEARNERS SAY LITTLE.
I HAVE TAUGHT HIM NOT TO STEAL, BUT HE IS A GENIUS AT FINDING WHAT OTHERS HAVE DISCARDED.
YOU WRITE THE WORDS OF TORAH?
THE WORDS OF ISAIAH MY FATHER HAD ME MEMORIZE AS A CHILD.
"HE WAS DESPISED AND REJECTED BY MEN; A MAN OF SORROWS, AND ACQUAINTED WITH GRIEF."
"SURELY HE HAS BORNE OUR GRIEFS AND CARRIED OUR SORROWS.
HE WAS WOUNDED FOR OUR TRANS-GRESSIONS.
HE WAS CRUSHED FOR OUR INIQUITIES."
YOU READ WELL FOR A SERVANT!
MY FATHER WAS LORD OMAR'S SCRIBE.
HE MADE ME STUDY, BRIBING ME WITH DATES AND RAISINS SCRAPED FROM THE PLATES OF OMAR'S FEASTS!

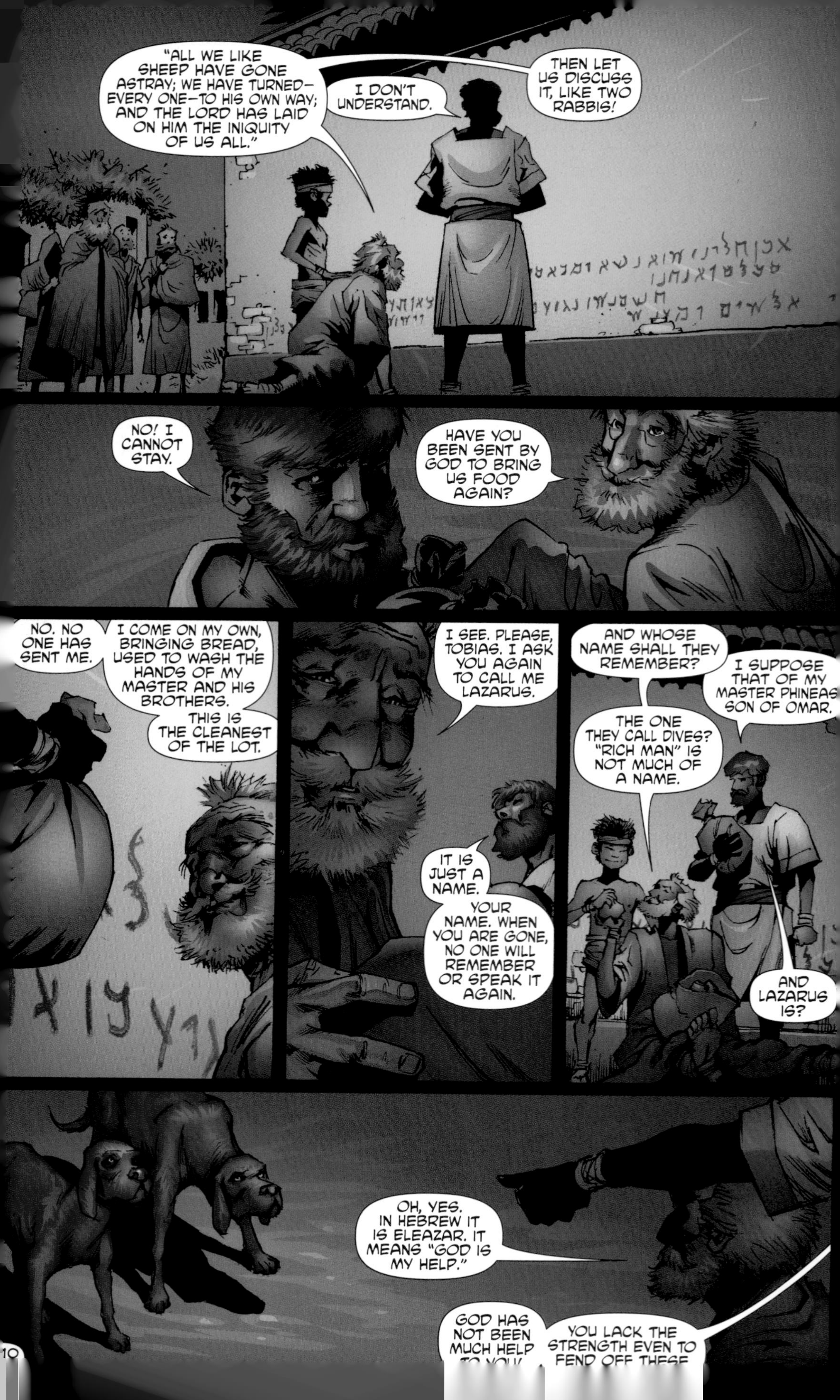

"ALL WE LIKE SHEEP HAVE GONE ASTRAY; WE HAVE TURNED— EVERY ONE—TO HIS OWN WAY; AND THE LORD HAS LAID ON HIM THE INIQUITY OF US ALL."
I DON'T UNDERSTAND.
THEN LET US DISCUSS IT, LIKE TWO RABBIS!
NO! I CANNOT STAY.
HAVE YOU BEEN SENT BY GOD TO BRING US FOOD AGAIN?
NO. NO ONE HAS SENT ME.
I COME ON MY OWN, BRINGING BREAD, USED TO WASH THE HANDS OF MY MASTER AND HIS BROTHERS.
THIS IS THE CLEANEST OF THE LOT.
I SEE. PLEASE, TOBIAS. I ASK YOU AGAIN TO CALL ME LAZARUS.
IT IS JUST A NAME.
YOUR NAME. WHEN YOU ARE GONE, NO ONE WILL REMEMBER OR SPEAK IT AGAIN.
AND WHOSE NAME SHALL THEY REMEMBER?
I SUPPOSE THAT OF MY MASTER PHINEAS SON OF OMAR.
THE ONE THEY CALL DIVES? "RICH MAN" IS NOT MUCH OF A NAME.
AND LAZARUS IS?
OH, YES. IN HEBREW IT IS ELEAZAR. IT MEANS "GOD IS MY HELP."
GOD HAS NOT BEEN MUCH HELP TO YOU!
YOU LACK THE STRENGTH EVEN TO FEND OFF THESE

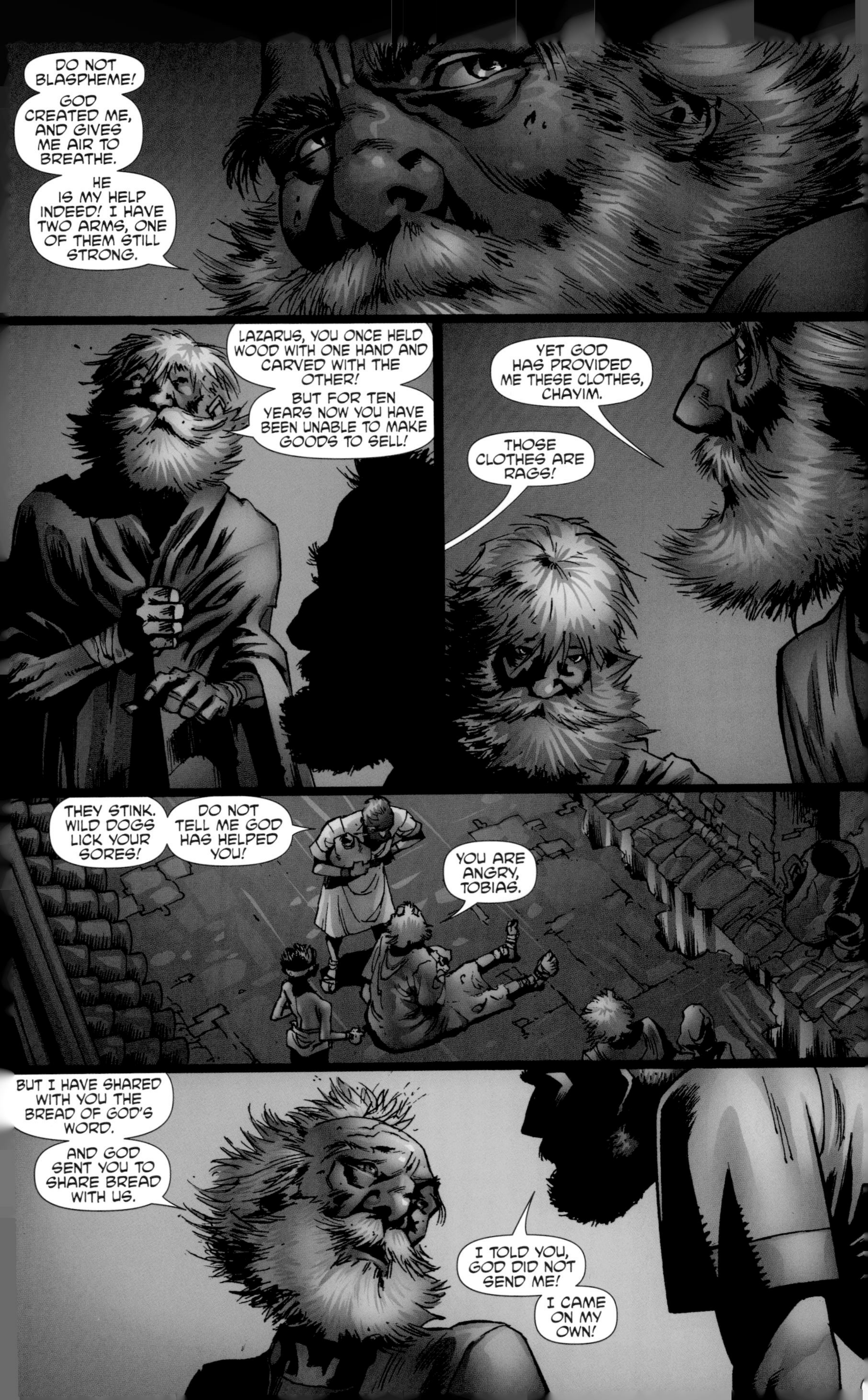
DO NOT BLASPHEME!
GOD CREATED ME, AND GIVES ME AIR TO BREATHE.
HE IS MY HELP INDEED! I HAVE TWO ARMS, ONE OF THEM STILL STRONG.
LAZARUS, YOU ONCE HELD WOOD WITH ONE HAND AND CARVED WITH THE OTHER!
BUT FOR TEN YEARS NOW YOU HAVE BEEN UNABLE TO MAKE GOODS TO SELL!
YET GOD HAS PROVIDED ME THESE CLOTHES, CHAYIM.
THOSE CLOTHES ARE RAGS!
THEY STINK. WILD DOGS LICK YOUR SORES!
DO NOT TELL ME GOD HAS HELPED YOU!
YOU ARE ANGRY, TOBIAS.
BUT I HAVE SHARED WITH YOU THE BREAD OF GOD'S WORD.
AND GOD SENT YOU TO SHARE BREAD WITH US.
I TOLD YOU, GOD DID NOT SEND ME!
I CAME ON MY OWN!

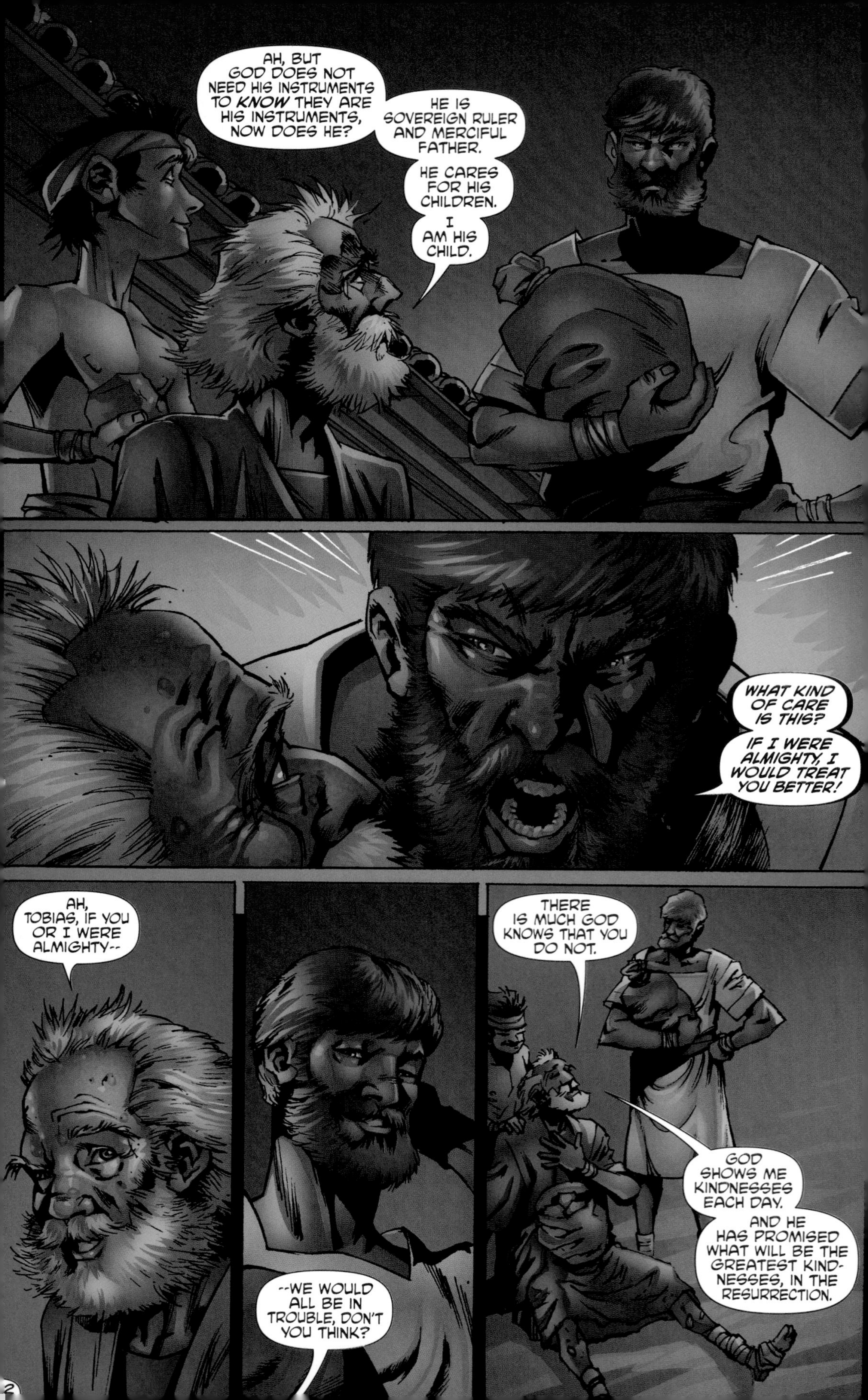
AH, BUT GOD DOES NOT NEED HIS INSTRUMENTS TO *KNOW* THEY ARE HIS INSTRUMENTS, NOW DOES HE?
HE IS SOVEREIGN RULER AND MERCIFUL FATHER.
HE CARES FOR HIS CHILDREN.
I AM HIS CHILD.
WHAT KIND OF CARE IS THIS?
IF I WERE ALMIGHTY, I WOULD TREAT YOU BETTER!
AH, TOBIAS, IF YOU OR I WERE ALMIGHTY--
--WE WOULD ALL BE IN TROUBLE, DON'T YOU THINK?
THERE IS MUCH GOD KNOWS THAT YOU DO NOT.
GOD SHOWS ME KINDNESSES EACH DAY.
AND HE HAS PROMISED WHAT WILL BE THE GREATEST KINDNESSES, IN THE RESURRECTION.

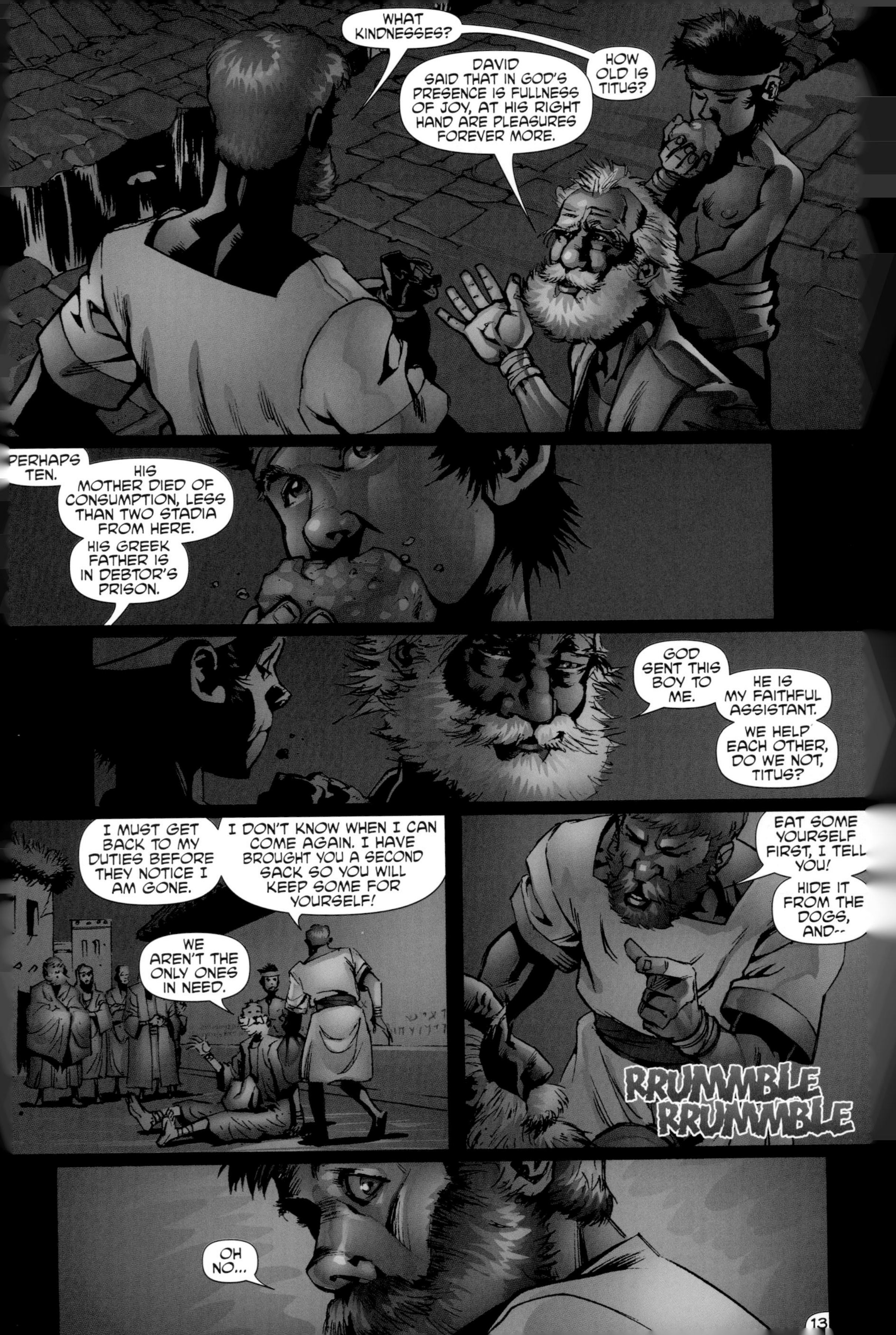
WHAT KINDNESSES?
DAVID SAID THAT IN GOD'S PRESENCE IS FULLNESS OF JOY, AT HIS RIGHT HAND ARE PLEASURES FOREVER MORE.
HOW OLD IS TITUS?
PERHAPS TEN.
HIS MOTHER DIED OF CONSUMPTION, LESS THAN TWO STADIA FROM HERE.
HIS GREEK FATHER IS IN DEBTOR'S PRISON.
GOD SENT THIS BOY TO ME.
HE IS MY FAITHFUL ASSISTANT.
WE HELP EACH OTHER, DO WE NOT, TITUS?
I MUST GET BACK TO MY DUTIES BEFORE THEY NOTICE I AM GONE.
I DON'T KNOW WHEN I CAN COME AGAIN. I HAVE BROUGHT YOU A SECOND SACK SO YOU WILL KEEP SOME FOR YOURSELF!
WE AREN'T THE ONLY ONES IN NEED.
EAT SOME YOURSELF FIRST, I TELL YOU!
HIDE IT FROM THE DOGS, AND--
RRUMMBLE RRUMMBLE
OH NO...

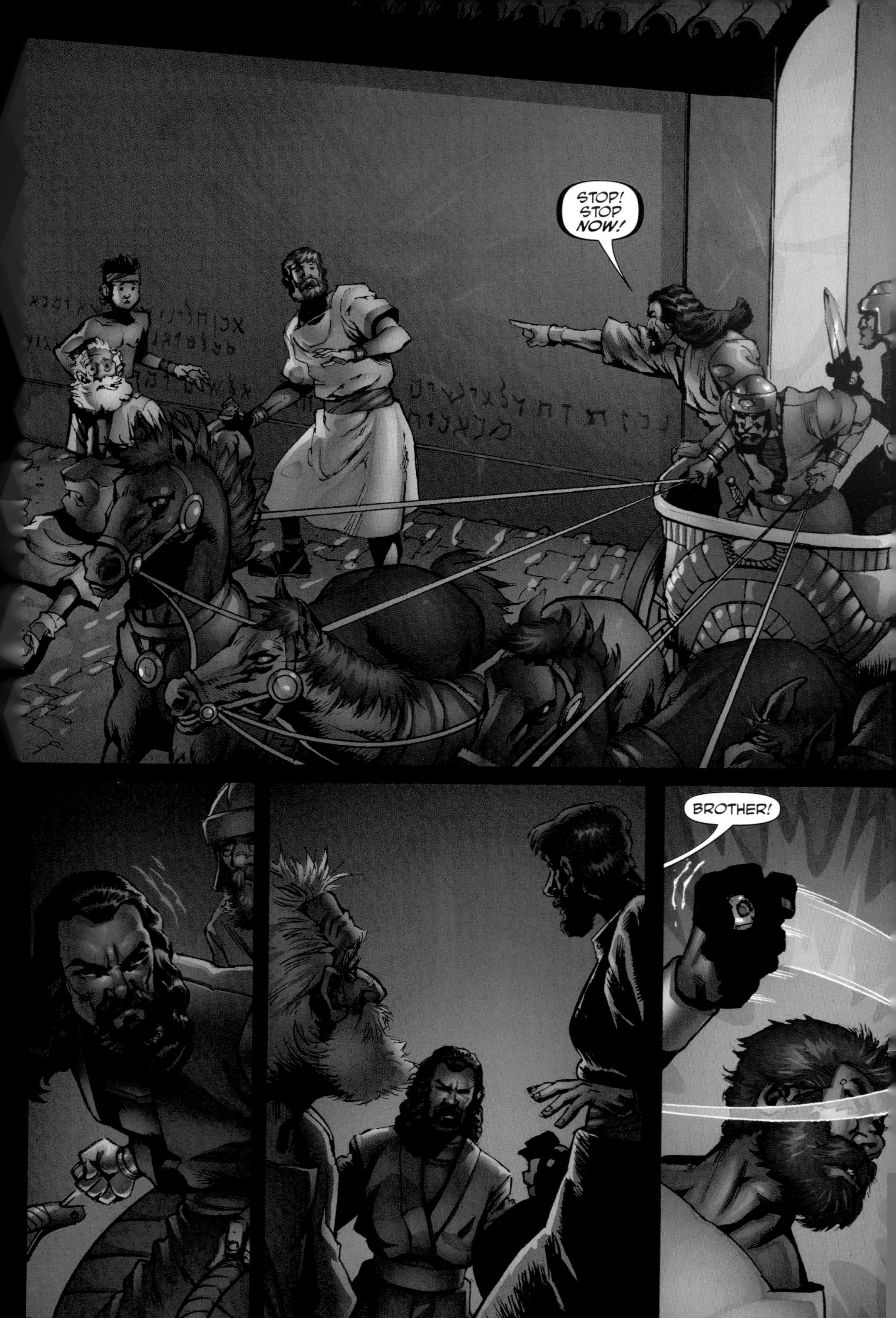
STOP! STOP NOW!
BROTHER!

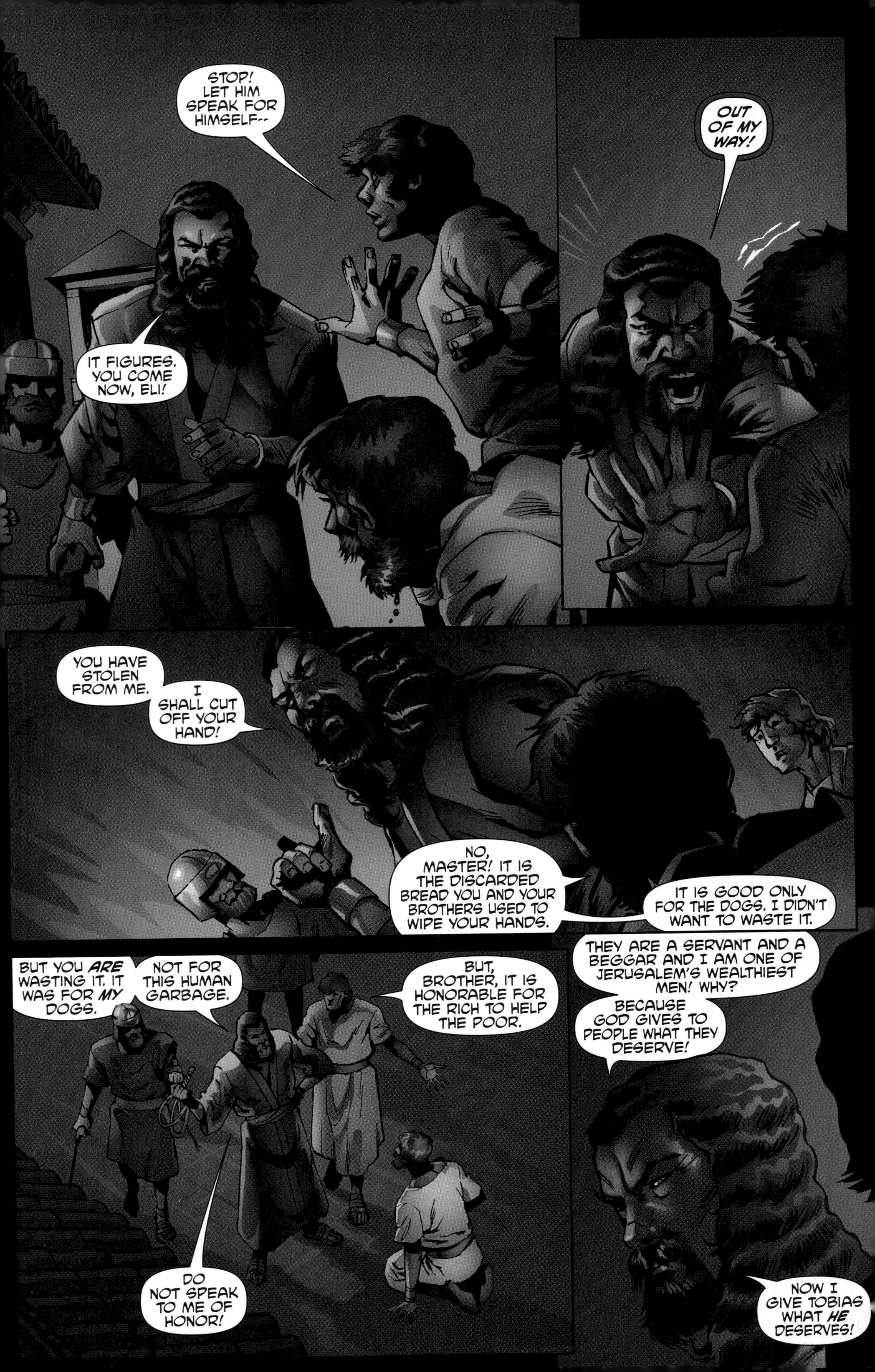
STOP! LET HIM SPEAK FOR HIMSELF--
IT FIGURES. YOU COME NOW, ELI!
OUT OF MY WAY!
YOU HAVE STOLEN FROM ME.
I SHALL CUT OFF YOUR HAND!
NO, MASTER! IT IS THE DISCARDED BREAD YOU AND YOUR BROTHERS USED TO WIPE YOUR HANDS.
IT IS GOOD ONLY FOR THE DOGS. I DIDN'T WANT TO WASTE IT.
BUT YOU *ARE* WASTING IT. IT WAS FOR *MY* DOGS.
NOT FOR THIS HUMAN GARBAGE.
BUT, BROTHER, IT IS HONORABLE FOR THE RICH TO HELP THE POOR.
DO NOT SPEAK TO ME OF HONOR!
THEY ARE A SERVANT AND A BEGGAR AND I AM ONE OF JERUSALEM'S WEALTHIEST MEN! WHY?
BECAUSE GOD GIVES TO PEOPLE WHAT THEY DESERVE!
NOW I GIVE TOBIAS WHAT *HE* DESERVES!

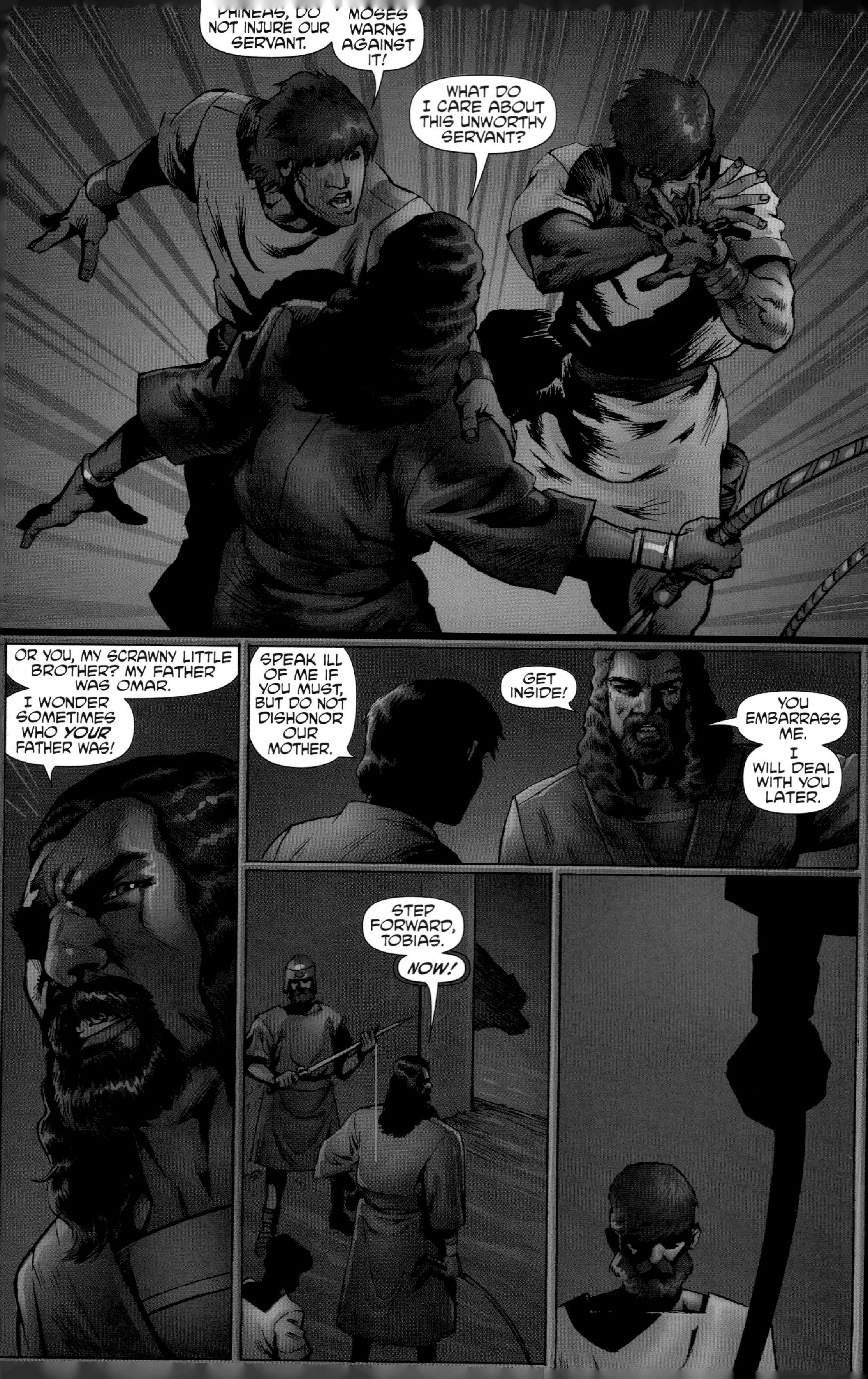
PHINEAS, DO NOT INJURE OUR SERVANT.
MOSES WARNS AGAINST IT!
WHAT DO I CARE ABOUT THIS UNWORTHY SERVANT?
OR YOU, MY SCRAWNY LITTLE BROTHER? MY FATHER WAS OMAR.
I WONDER SOMETIMES WHO *YOUR* FATHER WAS!
SPEAK ILL OF ME IF YOU MUST, BUT DO NOT DISHONOR OUR MOTHER.
GET INSIDE!
YOU EMBARRASS ME.
I WILL DEAL WITH YOU LATER.
STEP FORWARD, TOBIAS.
NOW!

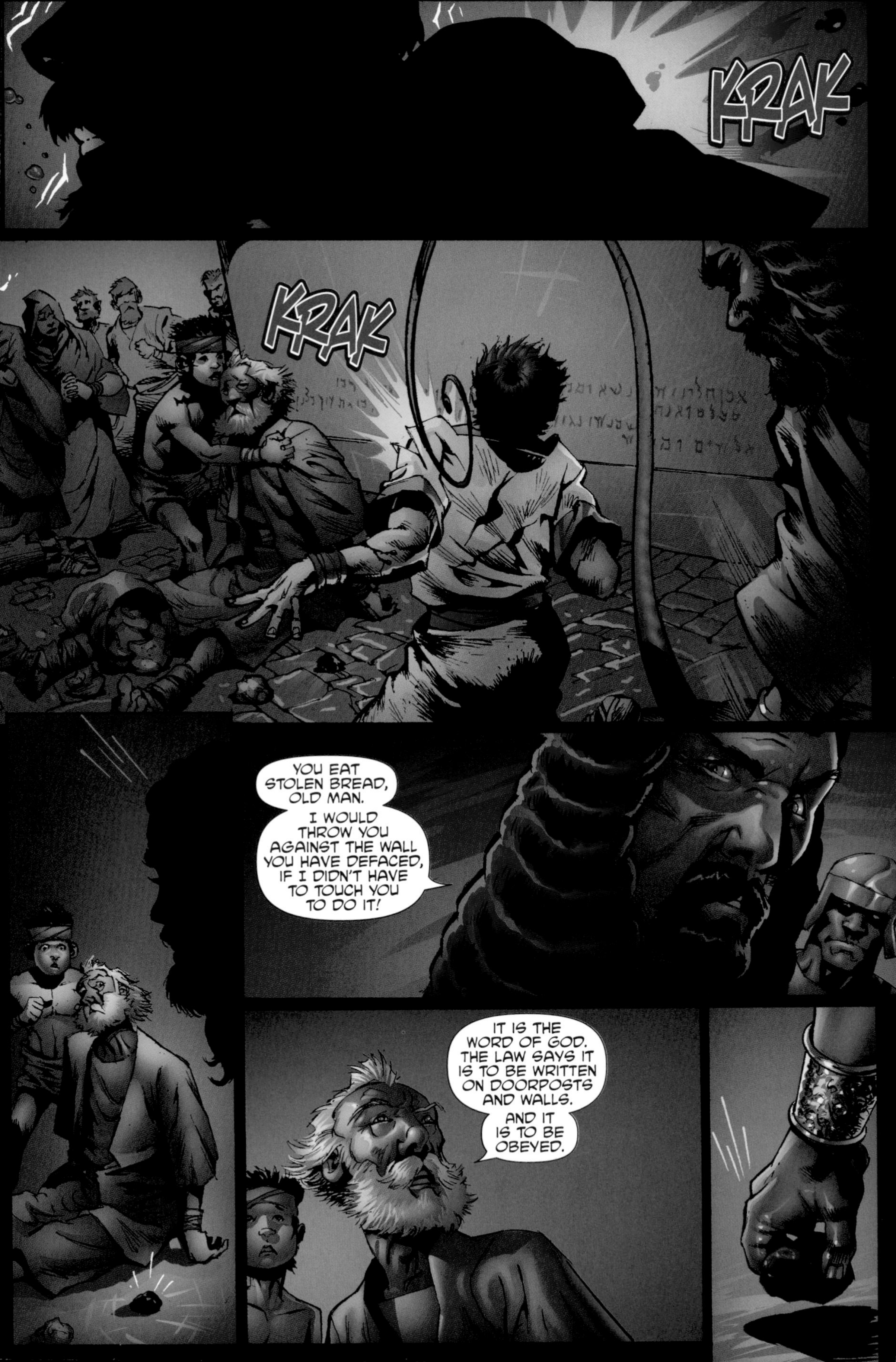
KRAK
KRAK
YOU EAT STOLEN BREAD, OLD MAN.
I WOULD THROW YOU AGAINST THE WALL YOU HAVE DEFACED, IF I DIDN'T HAVE TO TOUCH YOU TO DO IT!
IT IS THE WORD OF GOD. THE LAW SAYS IT IS TO BE WRITTEN ON DOORPOSTS AND WALLS.
AND IT IS TO BE OBEYED.

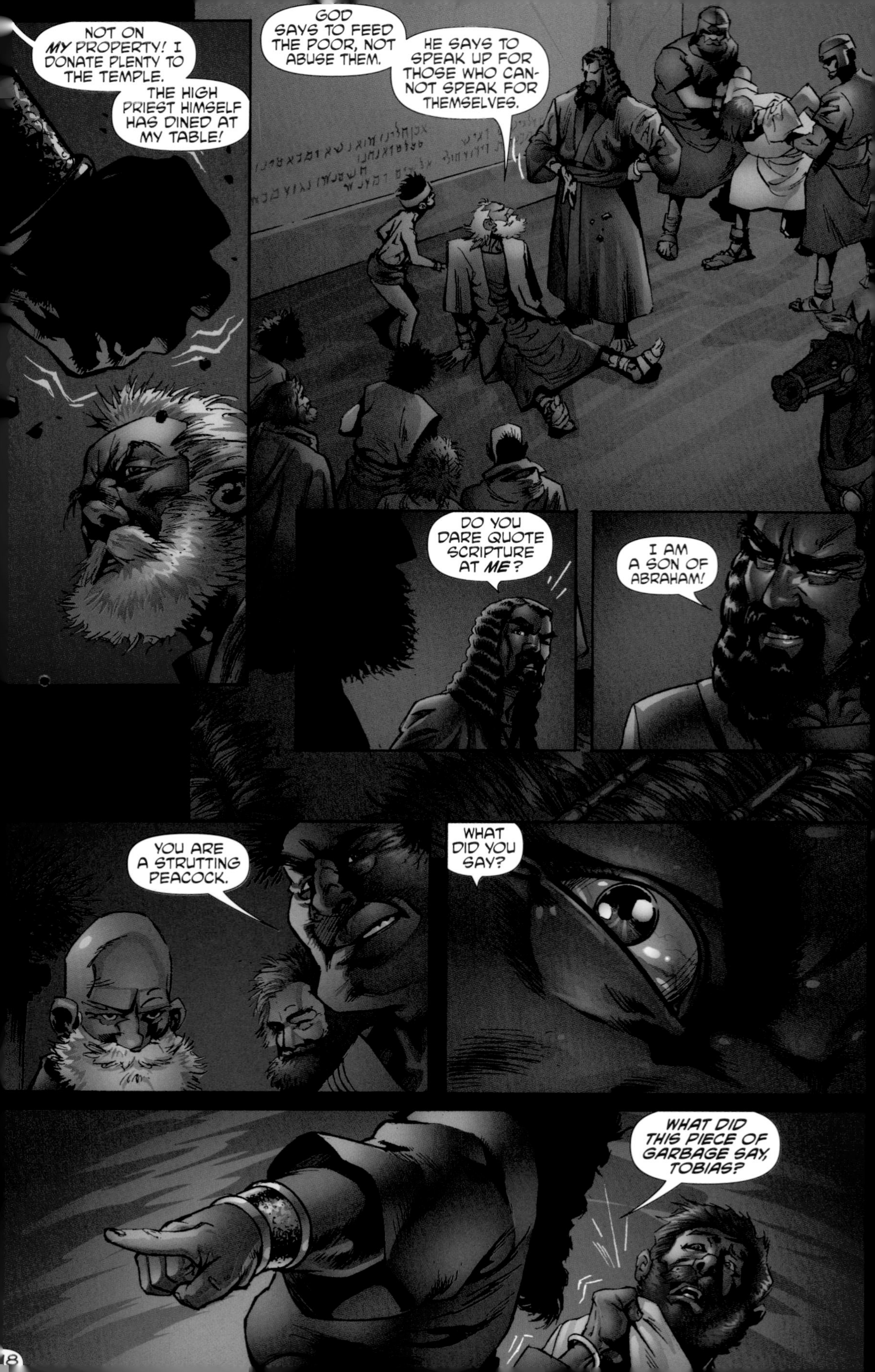
NOT ON MY PROPERTY! I DONATE PLENTY TO THE TEMPLE.
THE HIGH PRIEST HIMSELF HAS DINED AT MY TABLE!
GOD SAYS TO FEED THE POOR, NOT ABUSE THEM.
HE SAYS TO SPEAK UP FOR THOSE WHO CAN-NOT SPEAK FOR THEMSELVES.
DO YOU DARE QUOTE SCRIPTURE AT ME?
I AM A SON OF ABRAHAM!
YOU ARE A STRUTTING PEACOCK.
WHAT DID YOU SAY?
WHAT DID THIS PIECE OF GARBAGE SAY, TOBIAS?

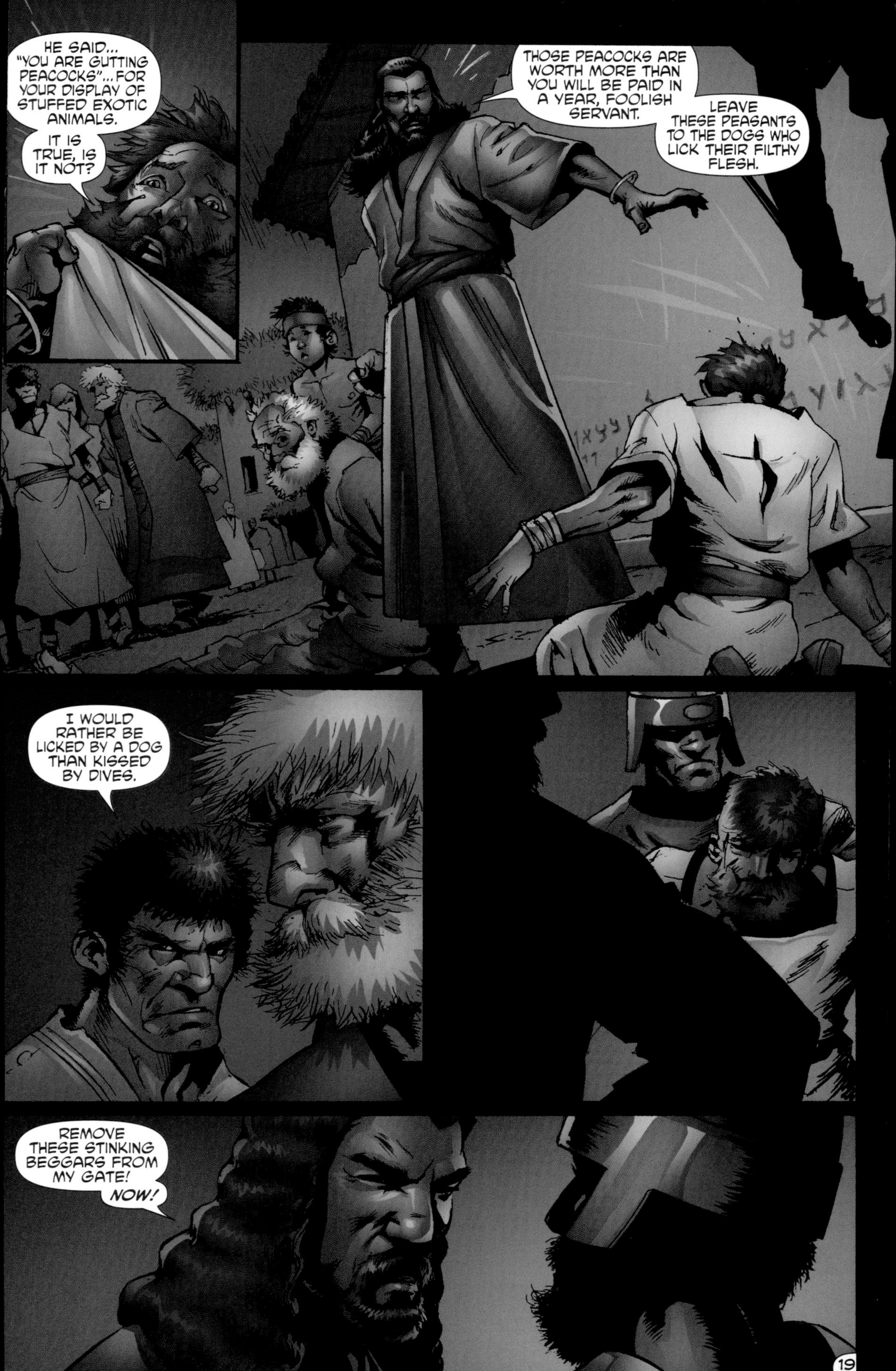
HE SAID... "YOU ARE GUTTING PEACOCKS"...FOR YOUR DISPLAY OF STUFFED EXOTIC ANIMALS.
IT IS TRUE, IS IT NOT?
THOSE PEACOCKS ARE WORTH MORE THAN YOU WILL BE PAID IN A YEAR, FOOLISH SERVANT.
LEAVE THESE PEASANTS TO THE DOGS WHO LICK THEIR FILTHY FLESH.
I WOULD RATHER BE LICKED BY A DOG THAN KISSED BY DIVES.
REMOVE THESE STINKING BEGGARS FROM MY GATE! *NOW!*

AND WASH THOSE WALLS! DO NOT LEAVE A SINGLE WORD OF IT!

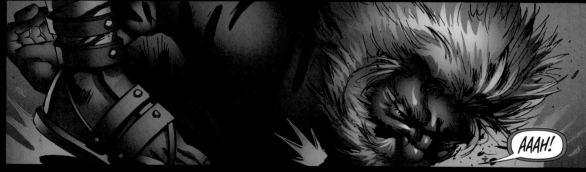

AAAH!

YOU ARE DOCKED A WEEK'S WAGES.

IF I CATCH YOU AGAIN SERVING THE UNCLEAN INSTEAD OF ME, YOUR ARMS AND LEGS SHALL BE BROKEN AND YOU WILL BE CAST OUT OF THE HOUSE OF OMAR!

SLAP

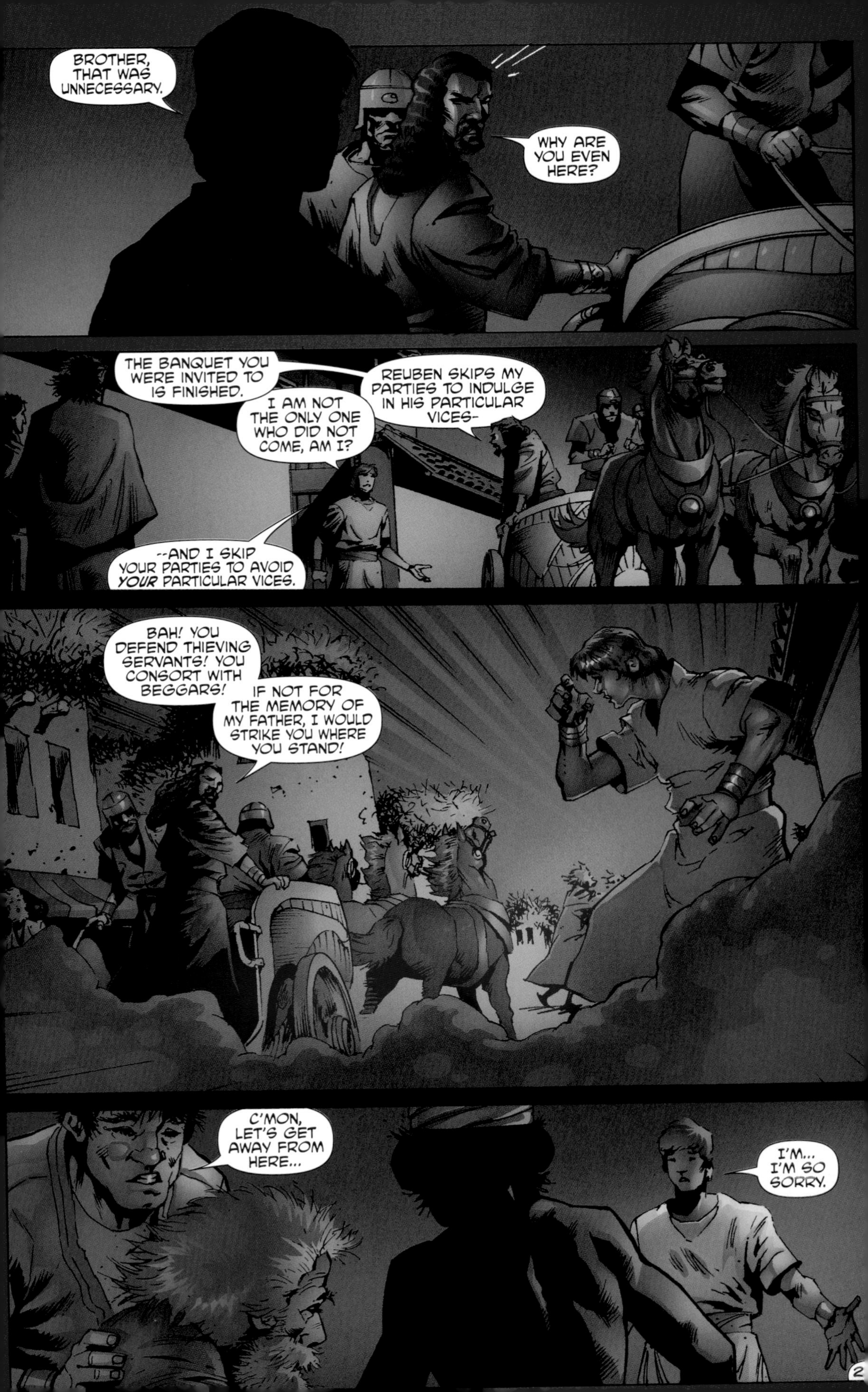
BROTHER, THAT WAS UNNECESSARY.
WHY ARE YOU EVEN HERE?
THE BANQUET YOU WERE INVITED TO IS FINISHED.
I AM NOT THE ONLY ONE WHO DID NOT COME, AM I?
REUBEN SKIPS MY PARTIES TO INDULGE IN HIS PARTICULAR VICES-
--AND I SKIP YOUR PARTIES TO AVOID *YOUR* PARTICULAR VICES.
BAH! YOU DEFEND THIEVING SERVANTS! YOU CONSORT WITH BEGGARS!
IF NOT FOR THE MEMORY OF MY FATHER, I WOULD STRIKE YOU WHERE YOU STAND!
C'MON, LET'S GET AWAY FROM HERE...
I'M... I'M SO SORRY.

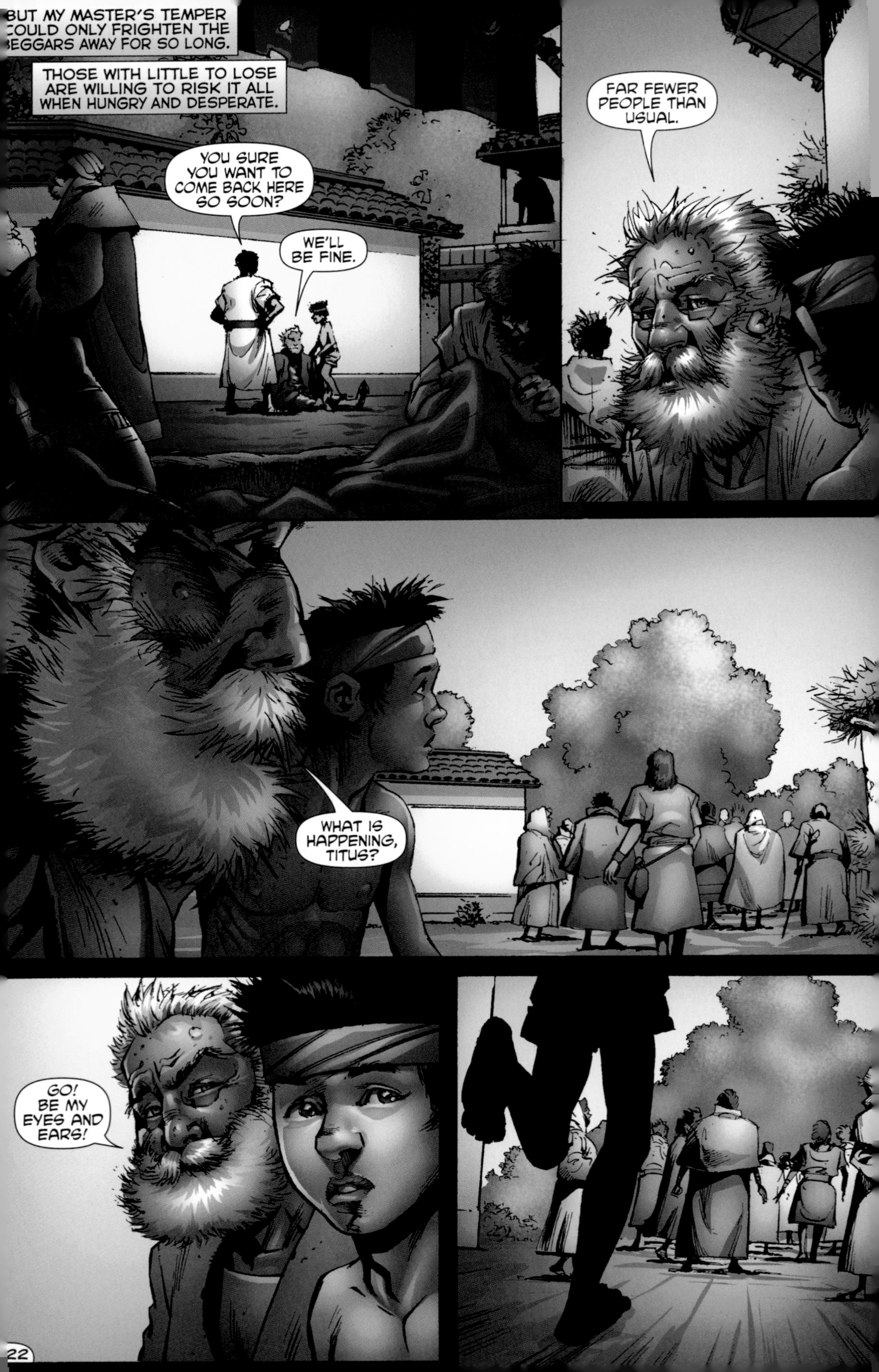
BUT MY MASTER'S TEMPER COULD ONLY FRIGHTEN THE BEGGARS AWAY FOR SO LONG.
THOSE WITH LITTLE TO LOSE ARE WILLING TO RISK IT ALL WHEN HUNGRY AND DESPERATE.
YOU SURE YOU WANT TO COME BACK HERE SO SOON?
WE'LL BE FINE.
FAR FEWER PEOPLE THAN USUAL.
WHAT IS HAPPENING, TITUS?
GO! BE MY EYES AND EARS!

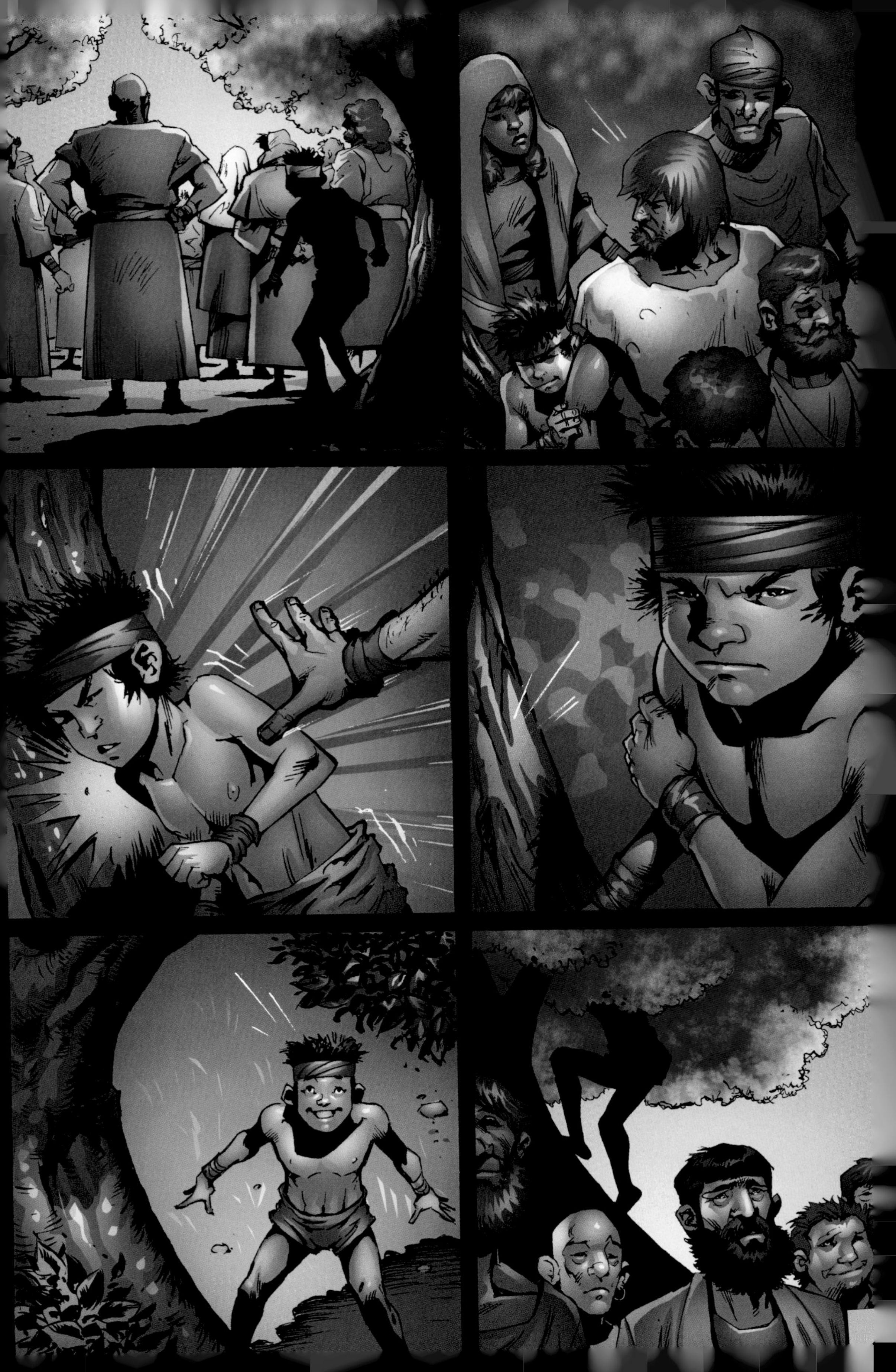

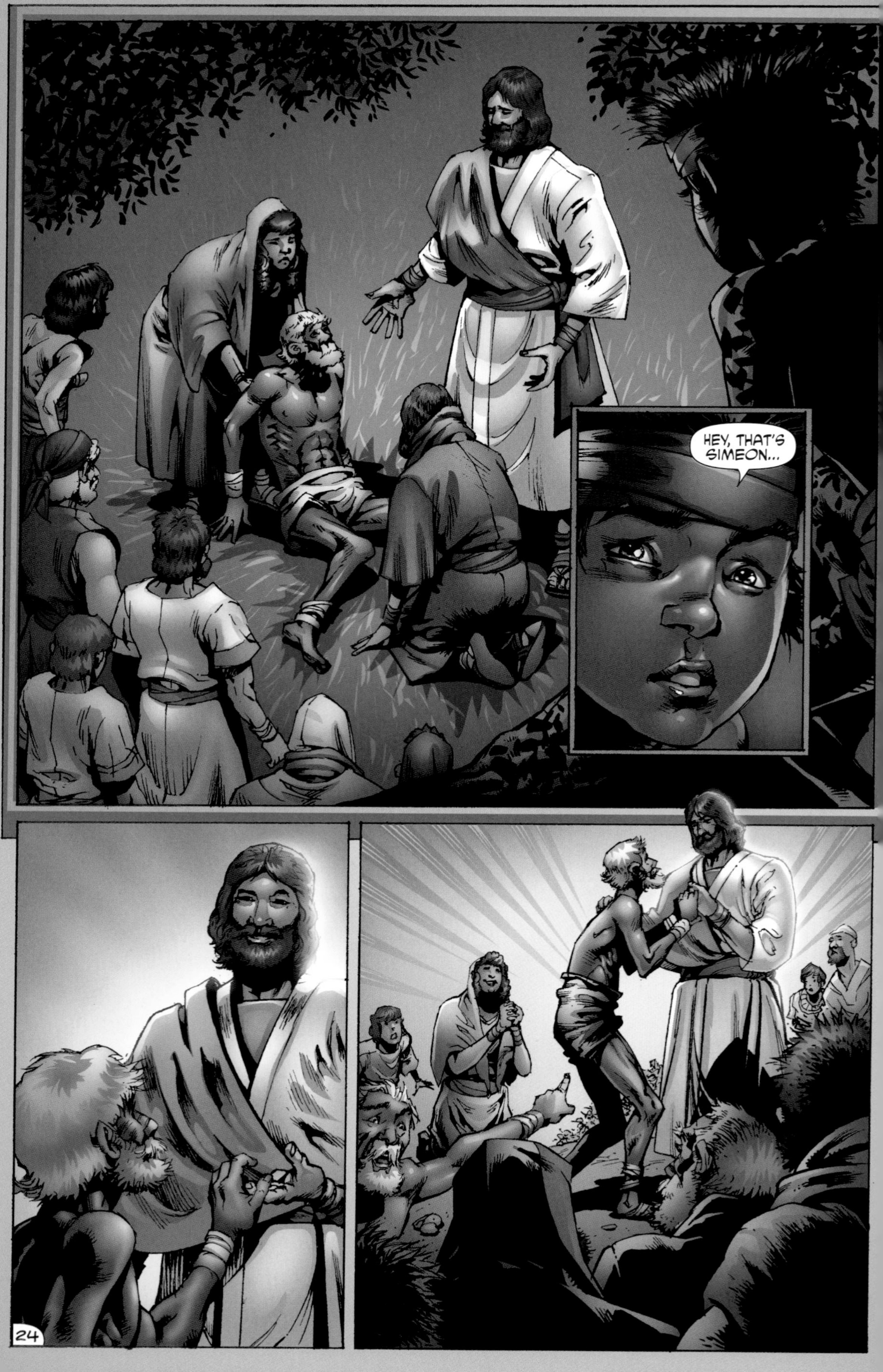
HEY, THAT'S SIMEON...

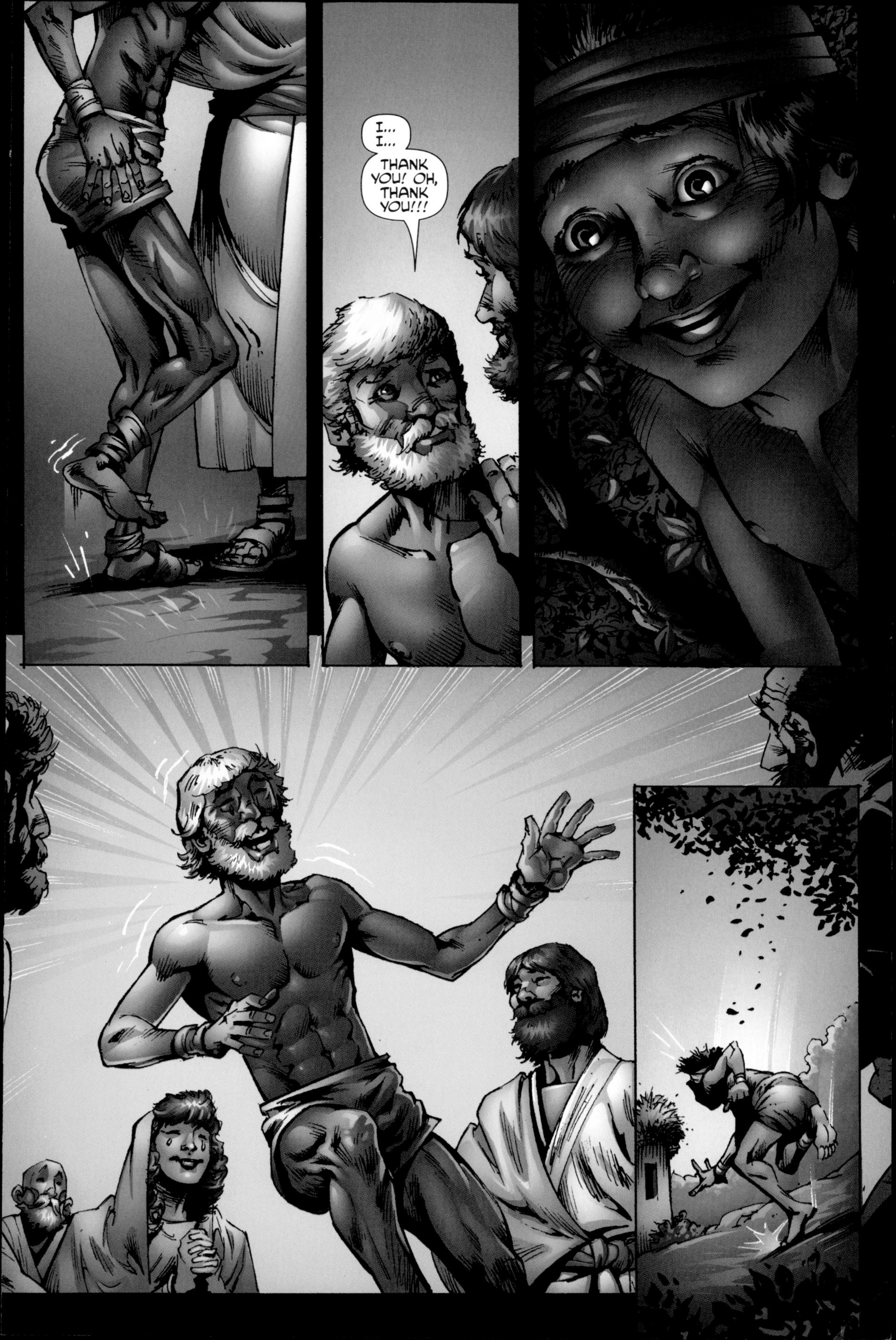
I... I... THANK YOU! OH, THANK YOU!!!

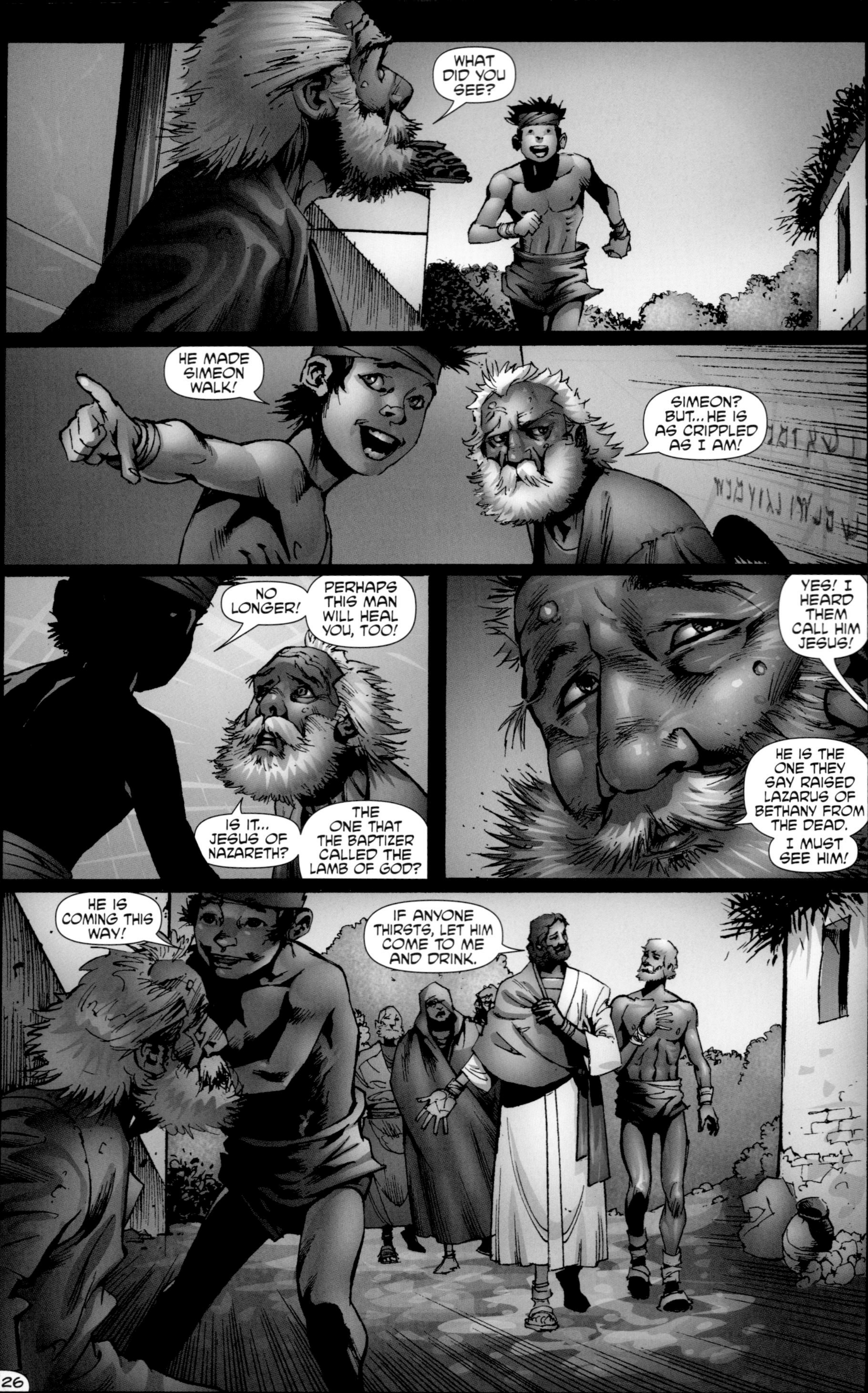
WHAT DID YOU SEE?
HE MADE SIMEON WALK!
SIMEON? BUT... HE IS AS CRIPPLED AS I AM!
NO LONGER!
PERHAPS THIS MAN WILL HEAL YOU, TOO!
IS IT... JESUS OF NAZARETH?
THE ONE THAT THE BAPTIZER CALLED THE LAMB OF GOD?
YES! I HEARD THEM CALL HIM JESUS!
HE IS THE ONE THEY SAY RAISED LAZARUS OF BETHANY FROM THE DEAD.
I MUST SEE HIM!
HE IS COMING THIS WAY!
IF ANYONE THIRSTS, LET HIM COME TO ME AND DRINK.

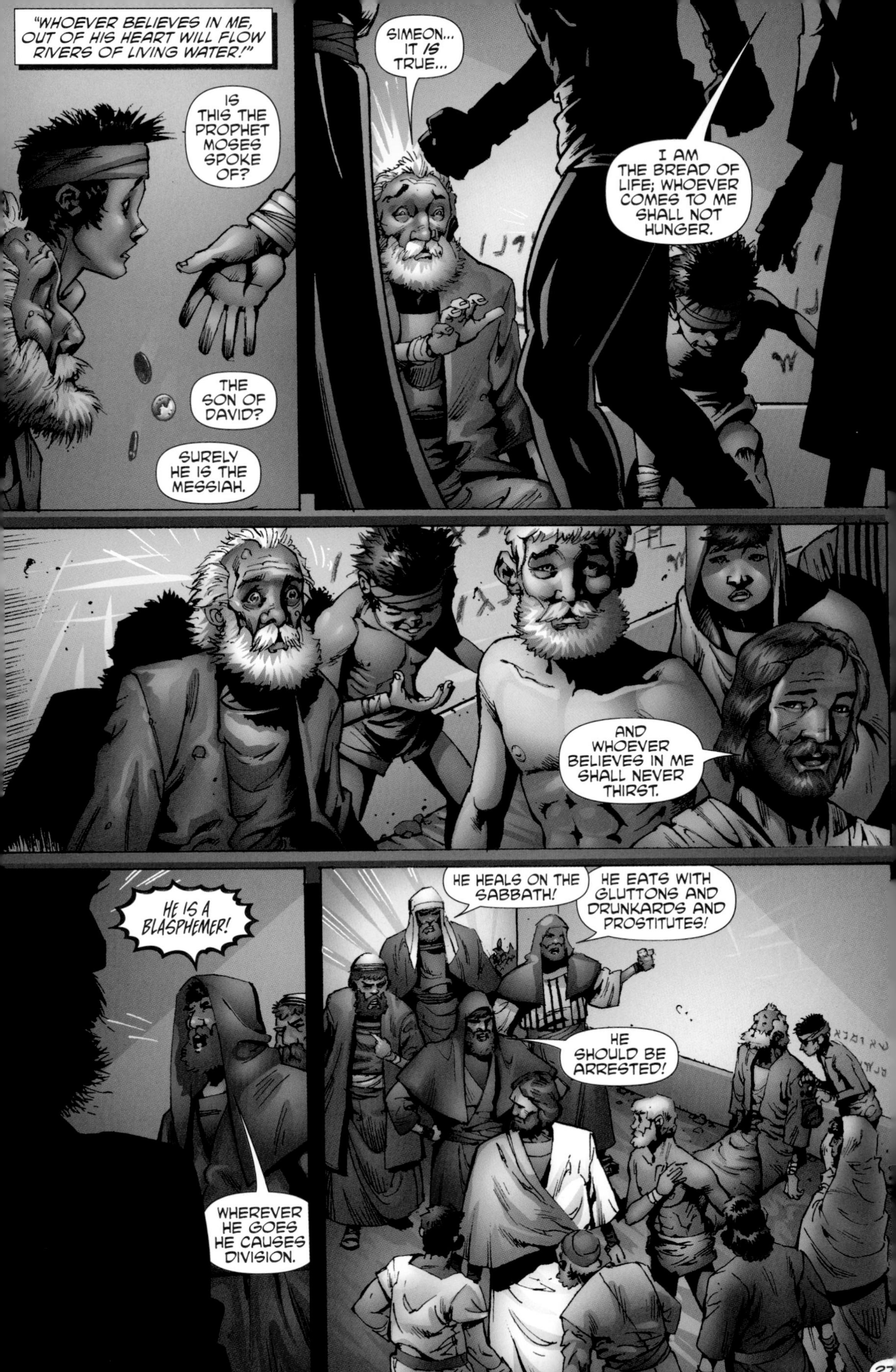
"WHOEVER BELIEVES IN ME, OUT OF HIS HEART WILL FLOW RIVERS OF LIVING WATER!"
IS THIS THE PROPHET MOSES SPOKE OF?
THE SON OF DAVID?
SURELY HE IS THE MESSIAH.
SIMEON... IT *IS* TRUE...
I AM THE BREAD OF LIFE; WHOEVER COMES TO ME SHALL NOT HUNGER.
AND WHOEVER BELIEVES IN ME SHALL NEVER THIRST.
HE IS A BLASPHEMER!
WHEREVER HE GOES HE CAUSES DIVISION.
HE HEALS ON THE SABBATH!
HE EATS WITH GLUTTONS AND DRUNKARDS AND PROSTITUTES!
HE SHOULD BE ARRESTED!

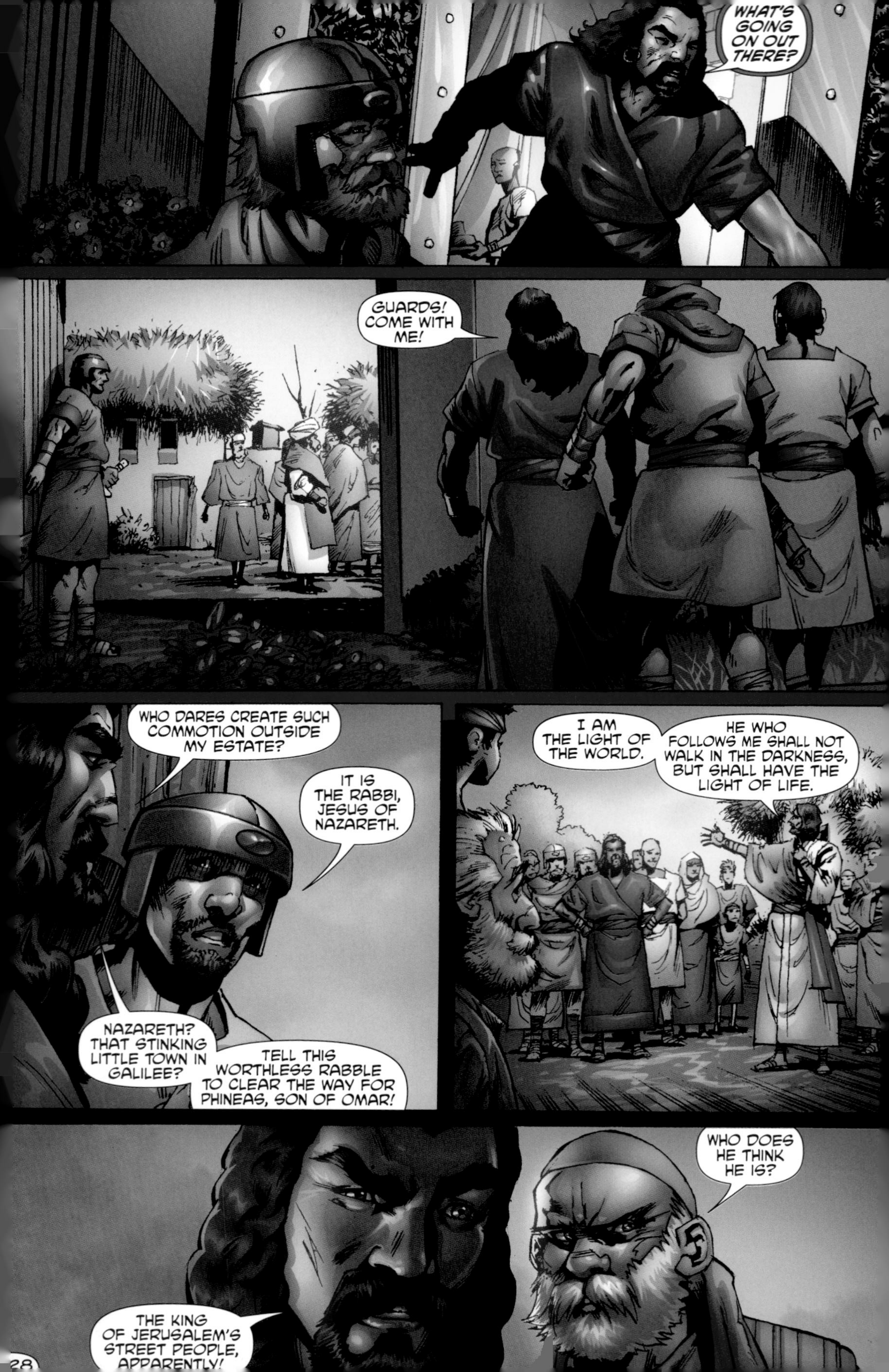
WHAT'S GOING ON OUT THERE?
GUARDS! COME WITH ME!
WHO DARES CREATE SUCH COMMOTION OUTSIDE MY ESTATE?
IT IS THE RABBI, JESUS OF NAZARETH.
NAZARETH? THAT STINKING LITTLE TOWN IN GALILEE?
TELL THIS WORTHLESS RABBLE TO CLEAR THE WAY FOR PHINEAS, SON OF OMAR!
I AM THE LIGHT OF THE WORLD.
HE WHO FOLLOWS ME SHALL NOT WALK IN THE DARKNESS, BUT SHALL HAVE THE LIGHT OF LIFE.
WHO DOES HE THINK HE IS?
THE KING OF JERUSALEM'S STREET PEOPLE, APPARENTLY!

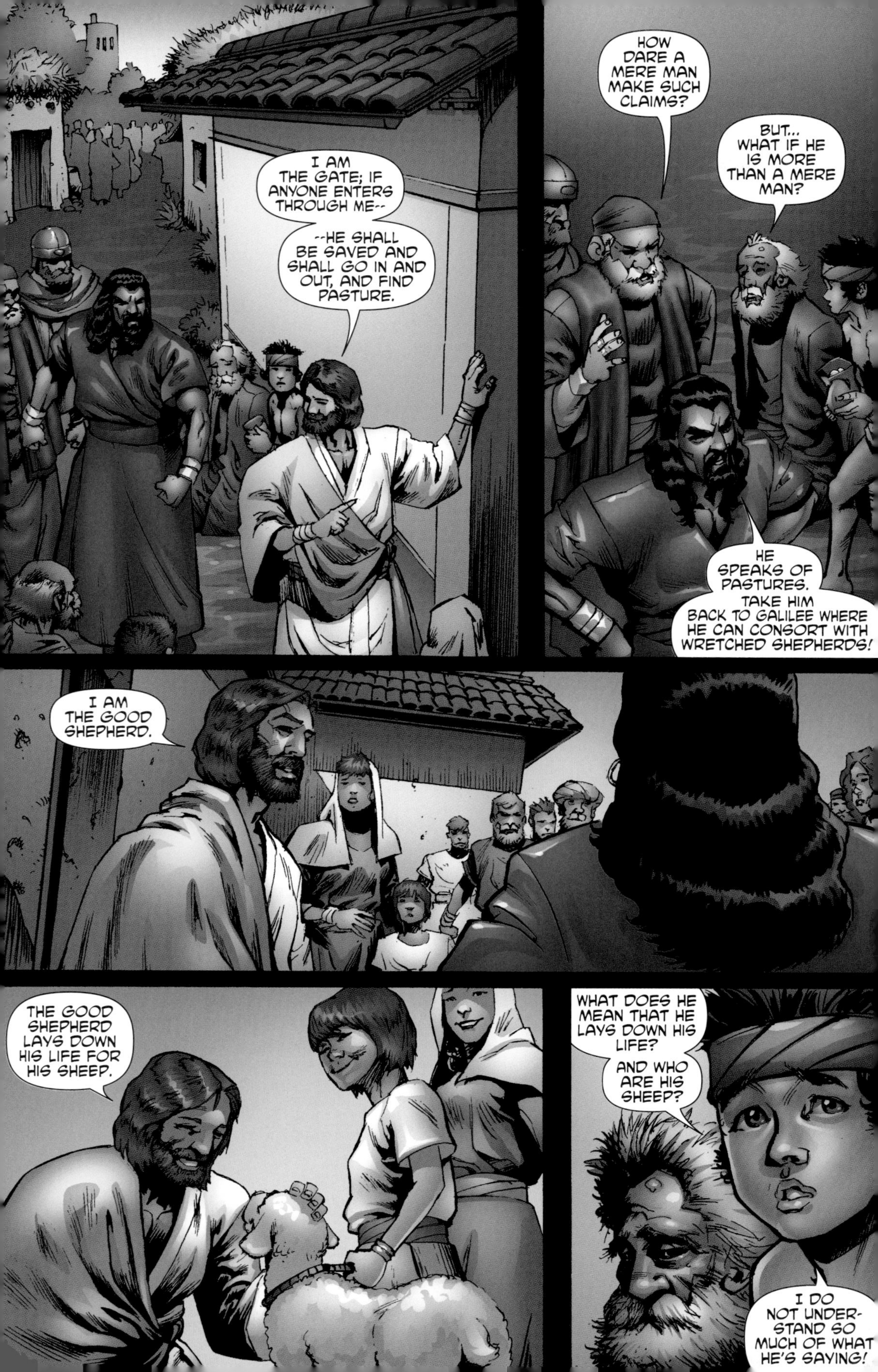
I AM THE GATE; IF ANYONE ENTERS THROUGH ME--
--HE SHALL BE SAVED AND SHALL GO IN AND OUT, AND FIND PASTURE.
HOW DARE A MERE MAN MAKE SUCH CLAIMS?
BUT... WHAT IF HE IS MORE THAN A MERE MAN?
HE SPEAKS OF PASTURES.
TAKE HIM BACK TO GALILEE WHERE HE CAN CONSORT WITH WRETCHED SHEPHERDS!
I AM THE GOOD SHEPHERD.
THE GOOD SHEPHERD LAYS DOWN HIS LIFE FOR HIS SHEEP.
WHAT DOES HE MEAN THAT HE LAYS DOWN HIS LIFE?
AND WHO ARE HIS SHEEP?
I DO NOT UNDERSTAND SO MUCH OF WHAT HE'S SAYING!

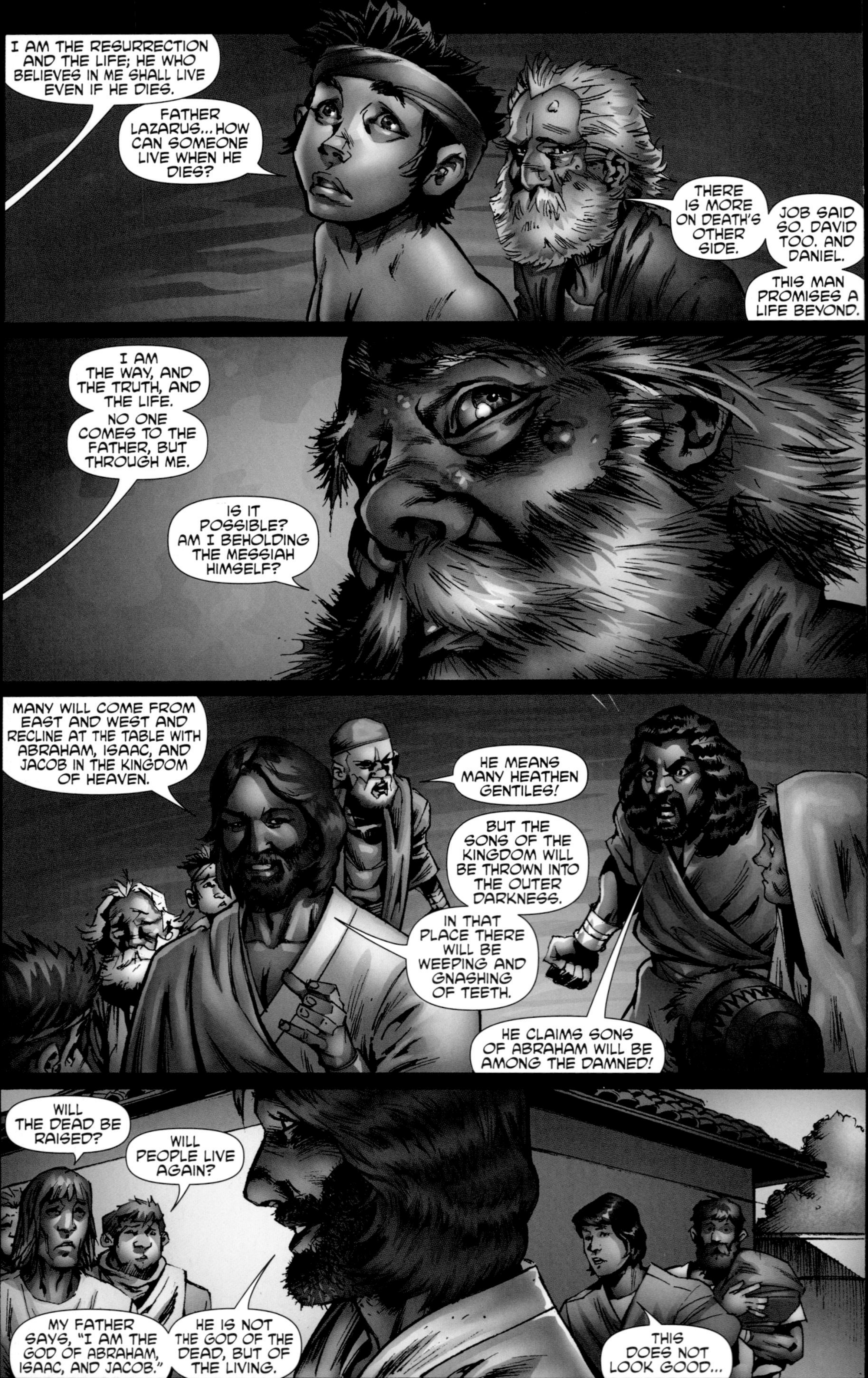
I AM THE RESURRECTION AND THE LIFE; HE WHO BELIEVES IN ME SHALL LIVE EVEN IF HE DIES.
FATHER LAZARUS... HOW CAN SOMEONE LIVE WHEN HE DIES?
THERE IS MORE ON DEATH'S OTHER SIDE.
JOB SAID SO. DAVID TOO. AND DANIEL.
THIS MAN PROMISES A LIFE BEYOND.
I AM THE WAY, AND THE TRUTH, AND THE LIFE.
NO ONE COMES TO THE FATHER, BUT THROUGH ME.
IS IT POSSIBLE? AM I BEHOLDING THE MESSIAH HIMSELF?
MANY WILL COME FROM EAST AND WEST AND RECLINE AT THE TABLE WITH ABRAHAM, ISAAC, AND JACOB IN THE KINGDOM OF HEAVEN.
HE MEANS MANY HEATHEN GENTILES!
BUT THE SONS OF THE KINGDOM WILL BE THROWN INTO THE OUTER DARKNESS.
IN THAT PLACE THERE WILL BE WEEPING AND GNASHING OF TEETH.
HE CLAIMS SONS OF ABRAHAM WILL BE AMONG THE DAMNED!
WILL THE DEAD BE RAISED?
WILL PEOPLE LIVE AGAIN?
MY FATHER SAYS, "I AM THE GOD OF ABRAHAM, ISAAC, AND JACOB."
HE IS NOT THE GOD OF THE DEAD, BUT OF THE LIVING.
THIS DOES NOT LOOK GOOD...

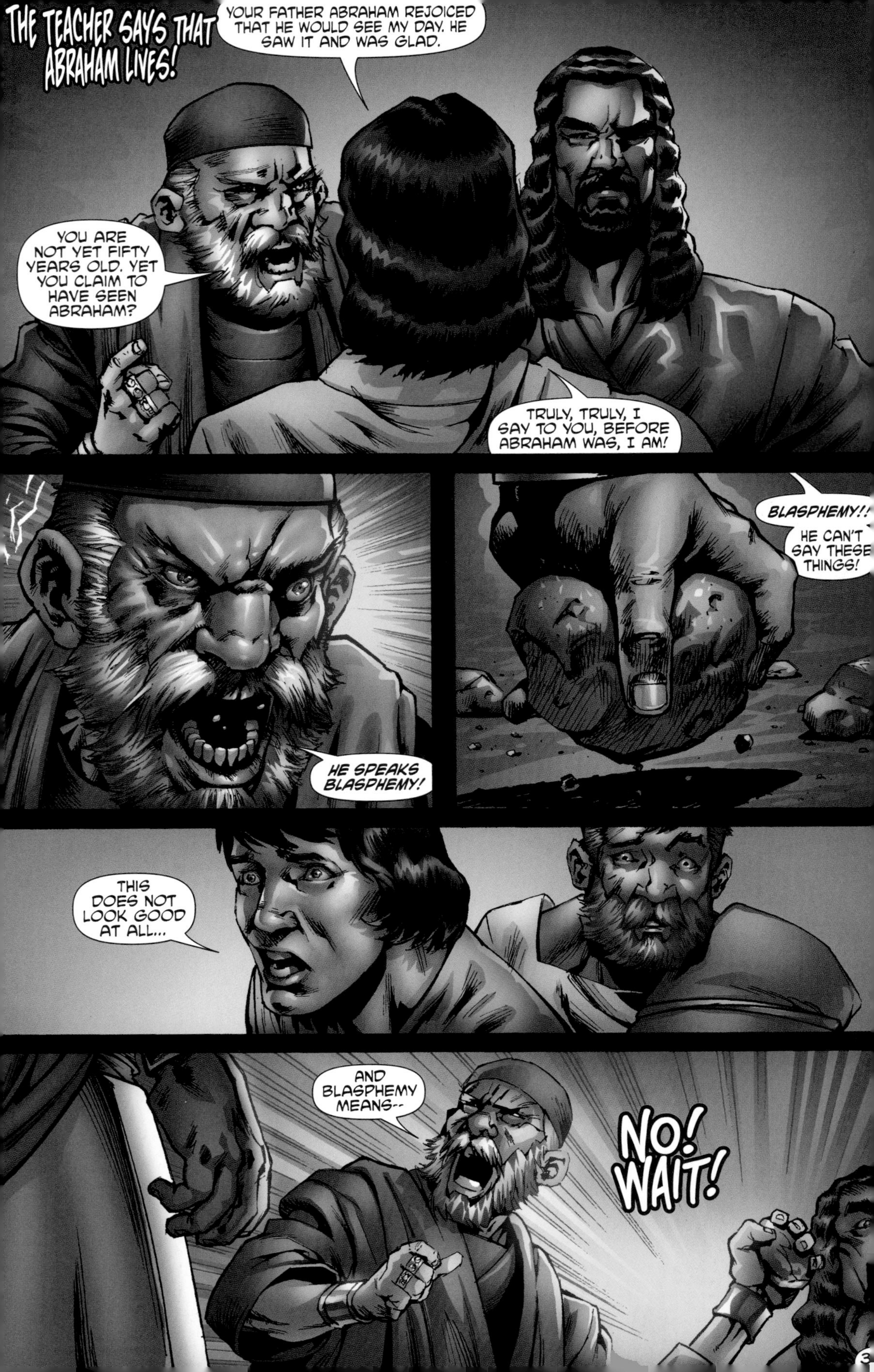
THE TEACHER SAYS THAT ABRAHAM LIVES!
YOUR FATHER ABRAHAM REJOICED THAT HE WOULD SEE MY DAY. HE SAW IT AND WAS GLAD.
YOU ARE NOT YET FIFTY YEARS OLD. YET YOU CLAIM TO HAVE SEEN ABRAHAM?
TRULY, TRULY, I SAY TO YOU, BEFORE ABRAHAM WAS, I AM!
HE SPEAKS BLASPHEMY!
BLASPHEMY!! HE CAN'T SAY THESE THINGS!
THIS DOES NOT LOOK GOOD AT ALL...
AND BLASPHEMY MEANS--
NO! WAIT!

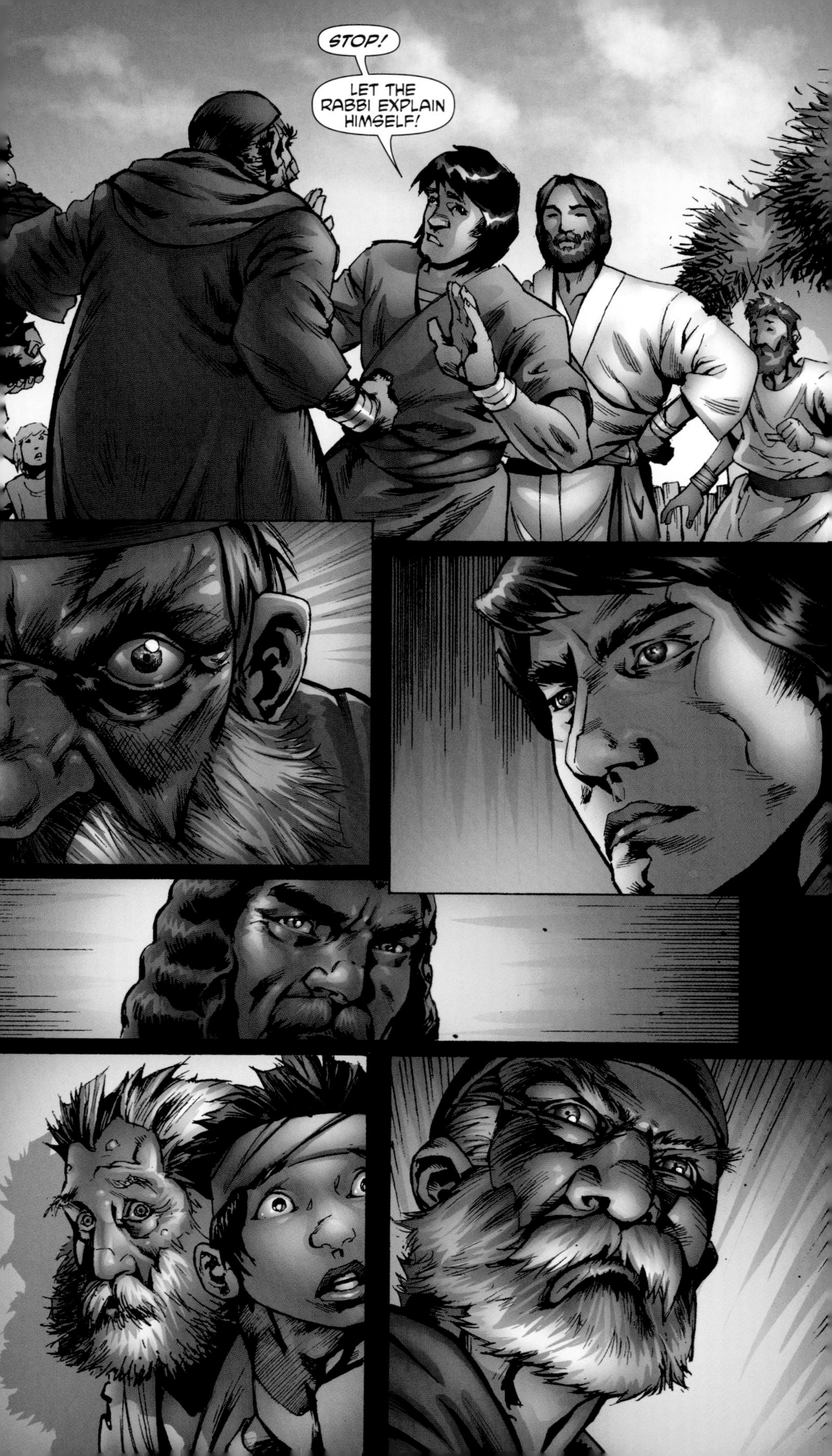
STOP!
LET THE RABBI EXPLAIN HIMSELF!

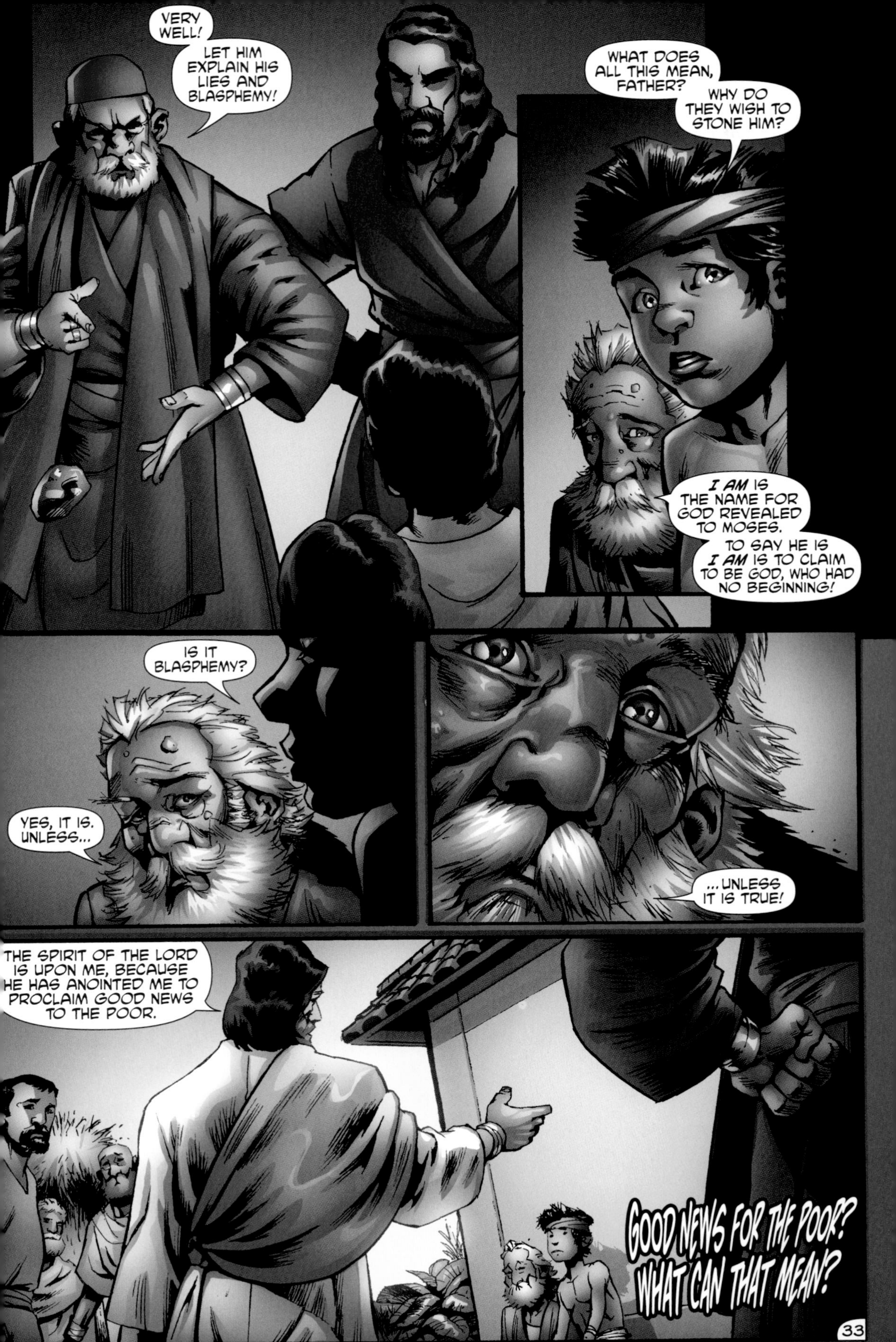

VERY WELL!
LET HIM EXPLAIN HIS LIES AND BLASPHEMY!
WHAT DOES ALL THIS MEAN, FATHER?
WHY DO THEY WISH TO STONE HIM?
I AM IS THE NAME FOR GOD REVEALED TO MOSES.
TO SAY HE IS *I AM* IS TO CLAIM TO BE GOD, WHO HAD NO BEGINNING!
IS IT BLASPHEMY?
YES, IT IS. UNLESS...
...UNLESS IT IS TRUE!
THE SPIRIT OF THE LORD IS UPON ME, BECAUSE HE HAS ANOINTED ME TO PROCLAIM GOOD NEWS TO THE POOR.
GOOD NEWS FOR THE POOR? WHAT CAN THAT MEAN?

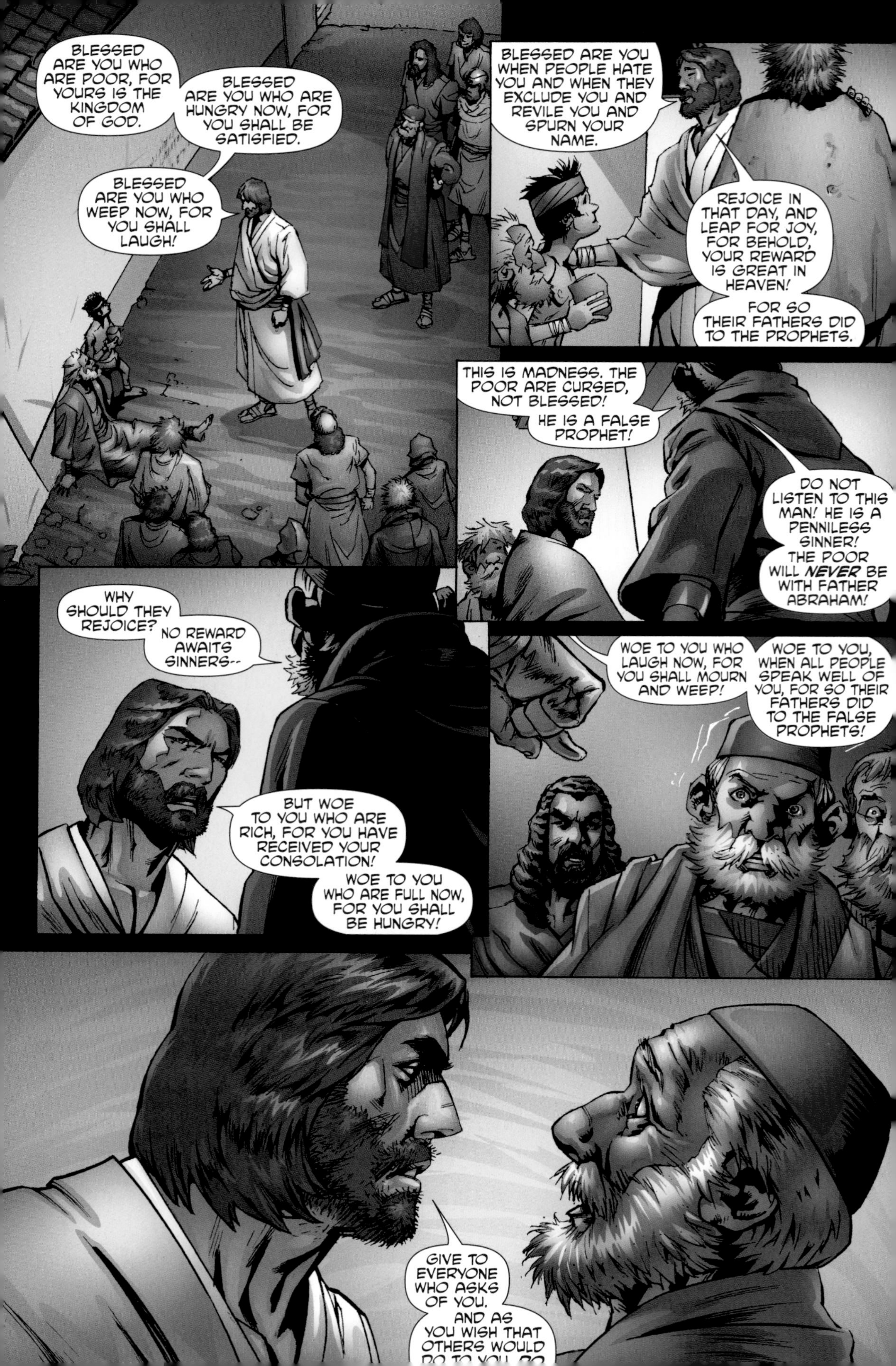
BLESSED ARE YOU WHO ARE POOR, FOR YOURS IS THE KINGDOM OF GOD.
BLESSED ARE YOU WHO ARE HUNGRY NOW, FOR YOU SHALL BE SATISFIED.
BLESSED ARE YOU WHO WEEP NOW, FOR YOU SHALL LAUGH!
BLESSED ARE YOU WHEN PEOPLE HATE YOU AND WHEN THEY EXCLUDE YOU AND REVILE YOU AND SPURN YOUR NAME.
REJOICE IN THAT DAY, AND LEAP FOR JOY, FOR BEHOLD, YOUR REWARD IS GREAT IN HEAVEN!
FOR SO THEIR FATHERS DID TO THE PROPHETS.
THIS IS MADNESS. THE POOR ARE CURSED, NOT BLESSED!
HE IS A FALSE PROPHET!
DO NOT LISTEN TO THIS MAN! HE IS A PENNILESS SINNER!
THE POOR WILL ***NEVER*** BE WITH FATHER ABRAHAM!
WHY SHOULD THEY REJOICE?
NO REWARD AWAITS SINNERS--
BUT WOE TO YOU WHO ARE RICH, FOR YOU HAVE RECEIVED YOUR CONSOLATION!
WOE TO YOU WHO ARE FULL NOW, FOR YOU SHALL BE HUNGRY!
WOE TO YOU WHO LAUGH NOW, FOR YOU SHALL MOURN AND WEEP!
WOE TO YOU, WHEN ALL PEOPLE SPEAK WELL OF YOU, FOR SO THEIR FATHERS DID TO THE FALSE PROPHETS!
GIVE TO EVERYONE WHO ASKS OF YOU.
AND AS YOU WISH THAT OTHERS WOULD

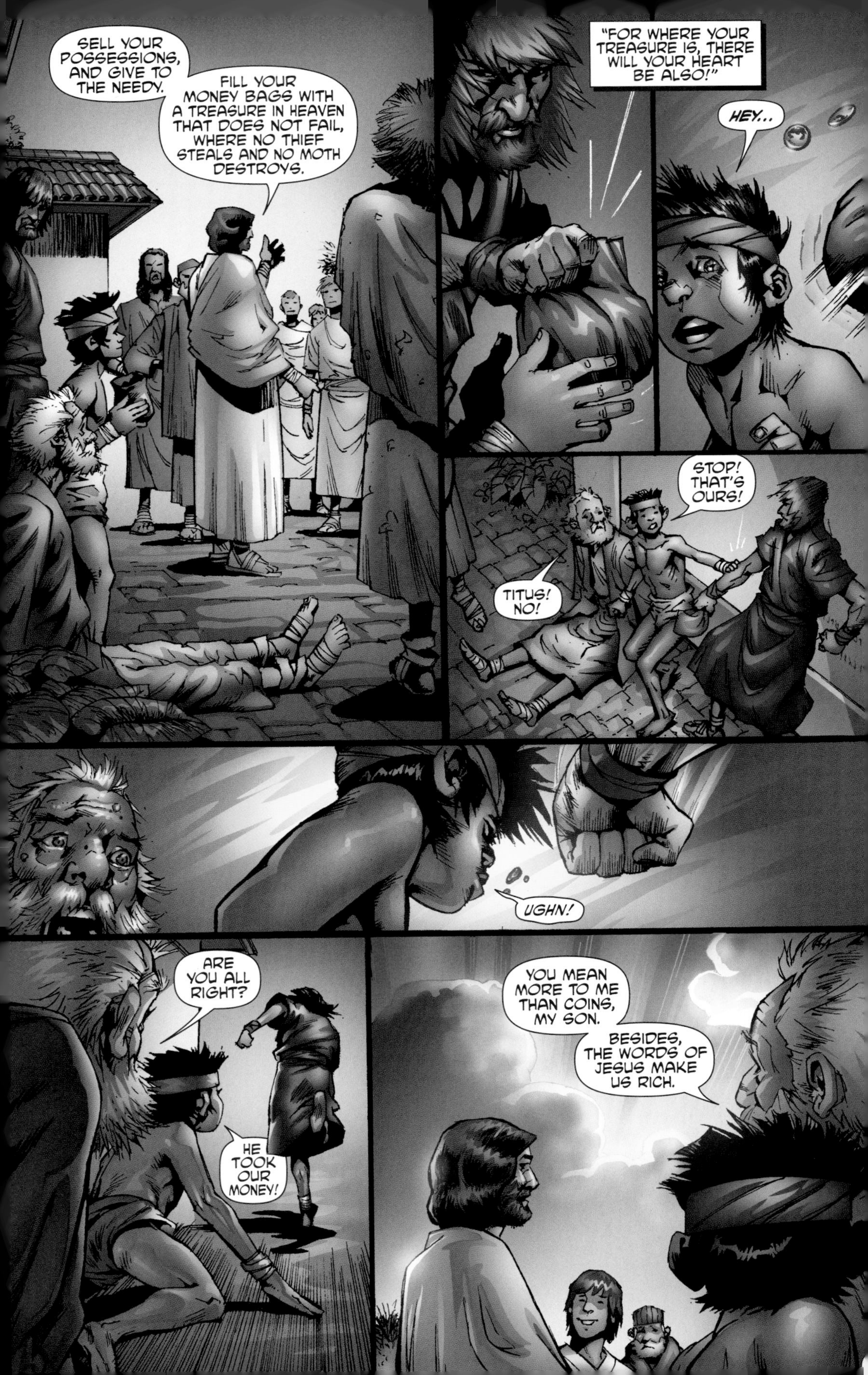
SELL YOUR POSSESSIONS, AND GIVE TO THE NEEDY.
FILL YOUR MONEY BAGS WITH A TREASURE IN HEAVEN THAT DOES NOT FAIL, WHERE NO THIEF STEALS AND NO MOTH DESTROYS.
"FOR WHERE YOUR TREASURE IS, THERE WILL YOUR HEART BE ALSO!"
HEY...
STOP! THAT'S OURS!
TITUS! NO!
UGHN!
ARE YOU ALL RIGHT?
HE TOOK OUR MONEY!
YOU MEAN MORE TO ME THAN COINS, MY SON.
BESIDES, THE WORDS OF JESUS MAKE US RICH.

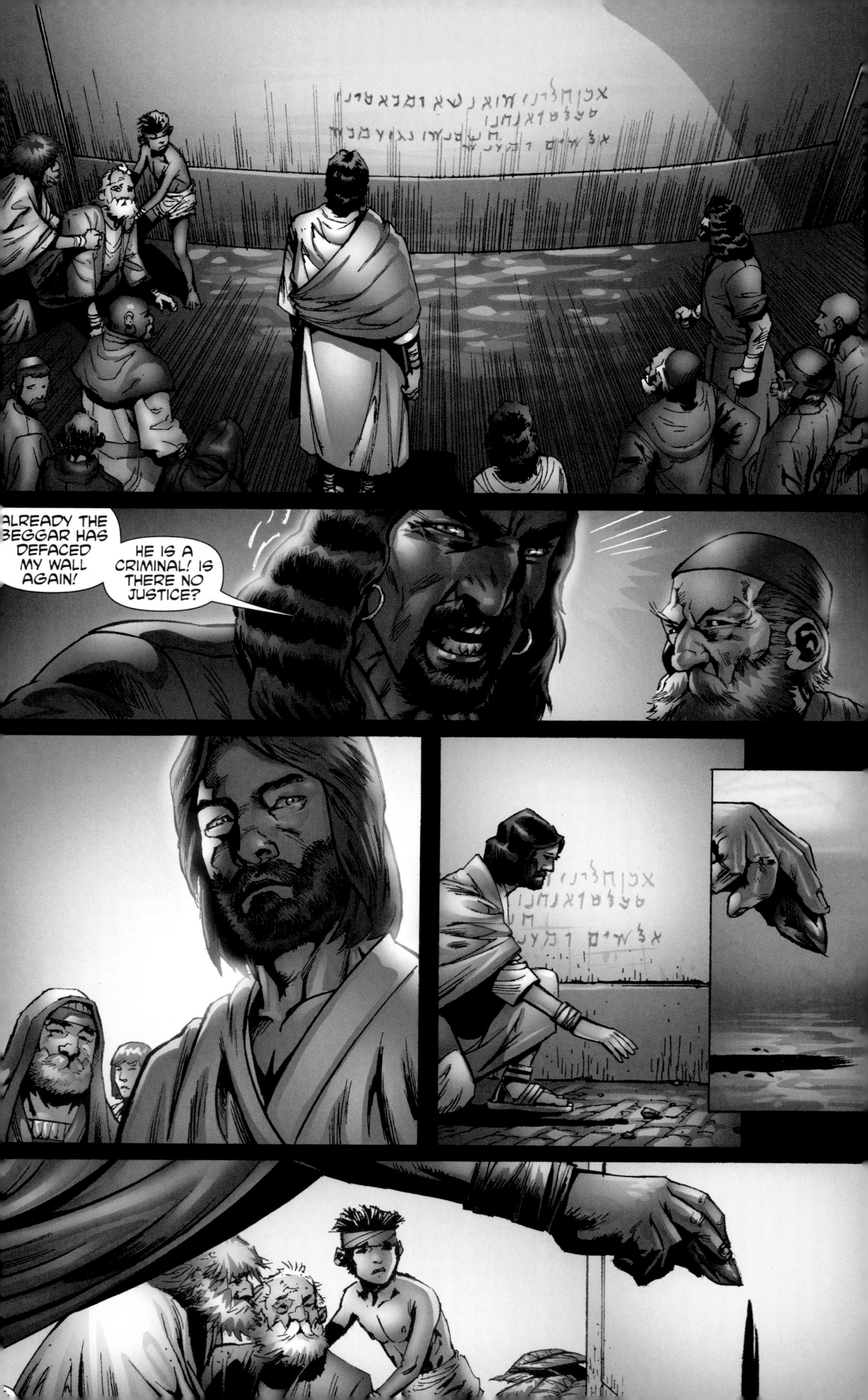
ALREADY THE BEGGAR HAS DEFACED MY WALL AGAIN!
HE IS A CRIMINAL! IS THERE NO JUSTICE?

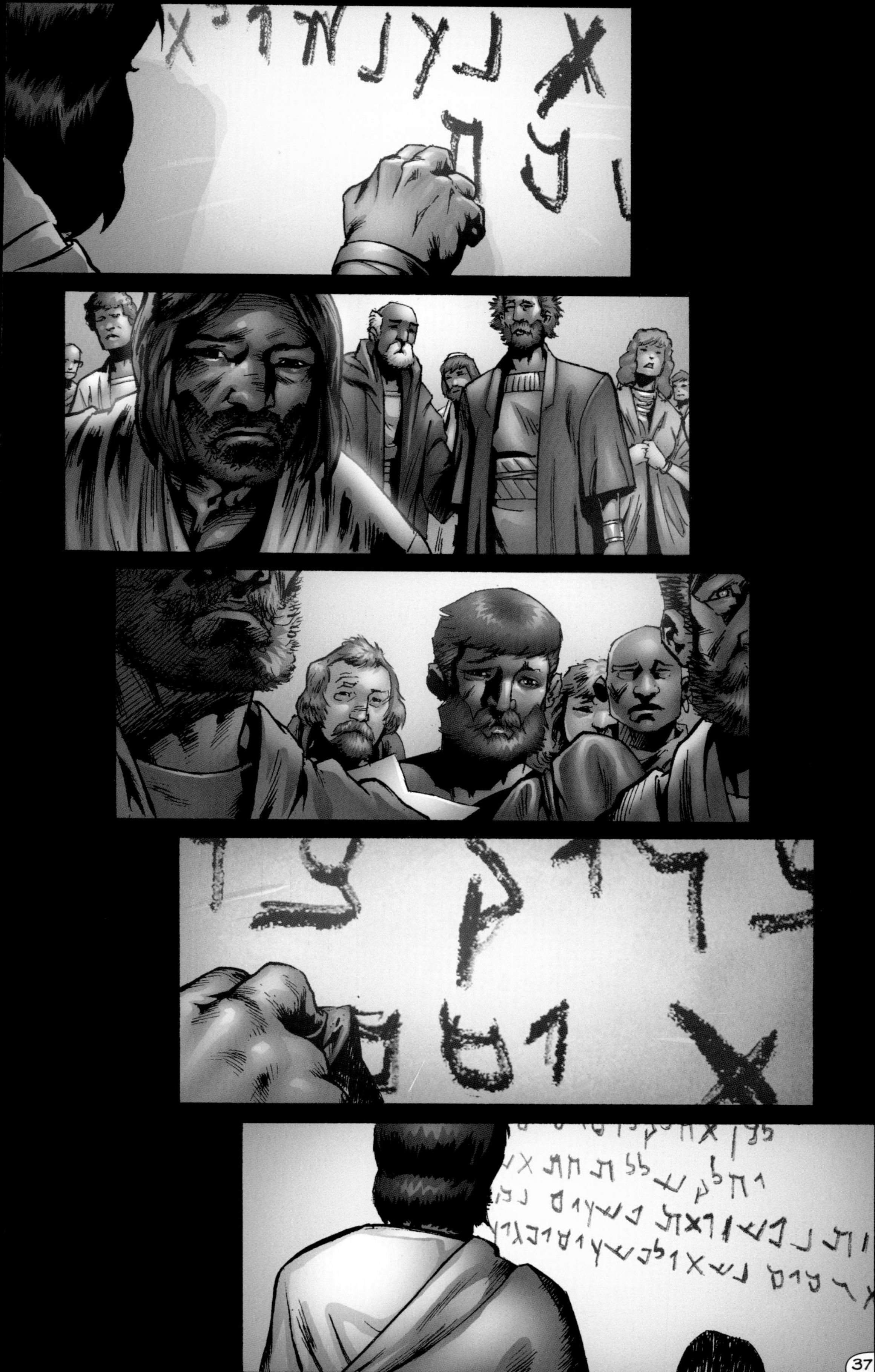

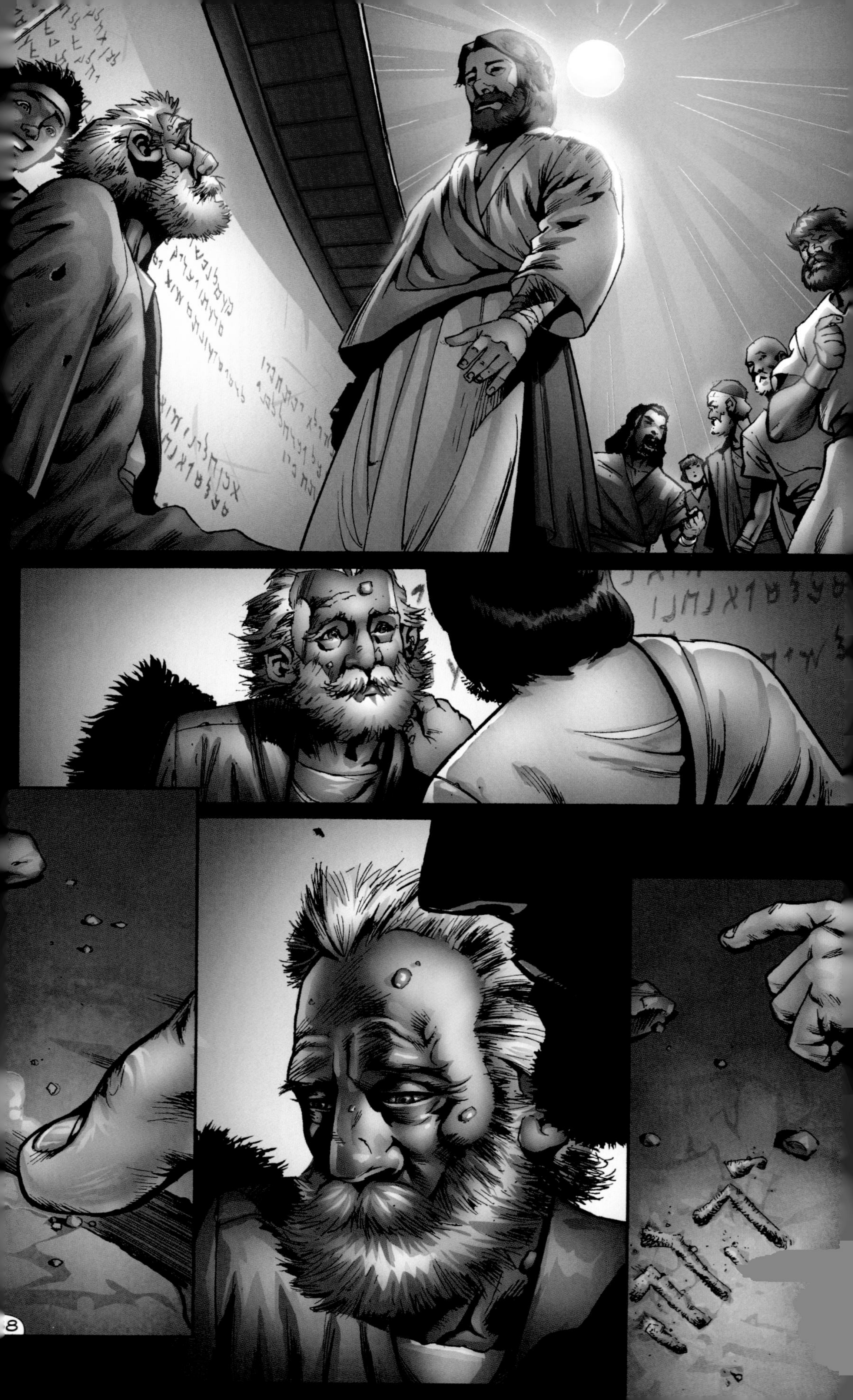

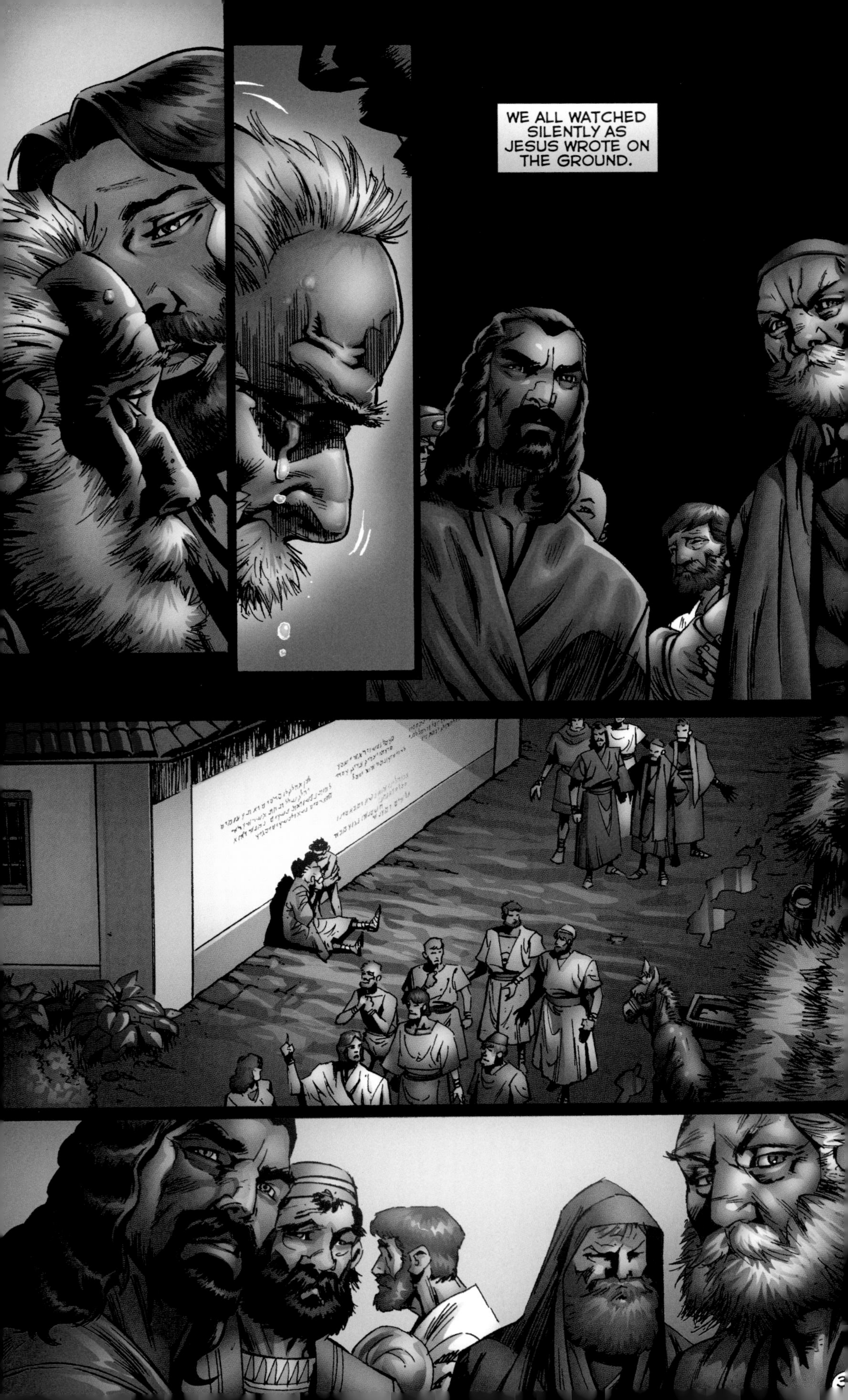
WE ALL WATCHED SILENTLY AS JESUS WROTE ON THE GROUND.

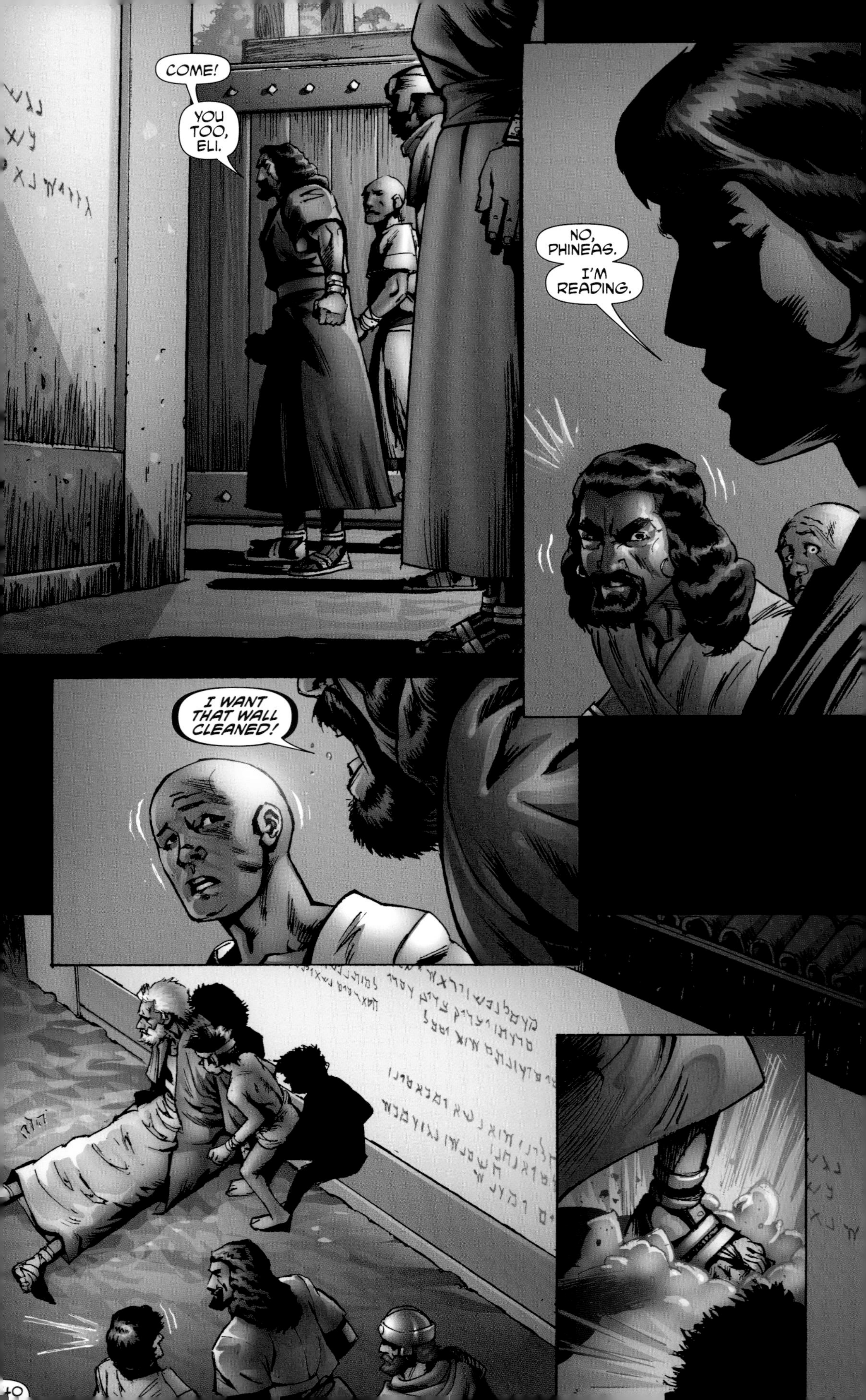
COME!
YOU TOO, ELI.
NO, PHINEAS.
I'M READING.
I WANT THAT WALL CLEANED!

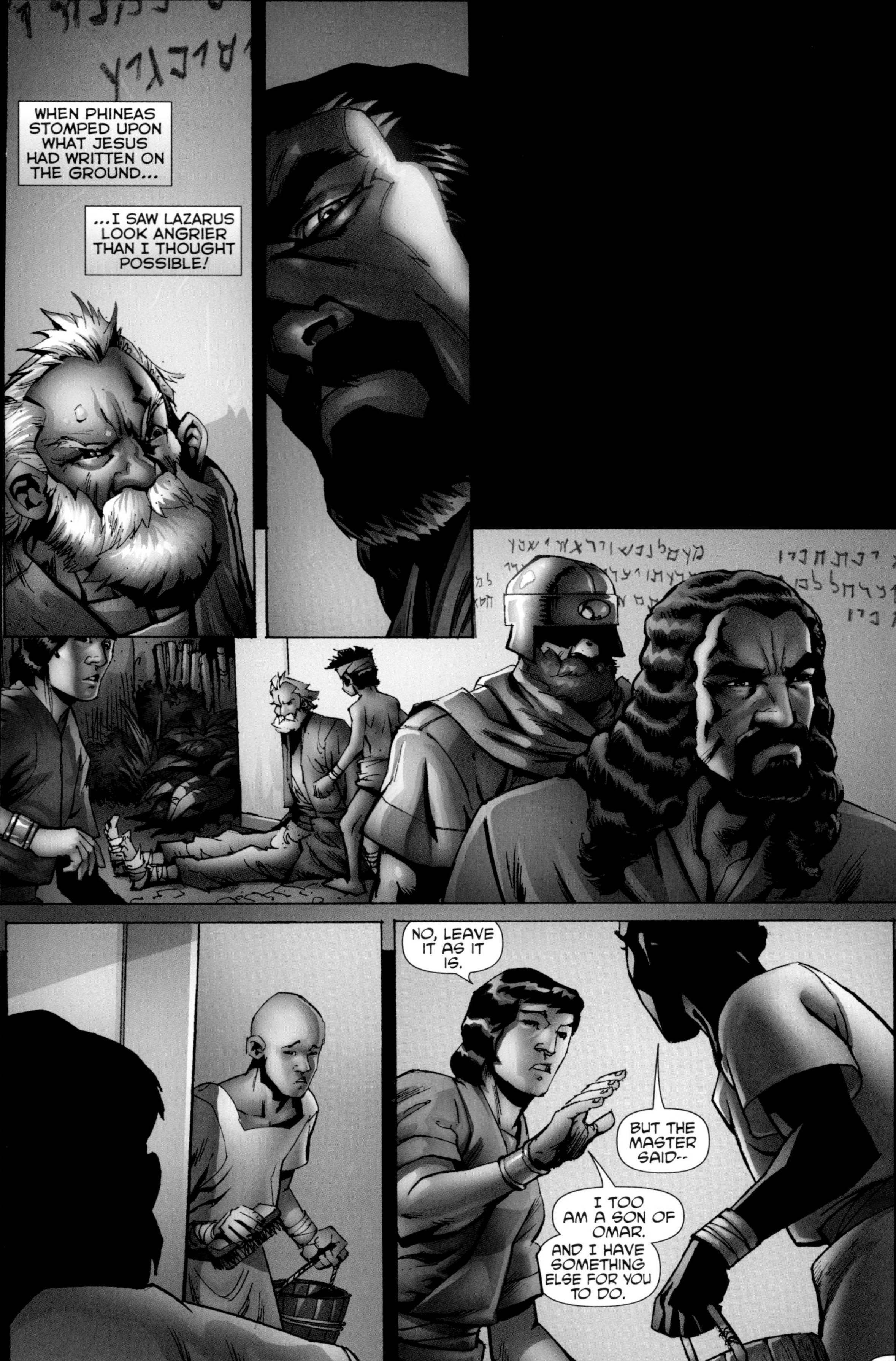
WHEN PHINEAS STOMPED UPON WHAT JESUS HAD WRITTEN ON THE GROUND...
...I SAW LAZARUS LOOK ANGRIER THAN I THOUGHT POSSIBLE!
NO, LEAVE IT AS IT IS.
BUT THE MASTER SAID--
I TOO AM A SON OF OMAR.
AND I HAVE SOMETHING ELSE FOR YOU TO DO.

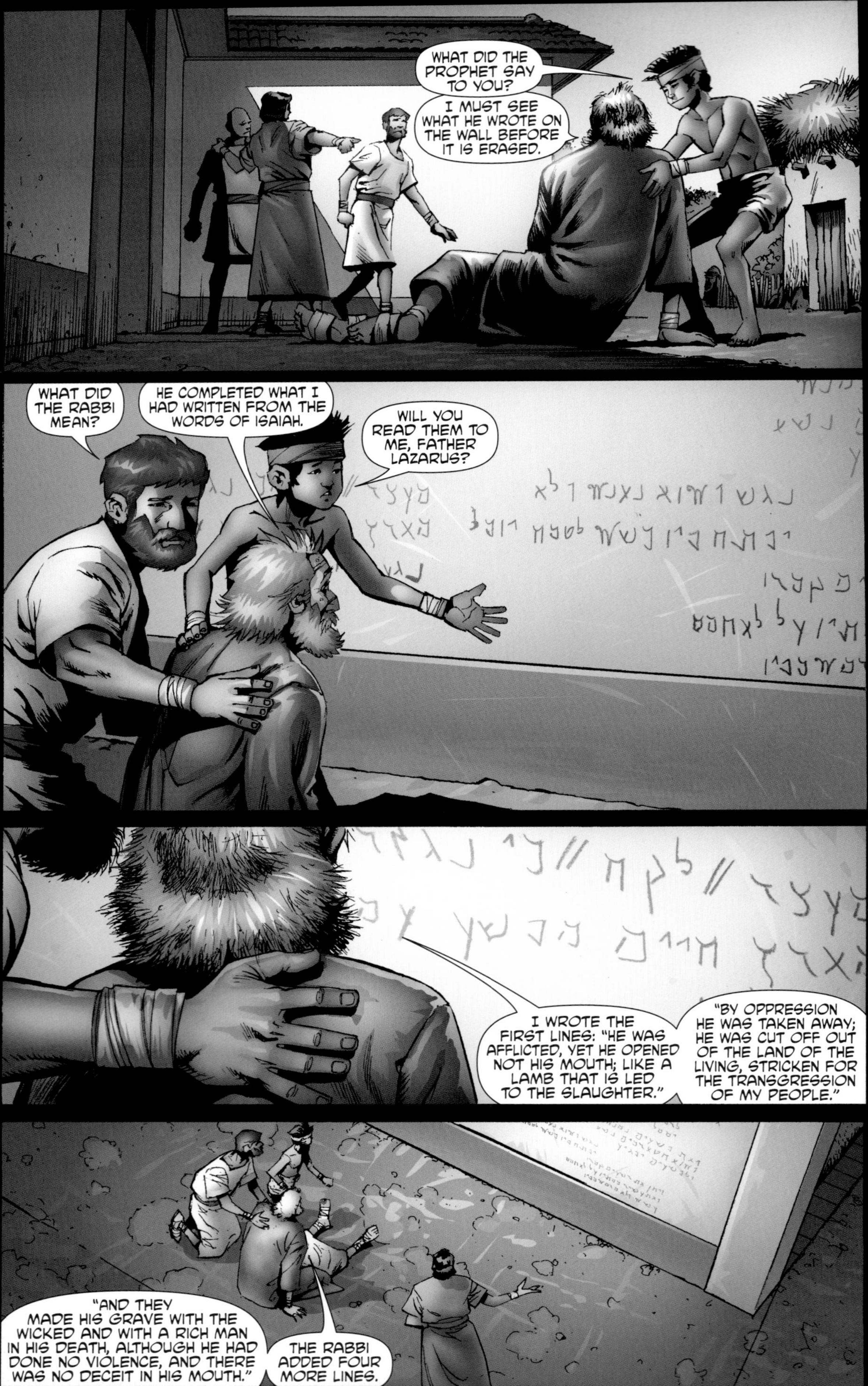
WHAT DID THE PROPHET SAY TO YOU?
I MUST SEE WHAT HE WROTE ON THE WALL BEFORE IT IS ERASED.
WHAT DID THE RABBI MEAN?
HE COMPLETED WHAT I HAD WRITTEN FROM THE WORDS OF ISAIAH.
WILL YOU READ THEM TO ME, FATHER LAZARUS?
I WROTE THE FIRST LINES: "HE WAS AFFLICTED, YET HE OPENED NOT HIS MOUTH; LIKE A LAMB THAT IS LED TO THE SLAUGHTER."
"BY OPPRESSION HE WAS TAKEN AWAY; HE WAS CUT OFF OUT OF THE LAND OF THE LIVING, STRICKEN FOR THE TRANSGRESSION OF MY PEOPLE."
THE RABBI ADDED FOUR MORE LINES.
"AND THEY MADE HIS GRAVE WITH THE WICKED AND WITH A RICH MAN IN HIS DEATH, ALTHOUGH HE HAD DONE NO VIOLENCE, AND THERE WAS NO DECEIT IN HIS MOUTH."

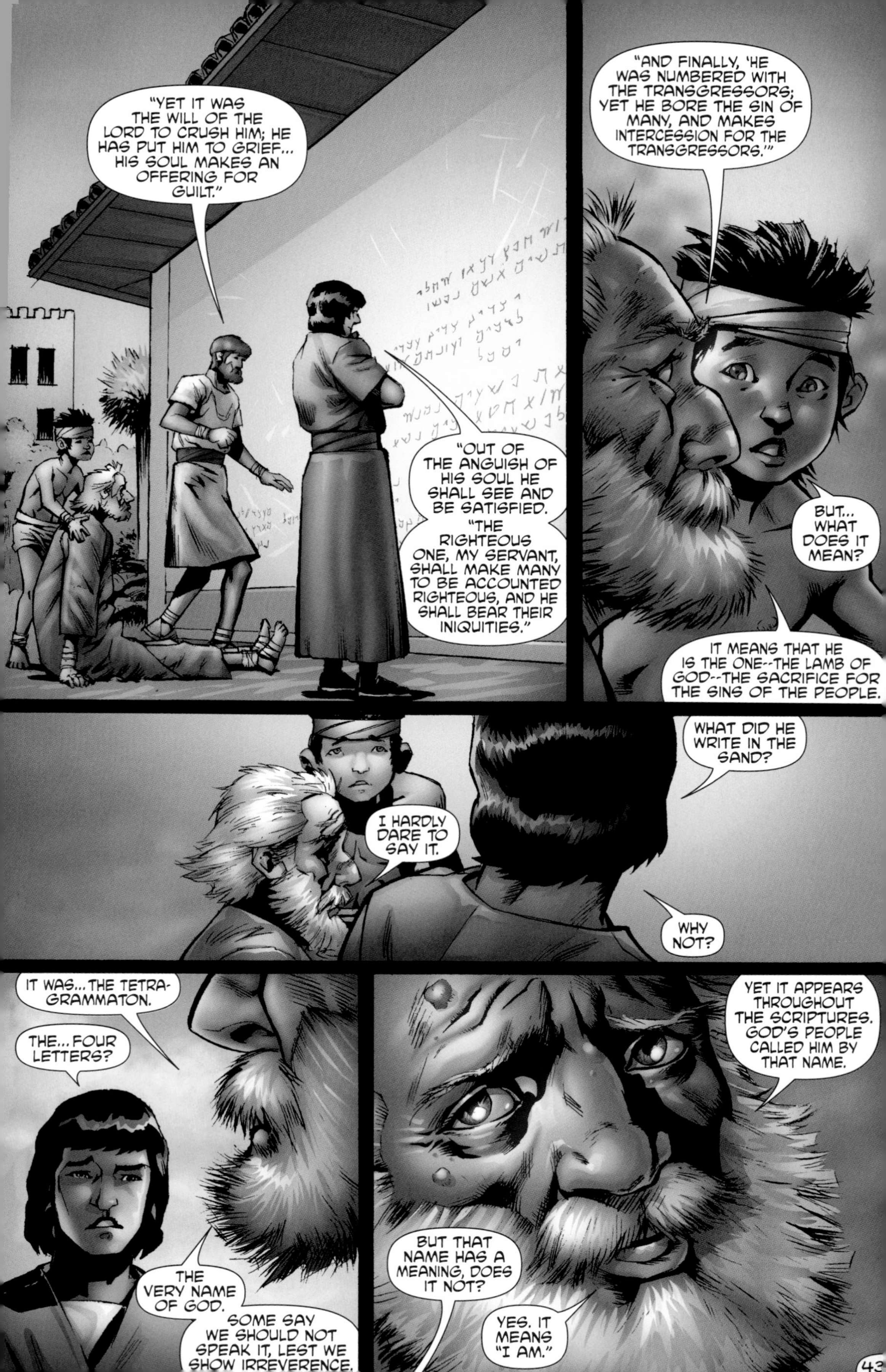
"YET IT WAS THE WILL OF THE LORD TO CRUSH HIM; HE HAS PUT HIM TO GRIEF... HIS SOUL MAKES AN OFFERING FOR GUILT."
"OUT OF THE ANGUISH OF HIS SOUL HE SHALL SEE AND BE SATISFIED.
"THE RIGHTEOUS ONE, MY SERVANT, SHALL MAKE MANY TO BE ACCOUNTED RIGHTEOUS, AND HE SHALL BEAR THEIR INIQUITIES."
"AND FINALLY, 'HE WAS NUMBERED WITH THE TRANSGRESSORS; YET HE BORE THE SIN OF MANY, AND MAKES INTERCESSION FOR THE TRANSGRESSORS.'"
BUT... WHAT DOES IT MEAN?
IT MEANS THAT HE IS THE ONE--THE LAMB OF GOD--THE SACRIFICE FOR THE SINS OF THE PEOPLE.
WHAT DID HE WRITE IN THE SAND?
I HARDLY DARE TO SAY IT.
WHY NOT?
IT WAS... THE TETRA-GRAMMATON.
THE... FOUR LETTERS?
THE VERY NAME OF GOD.
SOME SAY WE SHOULD NOT SPEAK IT, LEST WE SHOW IRREVERENCE.
YET IT APPEARS THROUGHOUT THE SCRIPTURES. GOD'S PEOPLE CALLED HIM BY THAT NAME.
BUT THAT NAME HAS A MEANING, DOES IT NOT?
YES. IT MEANS "I AM."

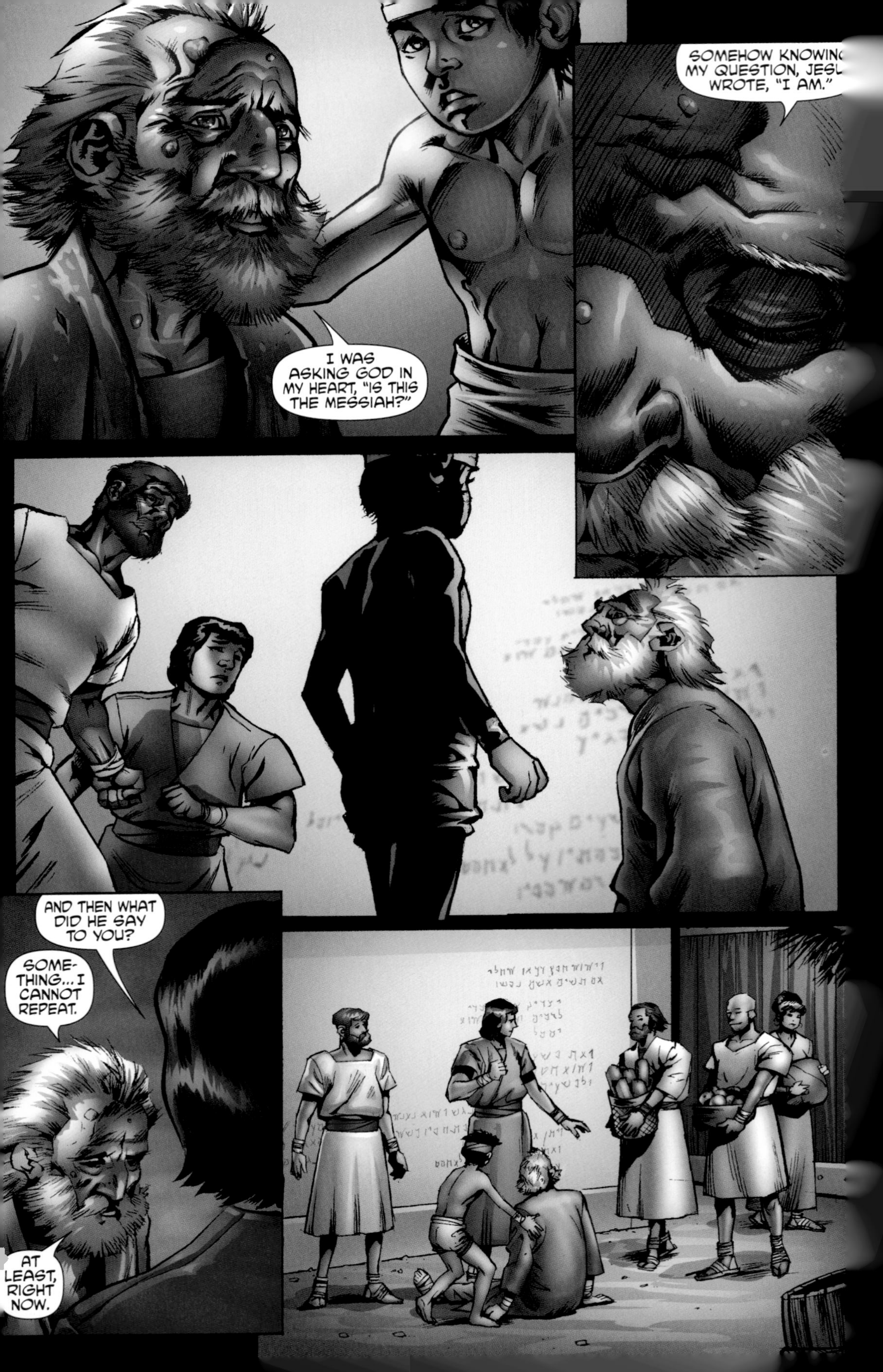
SOMEHOW KNOWING MY QUESTION, JESU WROTE, "I AM."
I WAS ASKING GOD IN MY HEART, "IS THIS THE MESSIAH?"
AND THEN WHAT DID HE SAY TO YOU?
SOME-THING... I CANNOT REPEAT.
AT LEAST, RIGHT NOW.

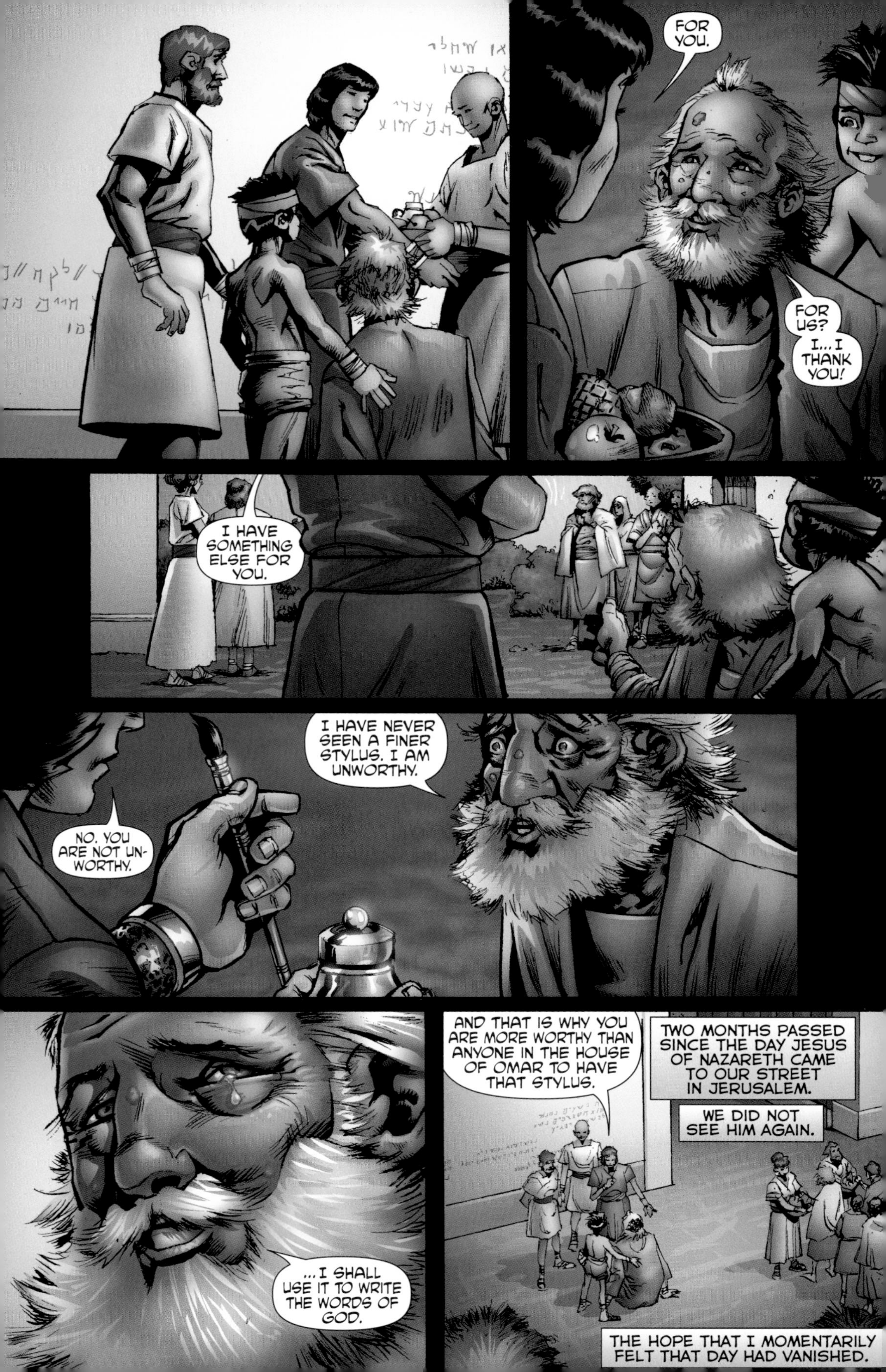
FOR YOU.
FOR US? I... I THANK YOU!
I HAVE SOMETHING ELSE FOR YOU.
I HAVE NEVER SEEN A FINER STYLUS. I AM UNWORTHY.
NO. YOU ARE NOT UN-WORTHY.
...I SHALL USE IT TO WRITE THE WORDS OF GOD.
AND THAT IS WHY YOU ARE MORE WORTHY THAN ANYONE IN THE HOUSE OF OMAR TO HAVE THAT STYLUS.
TWO MONTHS PASSED SINCE THE DAY JESUS OF NAZARETH CAME TO OUR STREET IN JERUSALEM.
WE DID NOT SEE HIM AGAIN.
THE HOPE THAT I MOMENTARILY FELT THAT DAY HAD VANISHED.

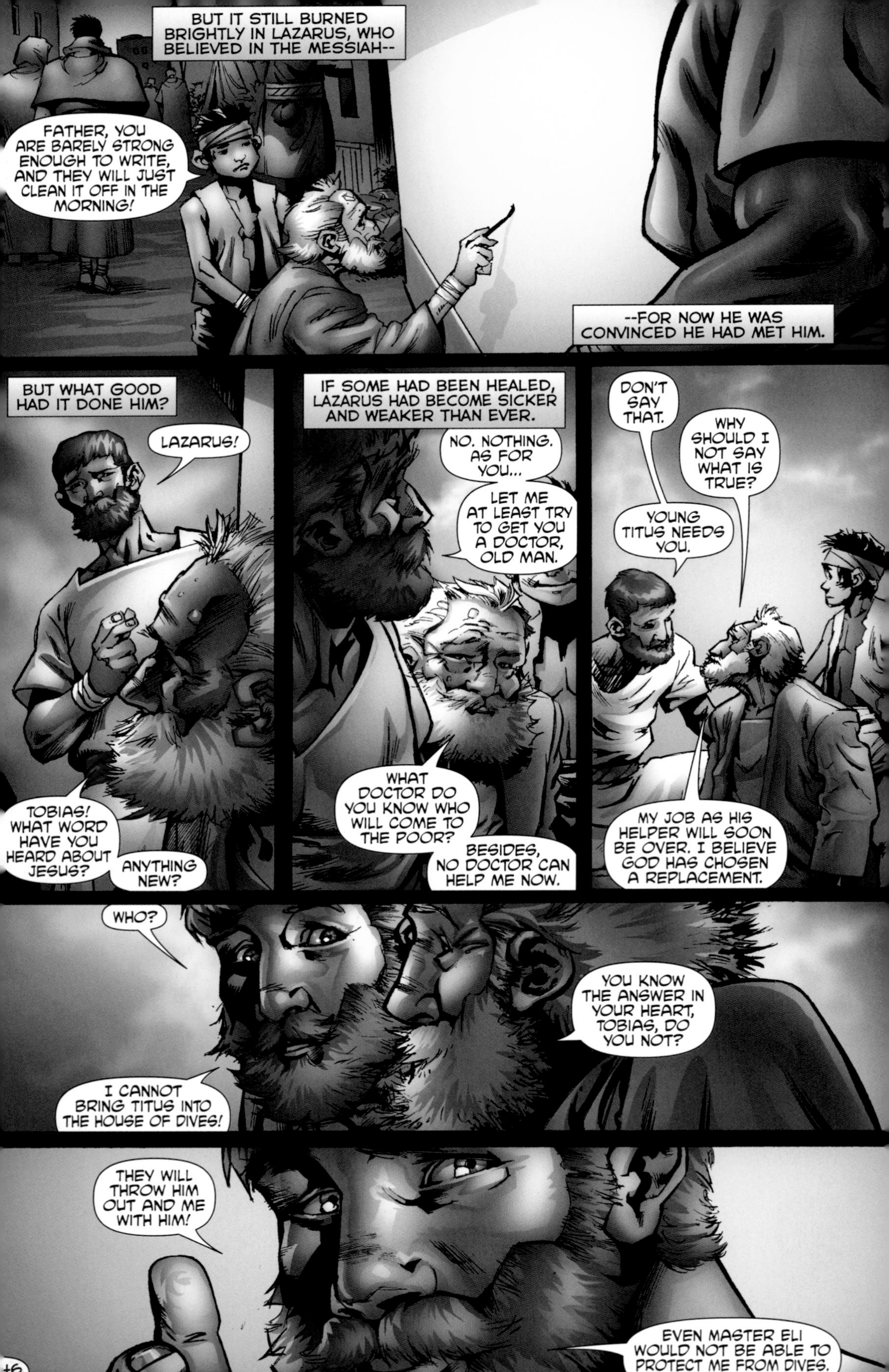

BUT IT STILL BURNED BRIGHTLY IN LAZARUS, WHO BELIEVED IN THE MESSIAH--
FATHER, YOU ARE BARELY STRONG ENOUGH TO WRITE, AND THEY WILL JUST CLEAN IT OFF IN THE MORNING!
--FOR NOW HE WAS CONVINCED HE HAD MET HIM.
BUT WHAT GOOD HAD IT DONE HIM?
LAZARUS!
TOBIAS! WHAT WORD HAVE YOU HEARD ABOUT JESUS?
ANYTHING NEW?
IF SOME HAD BEEN HEALED, LAZARUS HAD BECOME SICKER AND WEAKER THAN EVER.
NO. NOTHING. AS FOR YOU...
LET ME AT LEAST TRY TO GET YOU A DOCTOR, OLD MAN.
WHAT DOCTOR DO YOU KNOW WHO WILL COME TO THE POOR?
BESIDES, NO DOCTOR CAN HELP ME NOW.
DON'T SAY THAT.
WHY SHOULD I NOT SAY WHAT IS TRUE?
YOUNG TITUS NEEDS YOU.
MY JOB AS HIS HELPER WILL SOON BE OVER. I BELIEVE GOD HAS CHOSEN A REPLACEMENT.
WHO?
YOU KNOW THE ANSWER IN YOUR HEART, TOBIAS, DO YOU NOT?
I CANNOT BRING TITUS INTO THE HOUSE OF DIVES!
THEY WILL THROW HIM OUT AND ME WITH HIM!
EVEN MASTER ELI WOULD NOT BE ABLE TO PROTECT ME FROM DIVES.

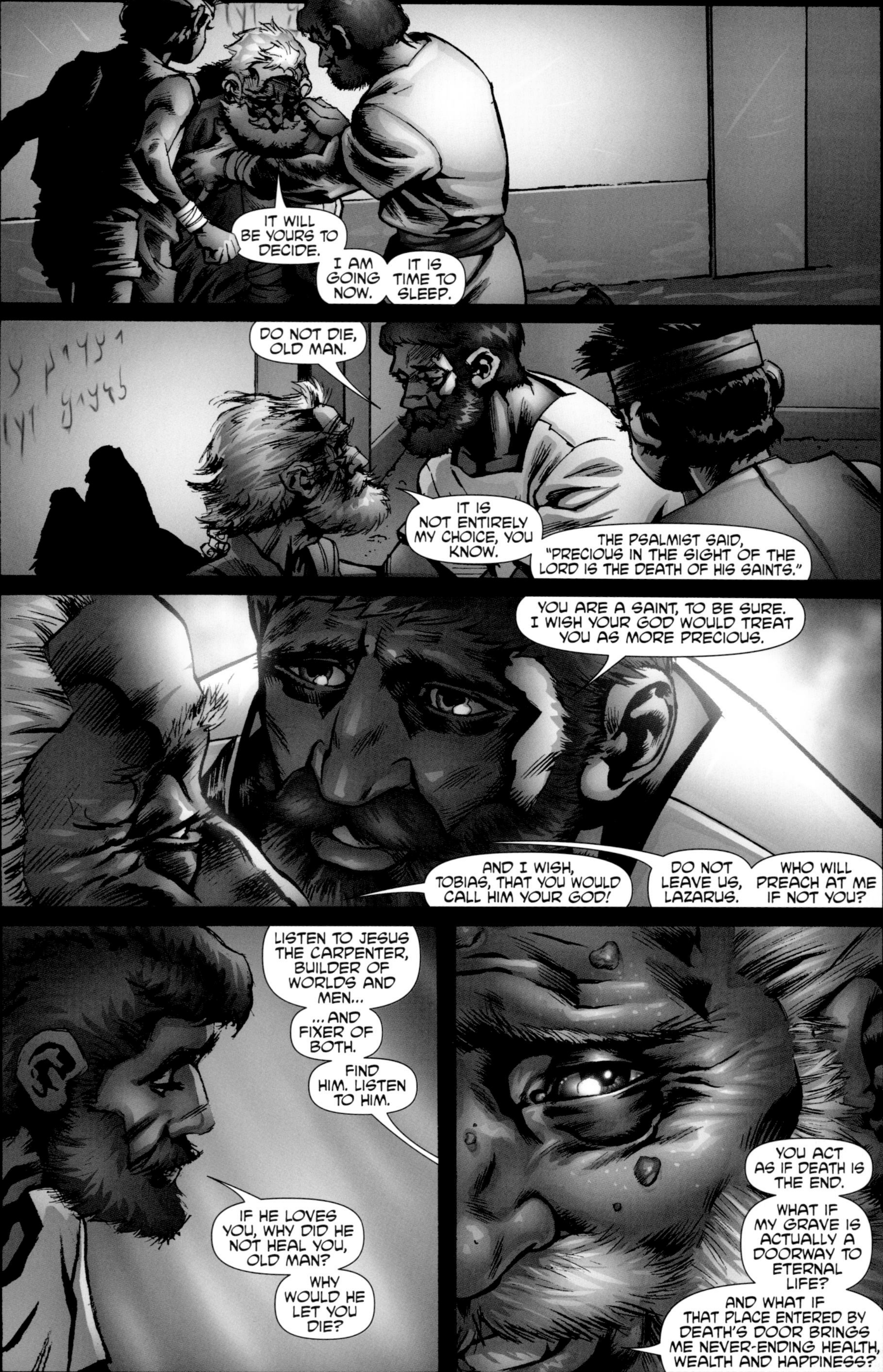
IT WILL BE YOURS TO DECIDE.
I AM GOING NOW.
IT IS TIME TO SLEEP.
DO NOT DIE, OLD MAN.
IT IS NOT ENTIRELY MY CHOICE, YOU KNOW.
THE PSALMIST SAID, "PRECIOUS IN THE SIGHT OF THE LORD IS THE DEATH OF HIS SAINTS."
YOU ARE A SAINT, TO BE SURE. I WISH YOUR GOD WOULD TREAT YOU AS MORE PRECIOUS.
AND I WISH, TOBIAS, THAT YOU WOULD CALL HIM YOUR GOD!
DO NOT LEAVE US, LAZARUS.
WHO WILL PREACH AT ME IF NOT YOU?
LISTEN TO JESUS THE CARPENTER, BUILDER OF WORLDS AND MEN...
...AND FIXER OF BOTH.
FIND HIM. LISTEN TO HIM.
IF HE LOVES YOU, WHY DID HE NOT HEAL YOU, OLD MAN?
WHY WOULD HE LET YOU DIE?
YOU ACT AS IF DEATH IS THE END.
WHAT IF MY GRAVE IS ACTUALLY A DOORWAY TO ETERNAL LIFE?
AND WHAT IF THAT PLACE ENTERED BY DEATH'S DOOR BRINGS ME NEVER-ENDING HEALTH, WEALTH AND HAPPINESS?

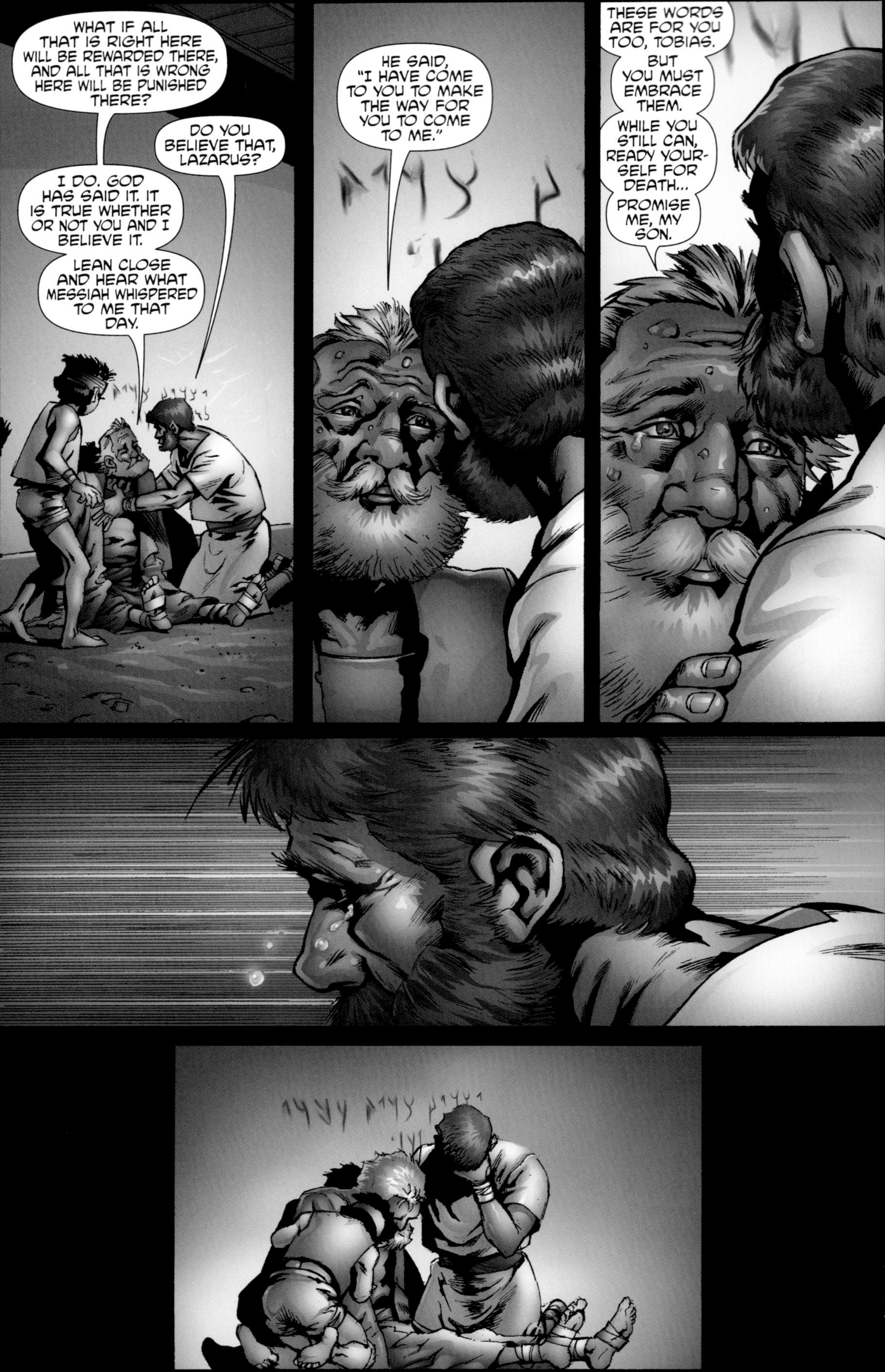

WHAT IF ALL THAT IS RIGHT HERE WILL BE REWARDED THERE, AND ALL THAT IS WRONG HERE WILL BE PUNISHED THERE?
DO YOU BELIEVE THAT, LAZARUS?
I DO. GOD HAS SAID IT. IT IS TRUE WHETHER OR NOT YOU AND I BELIEVE IT.
LEAN CLOSE AND HEAR WHAT MESSIAH WHISPERED TO ME THAT DAY.
HE SAID, "I HAVE COME TO YOU TO MAKE THE WAY FOR YOU TO COME TO ME."
THESE WORDS ARE FOR YOU TOO, TOBIAS.
BUT YOU MUST EMBRACE THEM.
WHILE YOU STILL CAN, READY YOUR-SELF FOR DEATH...
PROMISE ME, MY SON.

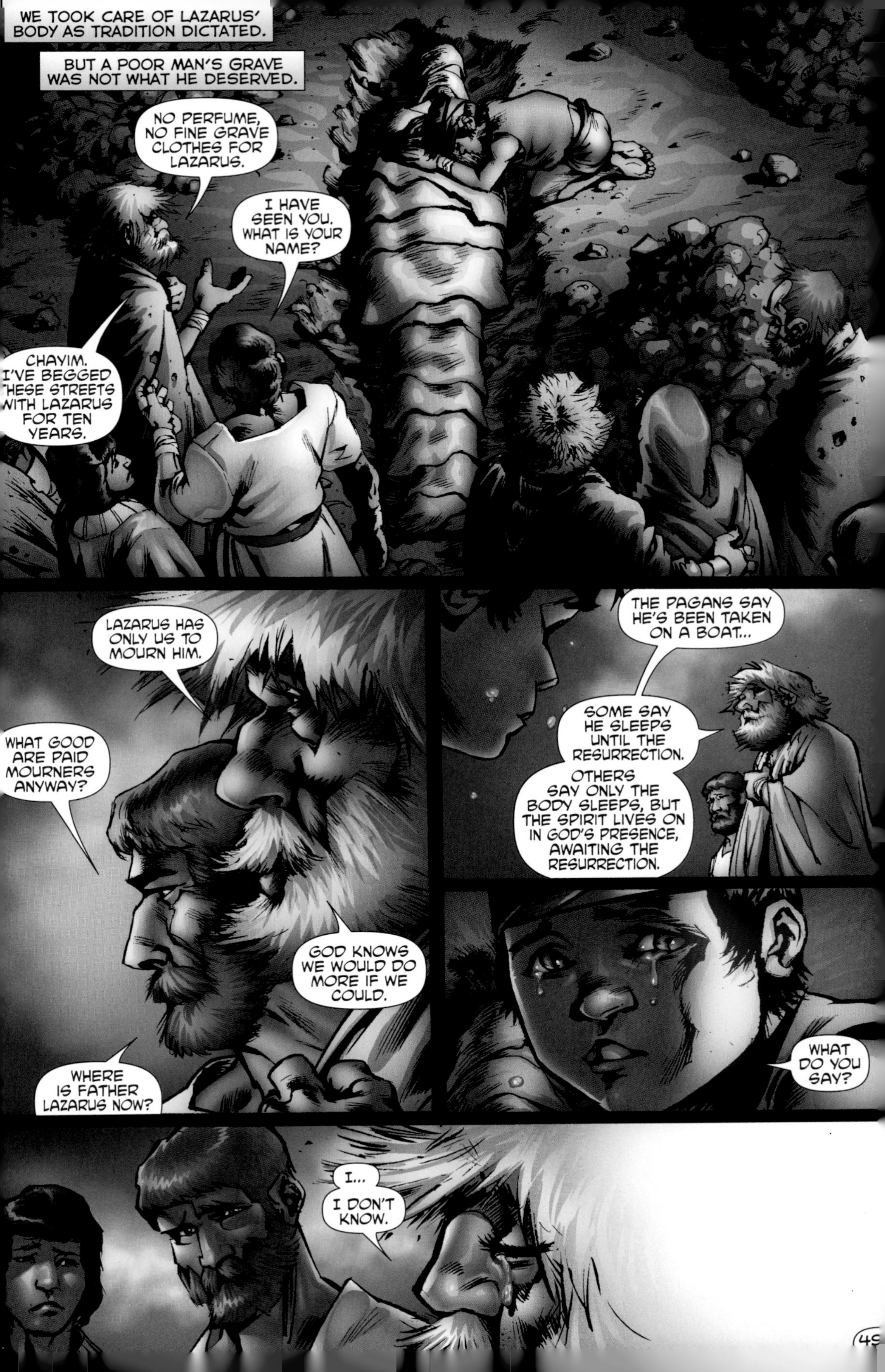

WE TOOK CARE OF LAZARUS' BODY AS TRADITION DICTATED.
BUT A POOR MAN'S GRAVE WAS NOT WHAT HE DESERVED.
NO PERFUME, NO FINE GRAVE CLOTHES FOR LAZARUS.
I HAVE SEEN YOU. WHAT IS YOUR NAME?
CHAYIM. I'VE BEGGED THESE STREETS WITH LAZARUS FOR TEN YEARS.
LAZARUS HAS ONLY US TO MOURN HIM.
WHAT GOOD ARE PAID MOURNERS ANYWAY?
GOD KNOWS WE WOULD DO MORE IF WE COULD.
WHERE IS FATHER LAZARUS NOW?
THE PAGANS SAY HE'S BEEN TAKEN ON A BOAT...
SOME SAY HE SLEEPS UNTIL THE RESURRECTION.
OTHERS SAY ONLY THE BODY SLEEPS, BUT THE SPIRIT LIVES ON IN GOD'S PRESENCE, AWAITING THE RESURRECTION.
WHAT DO YOU SAY?
I... I DON'T KNOW.

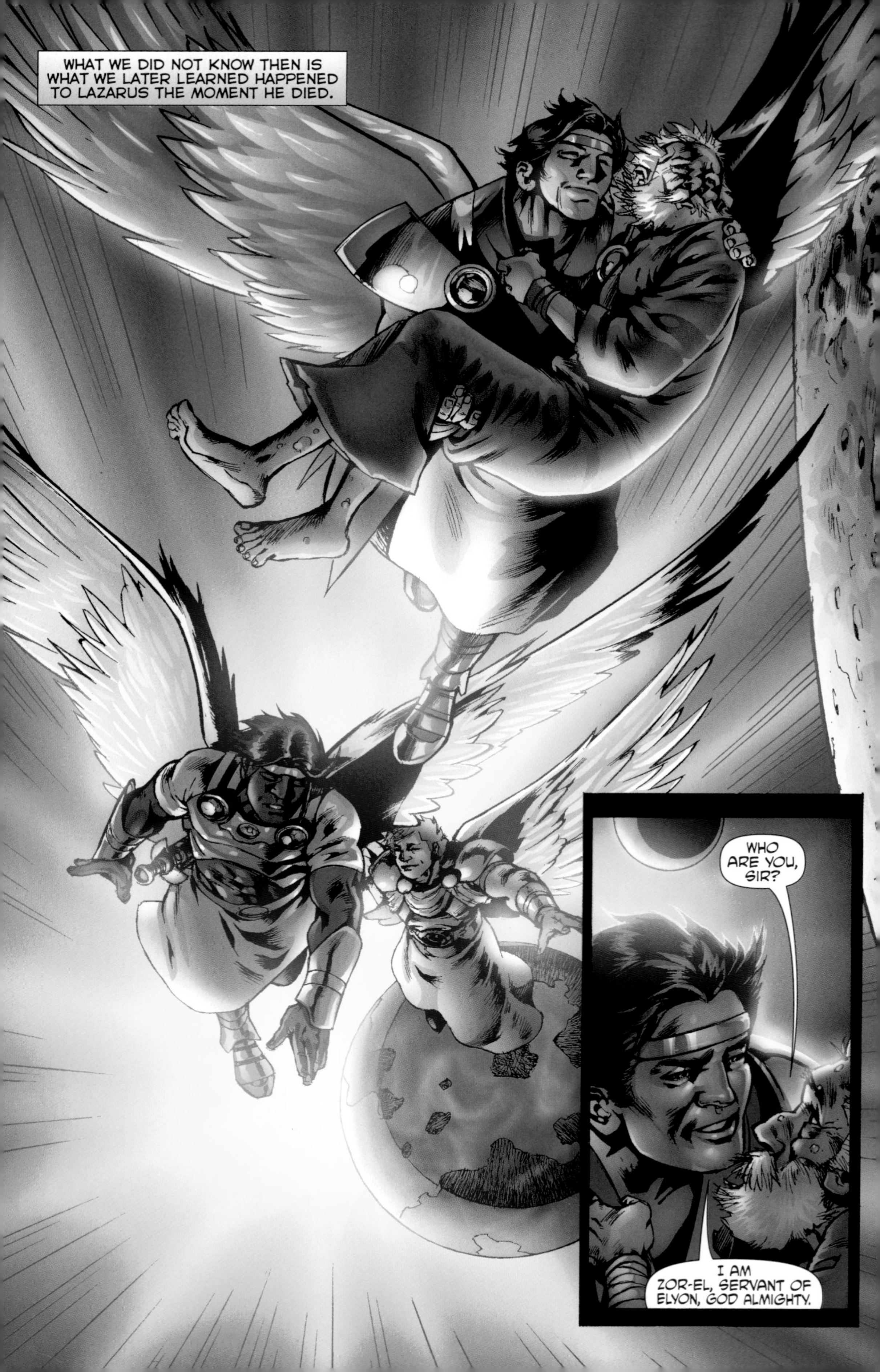
WHAT WE DID NOT KNOW THEN IS WHAT WE LATER LEARNED HAPPENED TO LAZARUS THE MOMENT HE DIED.
WHO ARE YOU, SIR?
I AM ZOR-EL, SERVANT OF ELYON, GOD ALMIGHTY.

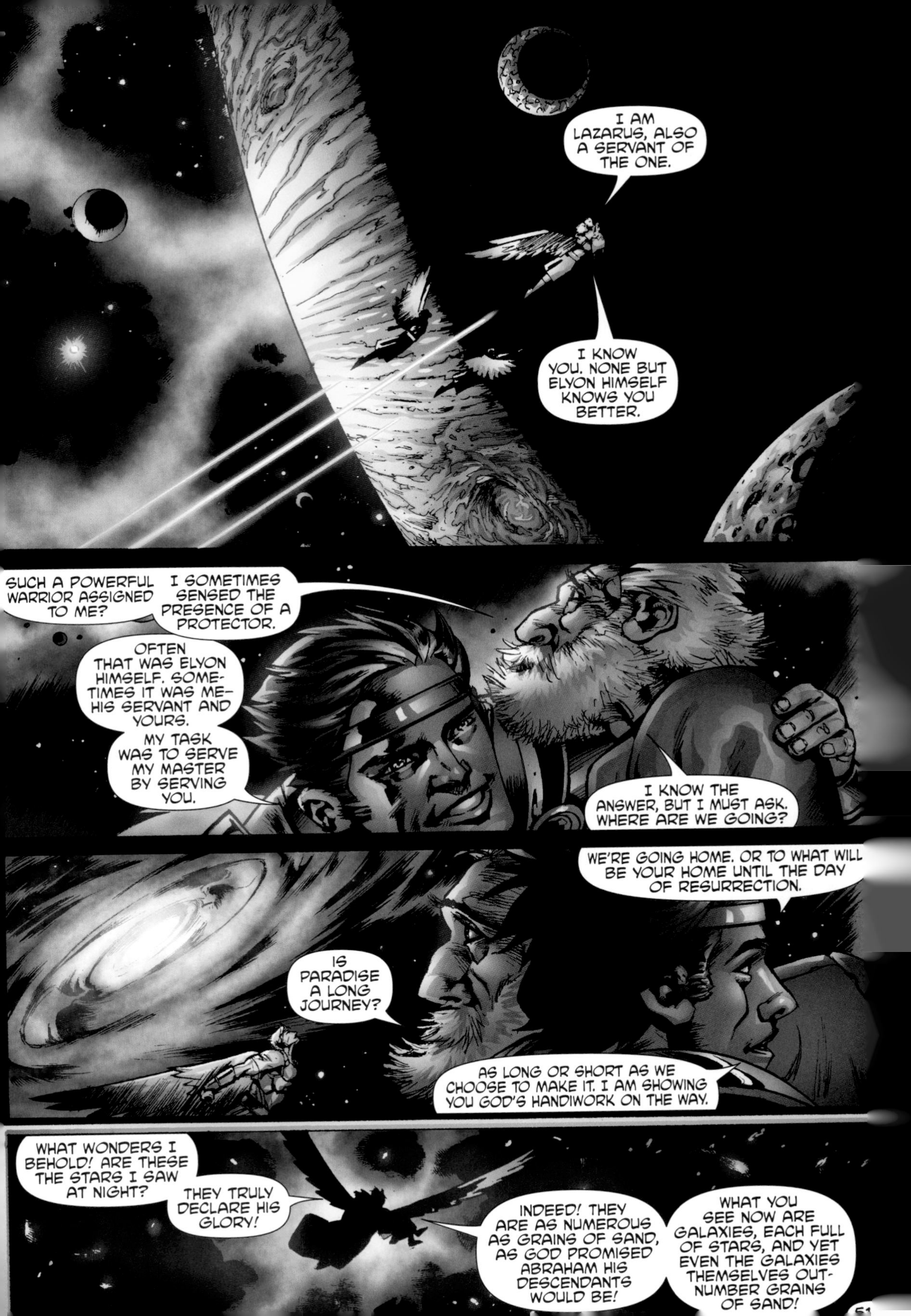
I AM LAZARUS, ALSO A SERVANT OF THE ONE.
I KNOW YOU. NONE BUT ELYON HIMSELF KNOWS YOU BETTER.
SUCH A POWERFUL WARRIOR ASSIGNED TO ME?
I SOMETIMES SENSED THE PRESENCE OF A PROTECTOR.
OFTEN THAT WAS ELYON HIMSELF. SOMETIMES IT WAS ME–HIS SERVANT AND YOURS.
MY TASK WAS TO SERVE MY MASTER BY SERVING YOU.
I KNOW THE ANSWER, BUT I MUST ASK. WHERE ARE WE GOING?
WE'RE GOING HOME. OR TO WHAT WILL BE YOUR HOME UNTIL THE DAY OF RESURRECTION.
IS PARADISE A LONG JOURNEY?
AS LONG OR SHORT AS WE CHOOSE TO MAKE IT. I AM SHOWING YOU GOD'S HANDIWORK ON THE WAY.
WHAT WONDERS I BEHOLD! ARE THESE THE STARS I SAW AT NIGHT?
THEY TRULY DECLARE HIS GLORY!
INDEED! THEY ARE AS NUMEROUS AS GRAINS OF SAND, AS GOD PROMISED ABRAHAM HIS DESCENDANTS WOULD BE!
WHAT YOU SEE NOW ARE GALAXIES, EACH FULL OF STARS, AND YET EVEN THE GALAXIES THEMSELVES OUT-NUMBER GRAINS OF SAND!

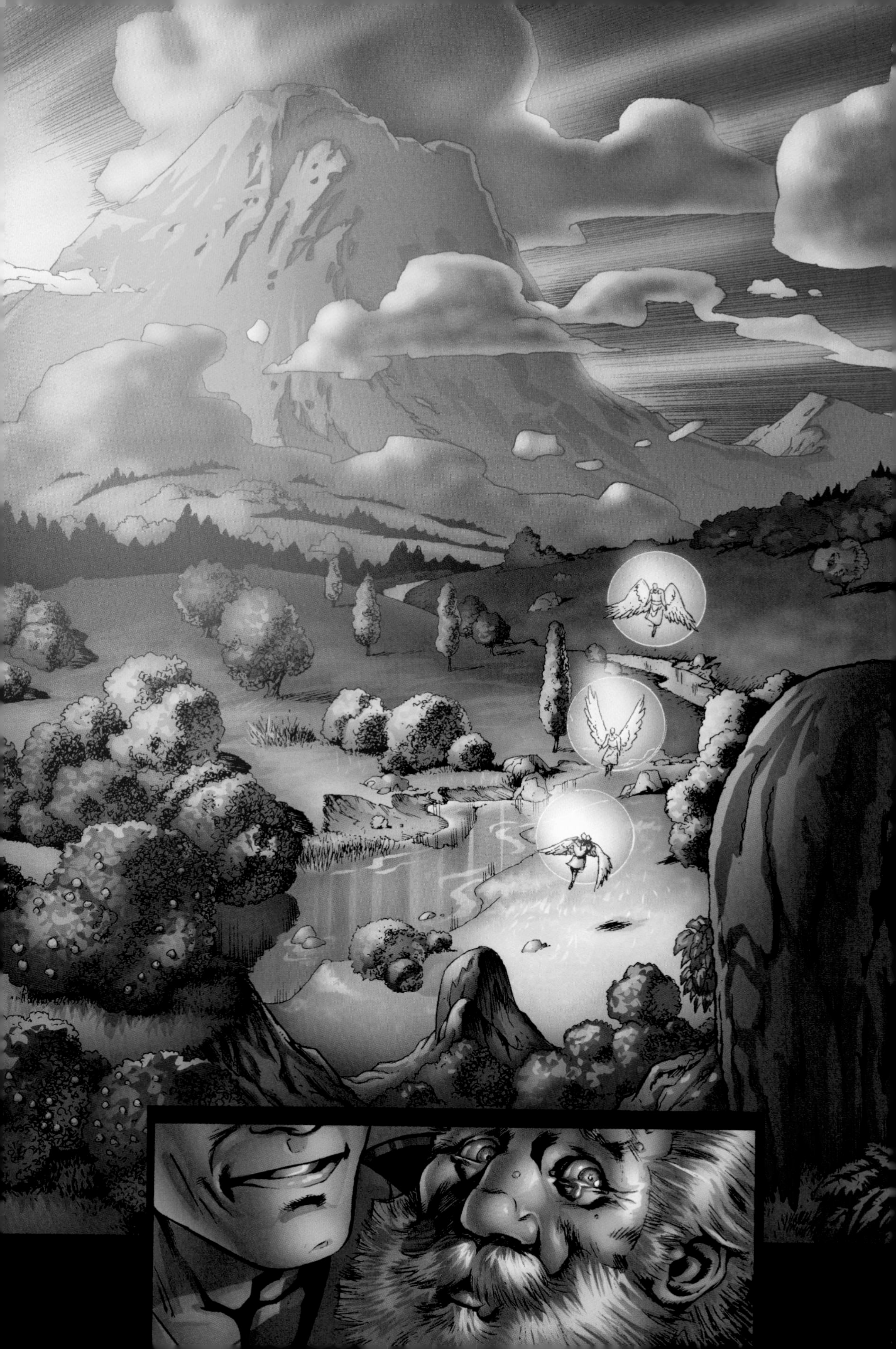

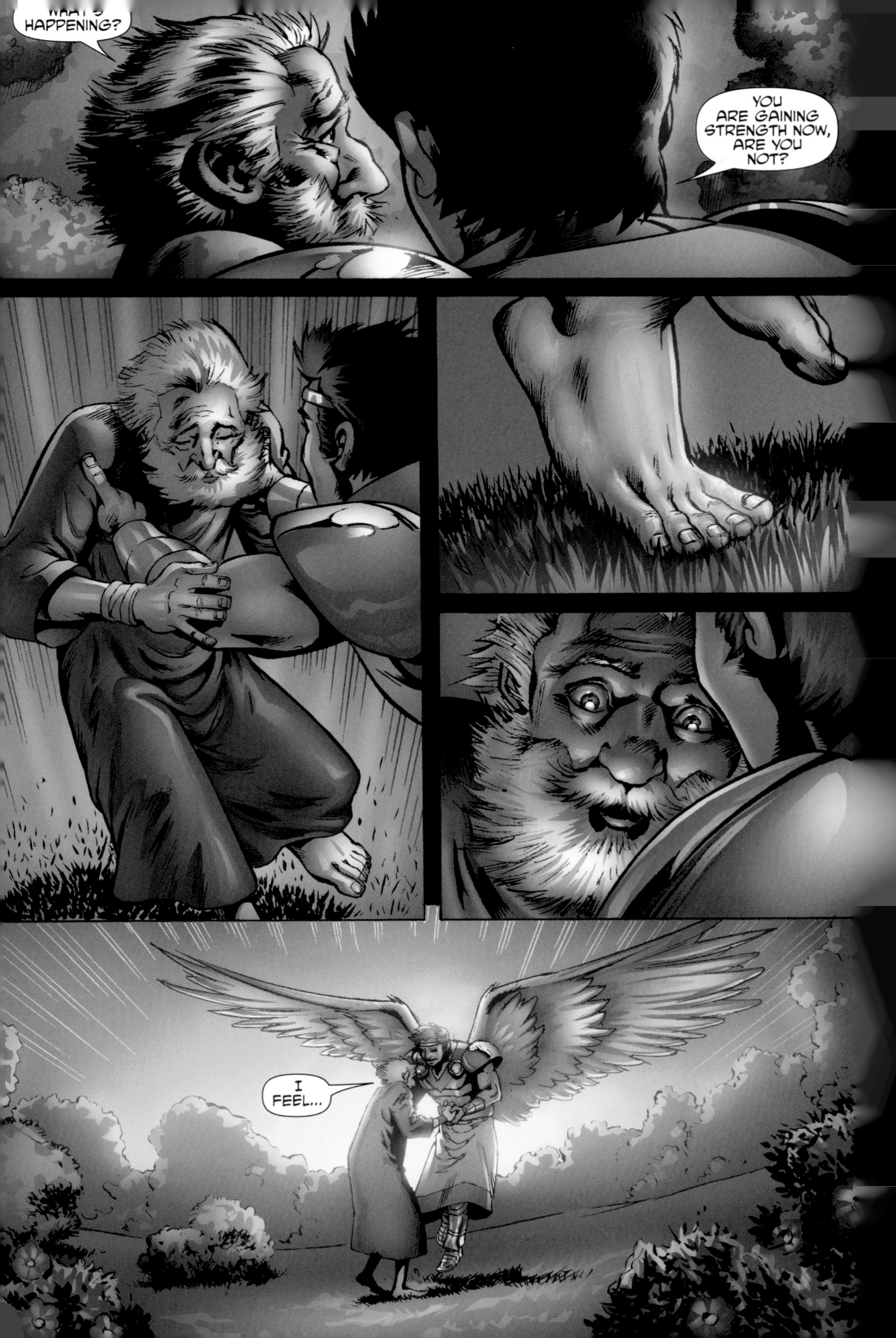
HAPPENING?
YOU ARE GAINING STRENGTH NOW, ARE YOU NOT?
I FEEL...

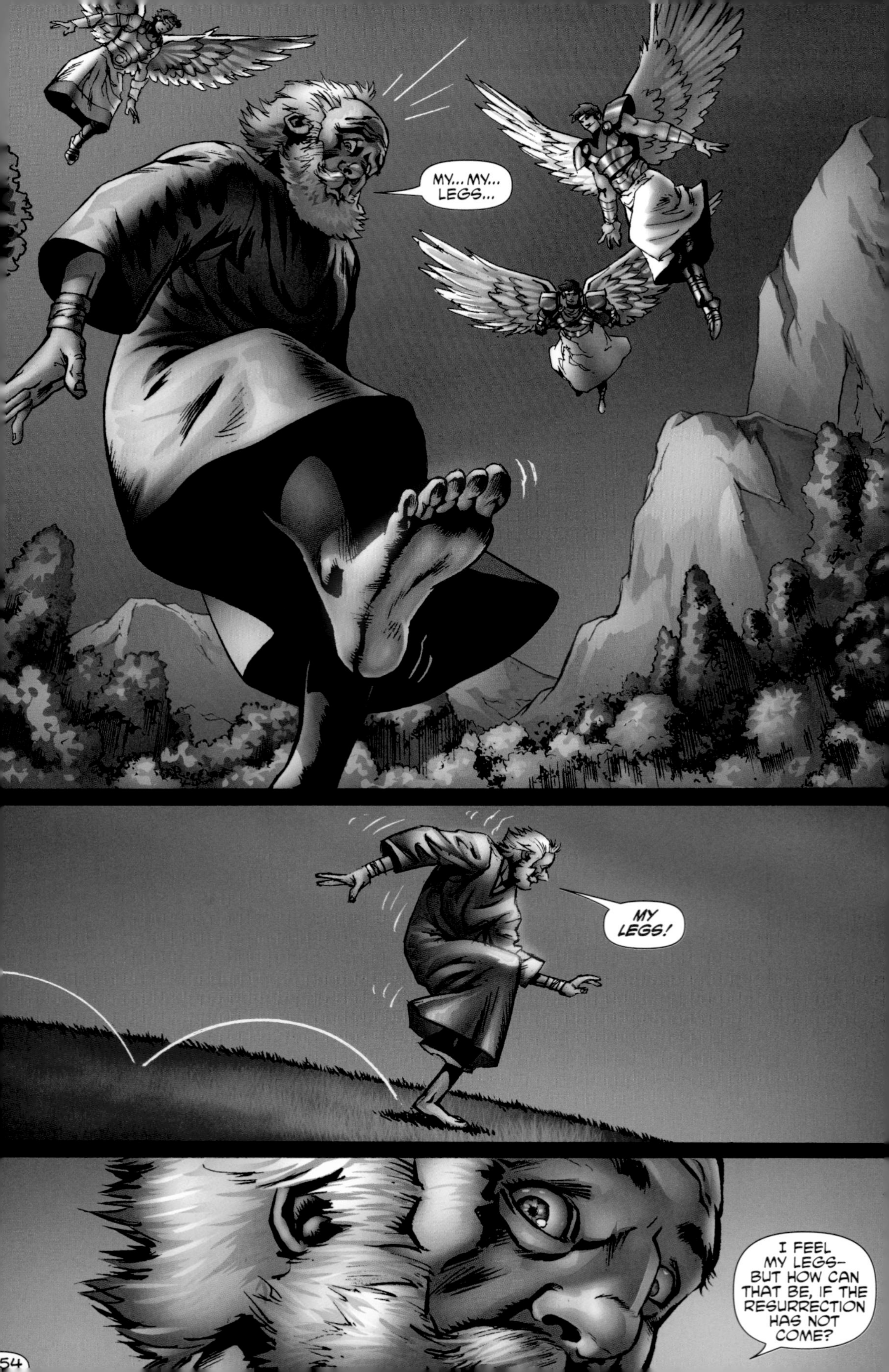
MY... MY... LEGS...
MY LEGS!
I FEEL MY LEGS– BUT HOW CAN THAT BE, IF THE RESURRECTION HAS NOT COME?

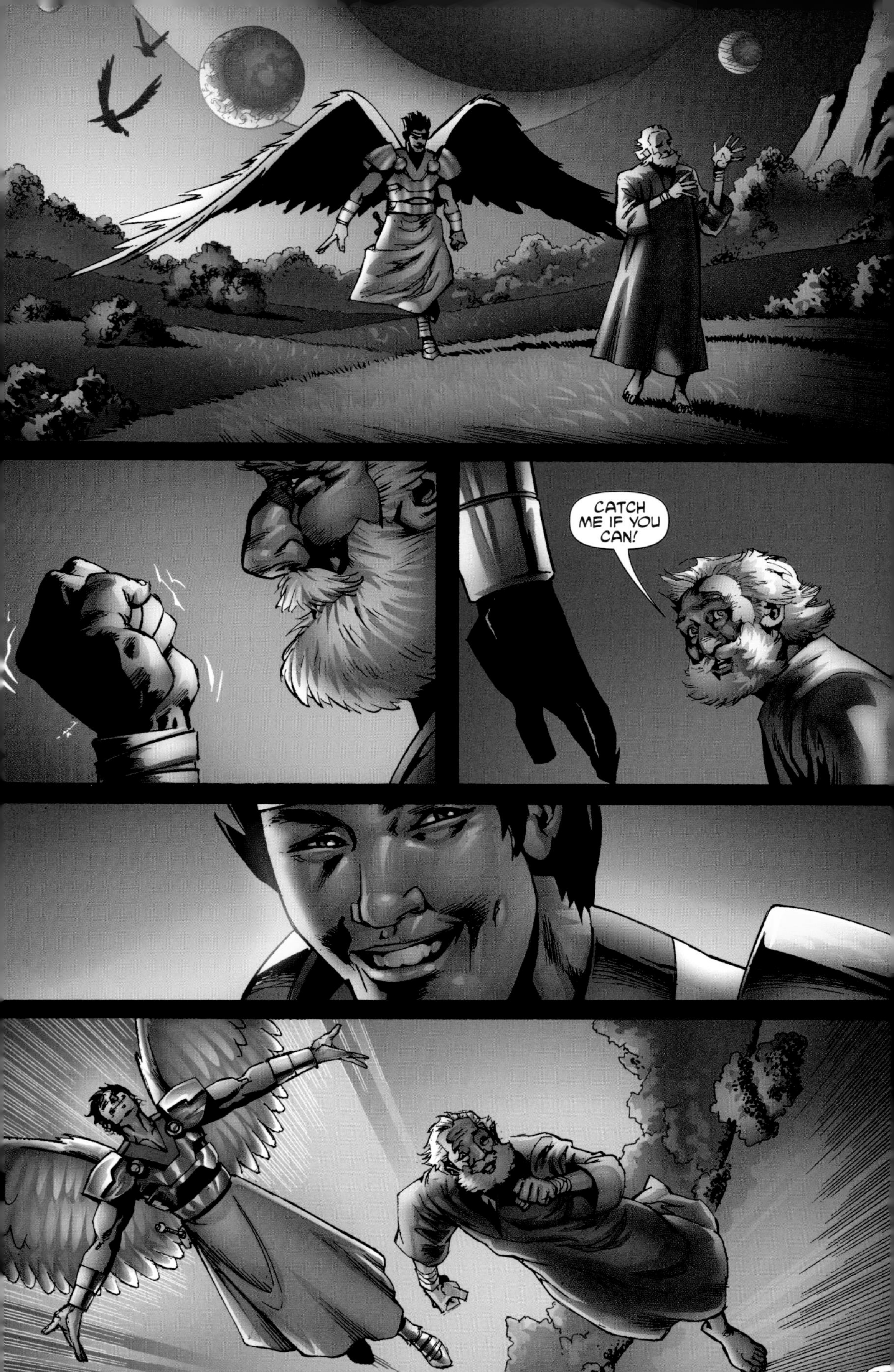
CATCH ME IF YOU CAN!

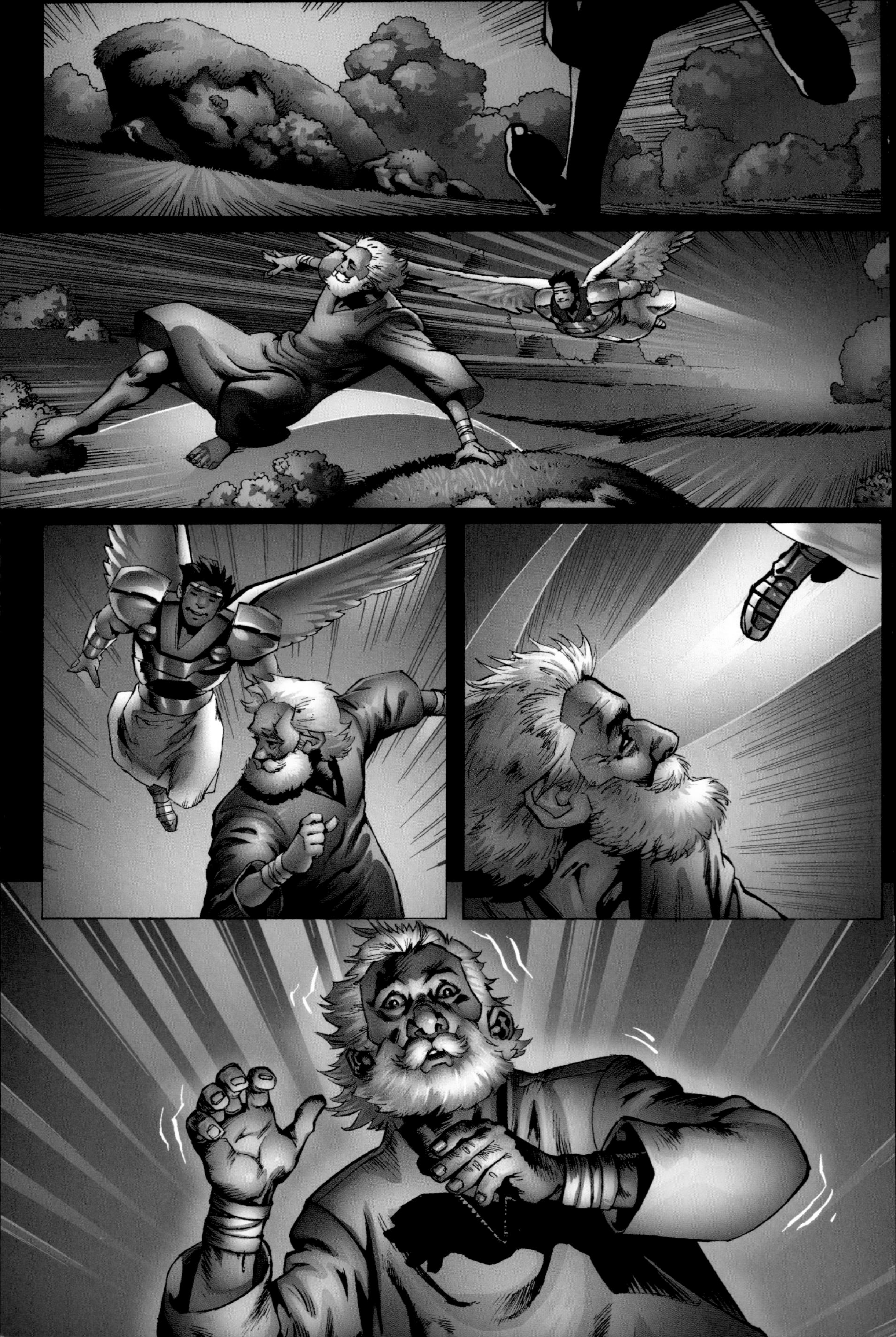

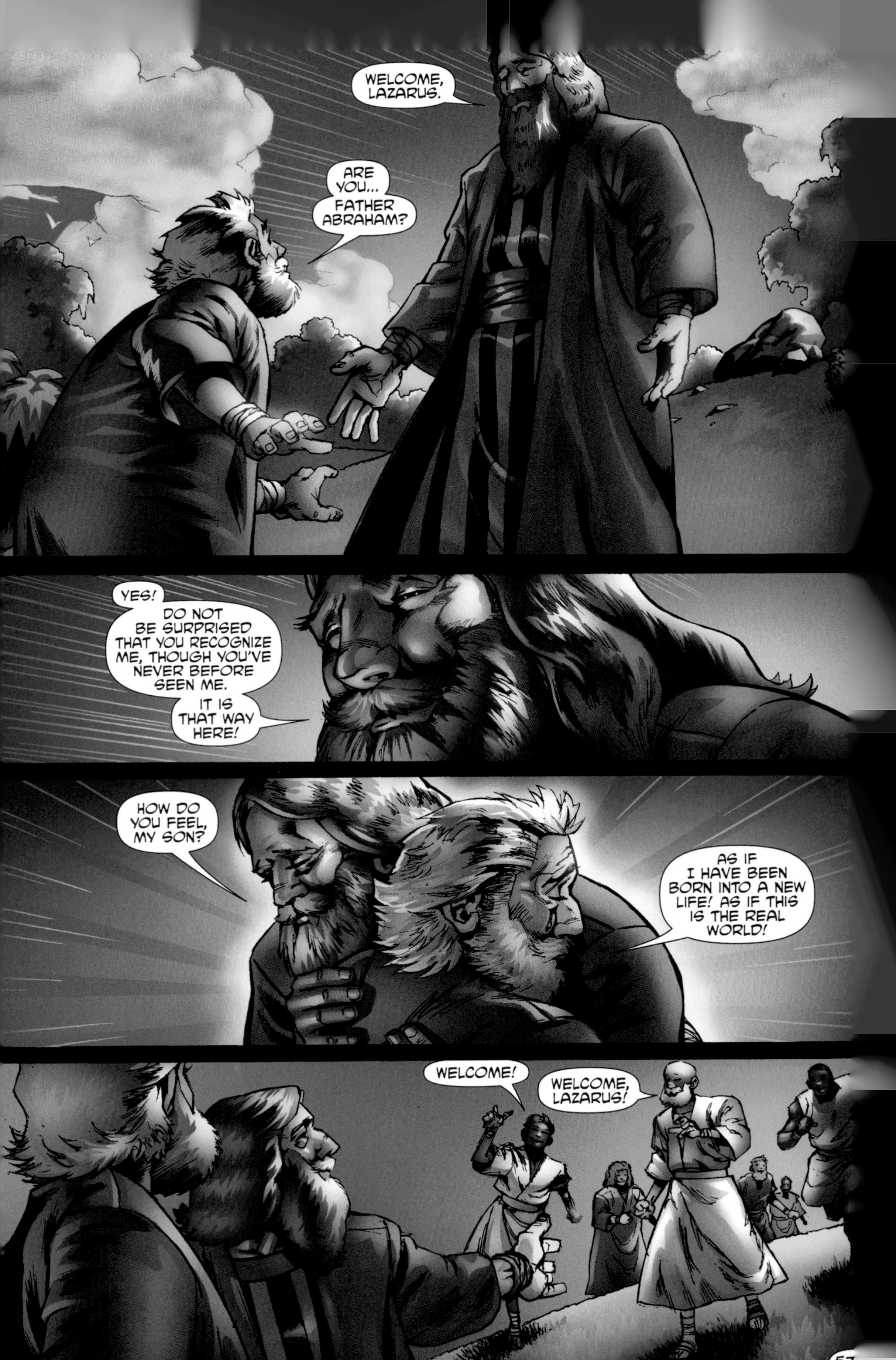
WELCOME, LAZARUS.
ARE YOU... FATHER ABRAHAM?
YES!
DO NOT BE SURPRISED THAT YOU RECOGNIZE ME, THOUGH YOU'VE NEVER BEFORE SEEN ME.
IT IS THAT WAY HERE!
HOW DO YOU FEEL, MY SON?
AS IF I HAVE BEEN BORN INTO A NEW LIFE! AS IF THIS IS THE REAL WORLD!
WELCOME!
WELCOME, LAZARUS!

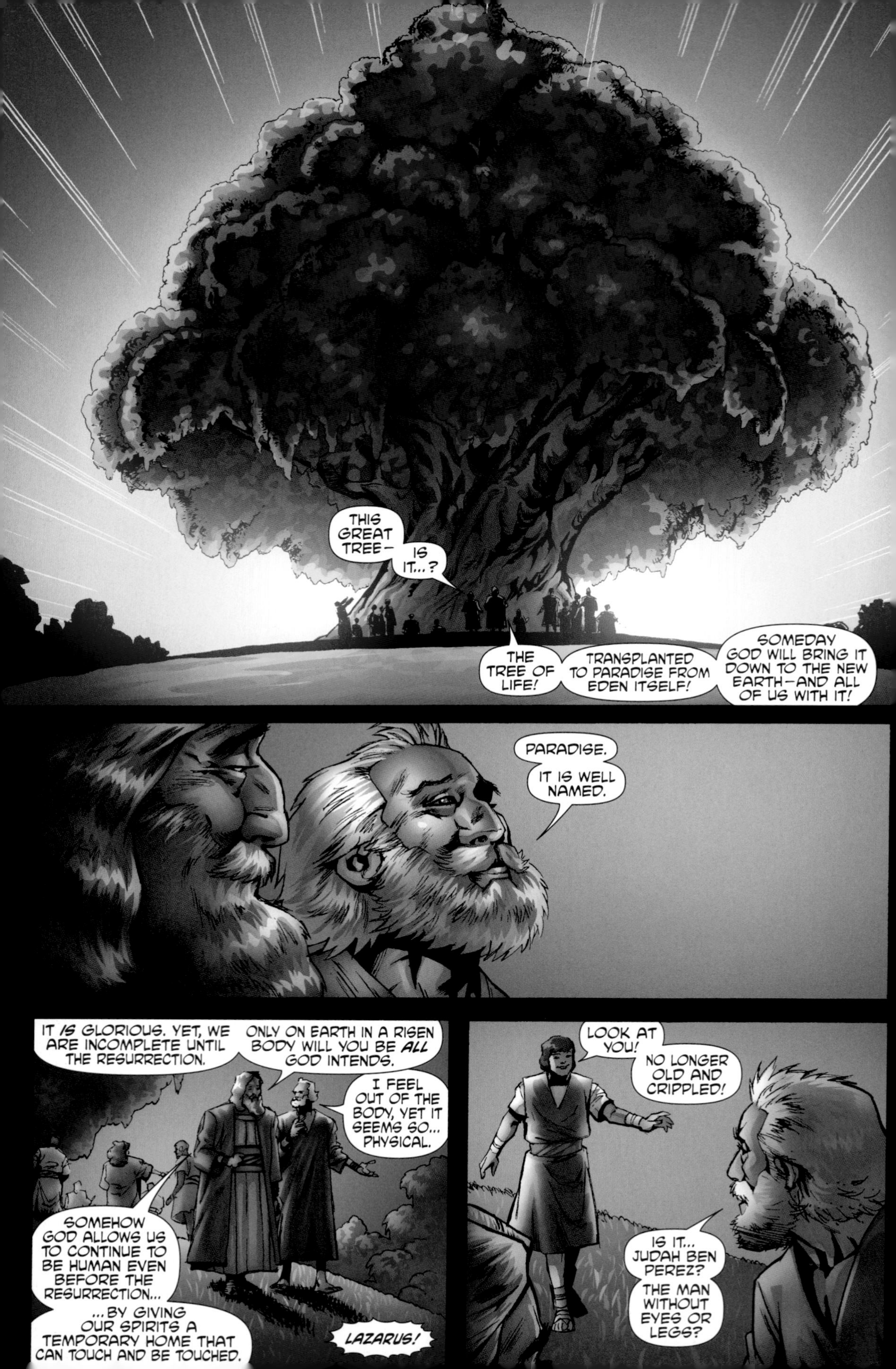
THIS GREAT TREE–
IS IT...?
THE TREE OF LIFE!
TRANSPLANTED TO PARADISE FROM EDEN ITSELF!
SOMEDAY GOD WILL BRING IT DOWN TO THE NEW EARTH—AND ALL OF US WITH IT!
PARADISE.
IT IS WELL NAMED.
IT *IS* GLORIOUS. YET, WE ARE INCOMPLETE UNTIL THE RESURRECTION.
ONLY ON EARTH IN A RISEN BODY WILL YOU BE *ALL* GOD INTENDS.
I FEEL OUT OF THE BODY, YET IT SEEMS SO... PHYSICAL.
SOMEHOW GOD ALLOWS US TO CONTINUE TO BE HUMAN EVEN BEFORE THE RESURRECTION...
...BY GIVING OUR SPIRITS A TEMPORARY HOME THAT CAN TOUCH AND BE TOUCHED.
LAZARUS!
LOOK AT YOU!
NO LONGER OLD AND CRIPPLED!
IS IT... JUDAH BEN PEREZ?
THE MAN WITHOUT EYES OR LEGS?

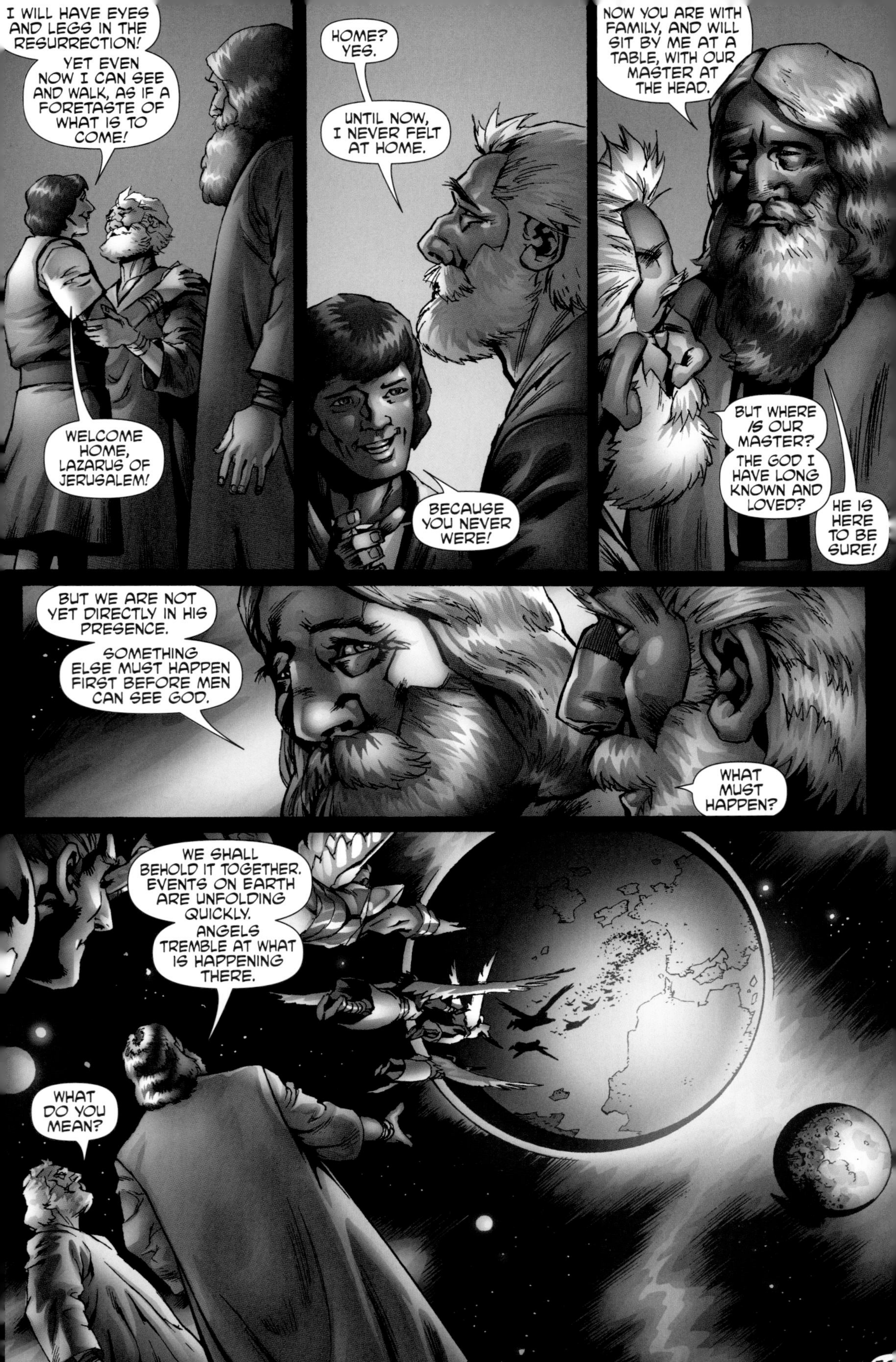
I WILL HAVE EYES AND LEGS IN THE RESURRECTION!
YET EVEN NOW I CAN SEE AND WALK, AS IF A FORETASTE OF WHAT IS TO COME!
WELCOME HOME, LAZARUS OF JERUSALEM!
HOME? YES.
UNTIL NOW, I NEVER FELT AT HOME.
BECAUSE YOU NEVER WERE!
NOW YOU ARE WITH FAMILY, AND WILL SIT BY ME AT A TABLE, WITH OUR MASTER AT THE HEAD.
BUT WHERE IS OUR MASTER? THE GOD I HAVE LONG KNOWN AND LOVED?
HE IS HERE TO BE SURE!
BUT WE ARE NOT YET DIRECTLY IN HIS PRESENCE.
SOMETHING ELSE MUST HAPPEN FIRST BEFORE MEN CAN SEE GOD.
WHAT MUST HAPPEN?
WE SHALL BEHOLD IT TOGETHER. EVENTS ON EARTH ARE UNFOLDING QUICKLY.
ANGELS TREMBLE AT WHAT IS HAPPENING THERE.
WHAT DO YOU MEAN?

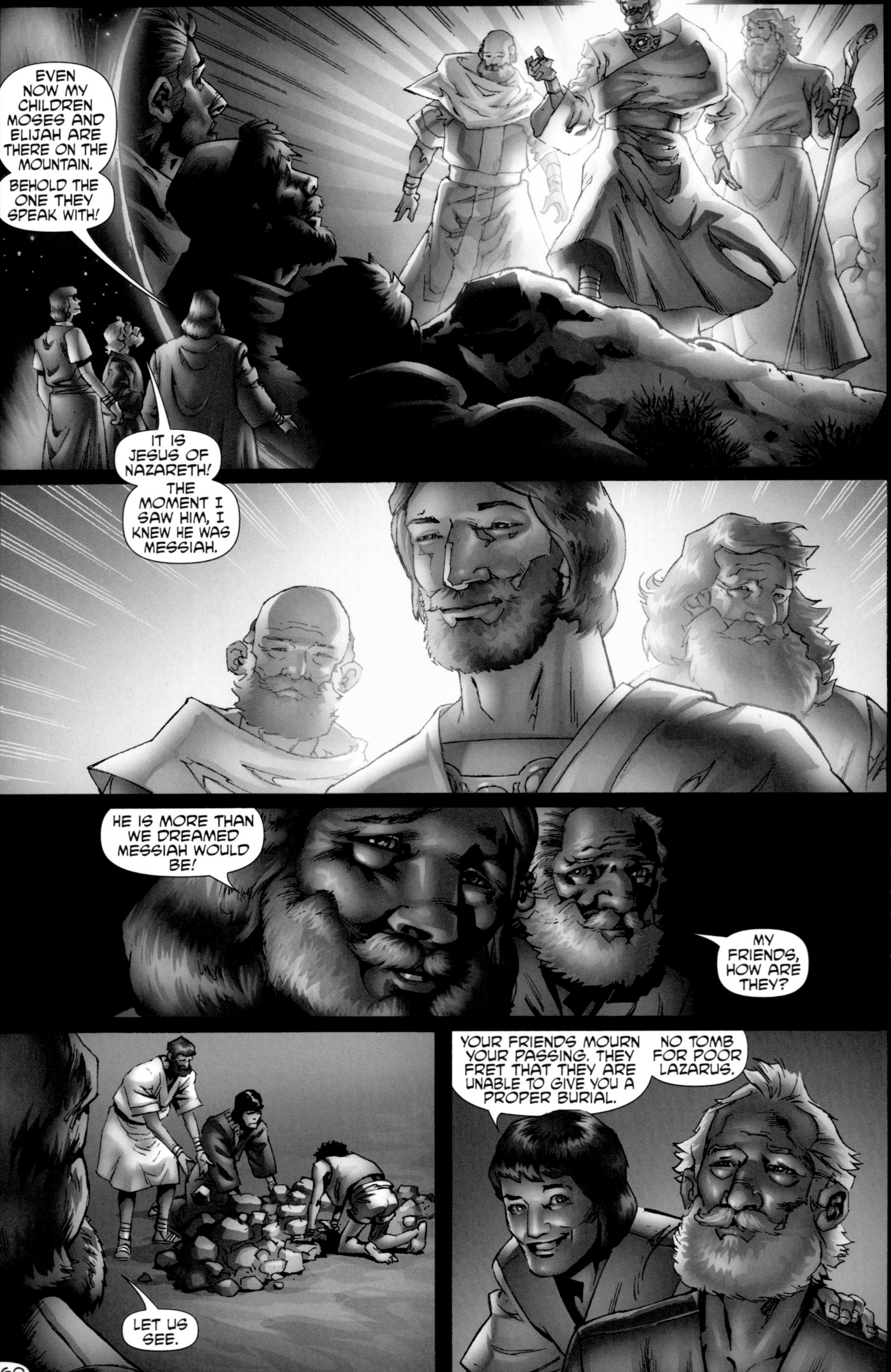
EVEN NOW MY CHILDREN MOSES AND ELIJAH ARE THERE ON THE MOUNTAIN.
BEHOLD THE ONE THEY SPEAK WITH!
IT IS JESUS OF NAZARETH!
THE MOMENT I SAW HIM, I KNEW HE WAS MESSIAH.
HE IS MORE THAN WE DREAMED MESSIAH WOULD BE!
MY FRIENDS, HOW ARE THEY?
LET US SEE.
YOUR FRIENDS MOURN YOUR PASSING. THEY FRET THAT THEY ARE UNABLE TO GIVE YOU A PROPER BURIAL.
NO TOMB FOR POOR LAZARUS.

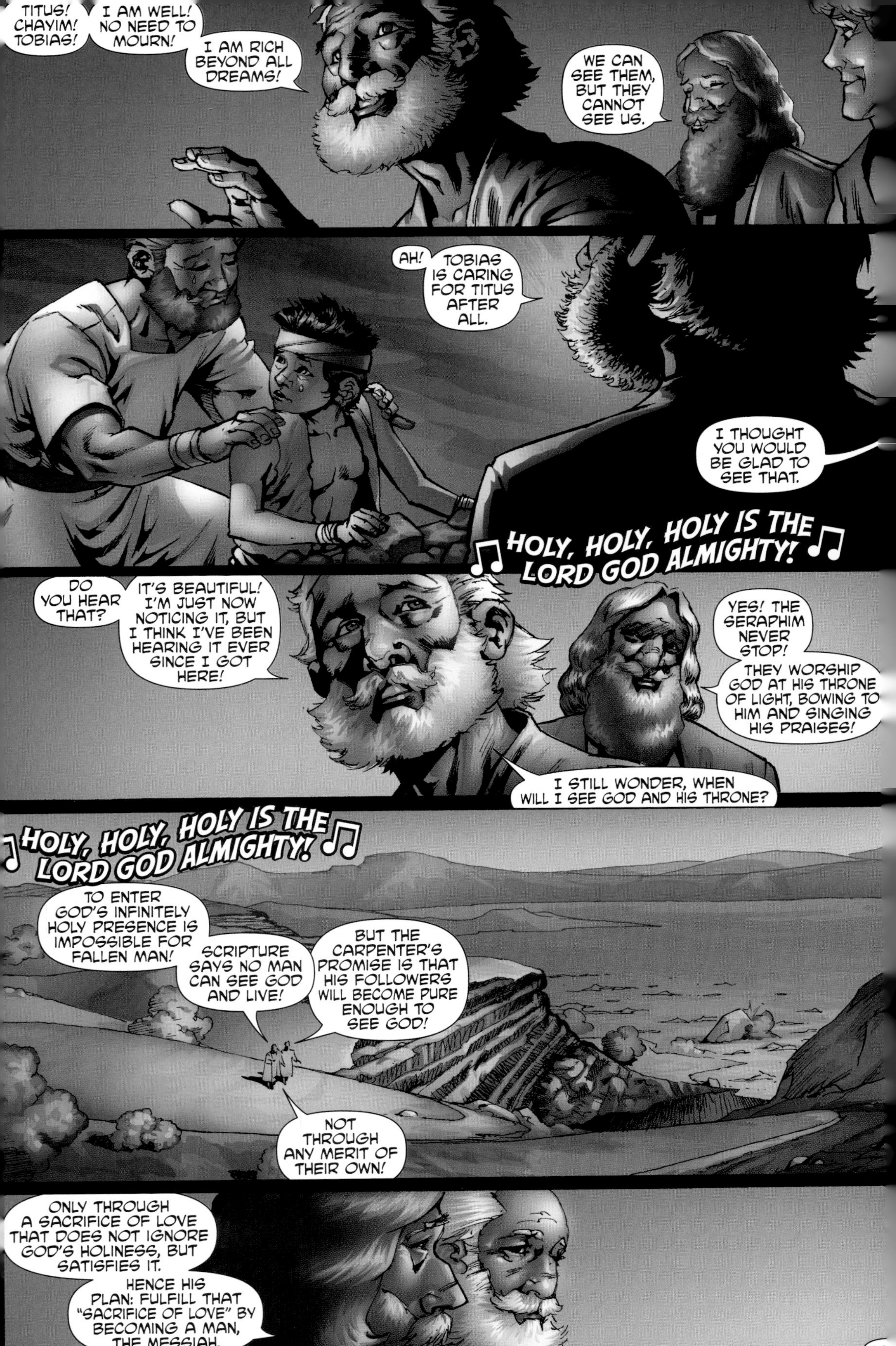

TITUS! CHAYIM! TOBIAS!
I AM WELL! NO NEED TO MOURN!
I AM RICH BEYOND ALL DREAMS!
WE CAN SEE THEM, BUT THEY CANNOT SEE US.
AH!
TOBIAS IS CARING FOR TITUS AFTER ALL.
I THOUGHT YOU WOULD BE GLAD TO SEE THAT.
♫ HOLY, HOLY, HOLY IS THE LORD GOD ALMIGHTY! ♫
DO YOU HEAR THAT?
IT'S BEAUTIFUL! I'M JUST NOW NOTICING IT, BUT I THINK I'VE BEEN HEARING IT EVER SINCE I GOT HERE!
YES! THE SERAPHIM NEVER STOP!
THEY WORSHIP GOD AT HIS THRONE OF LIGHT, BOWING TO HIM AND SINGING HIS PRAISES!
I STILL WONDER, WHEN WILL I SEE GOD AND HIS THRONE?
♫ HOLY, HOLY, HOLY IS THE LORD GOD ALMIGHTY! ♫
TO ENTER GOD'S INFINITELY HOLY PRESENCE IS IMPOSSIBLE FOR FALLEN MAN!
SCRIPTURE SAYS NO MAN CAN SEE GOD AND LIVE!
BUT THE CARPENTER'S PROMISE IS THAT HIS FOLLOWERS WILL BECOME PURE ENOUGH TO SEE GOD!
NOT THROUGH ANY MERIT OF THEIR OWN!
ONLY THROUGH A SACRIFICE OF LOVE THAT DOES NOT IGNORE GOD'S HOLINESS, BUT SATISFIES IT.
HENCE HIS PLAN: FULFILL THAT "SACRIFICE OF LOVE" BY BECOMING A MAN, THE MESSIAH.

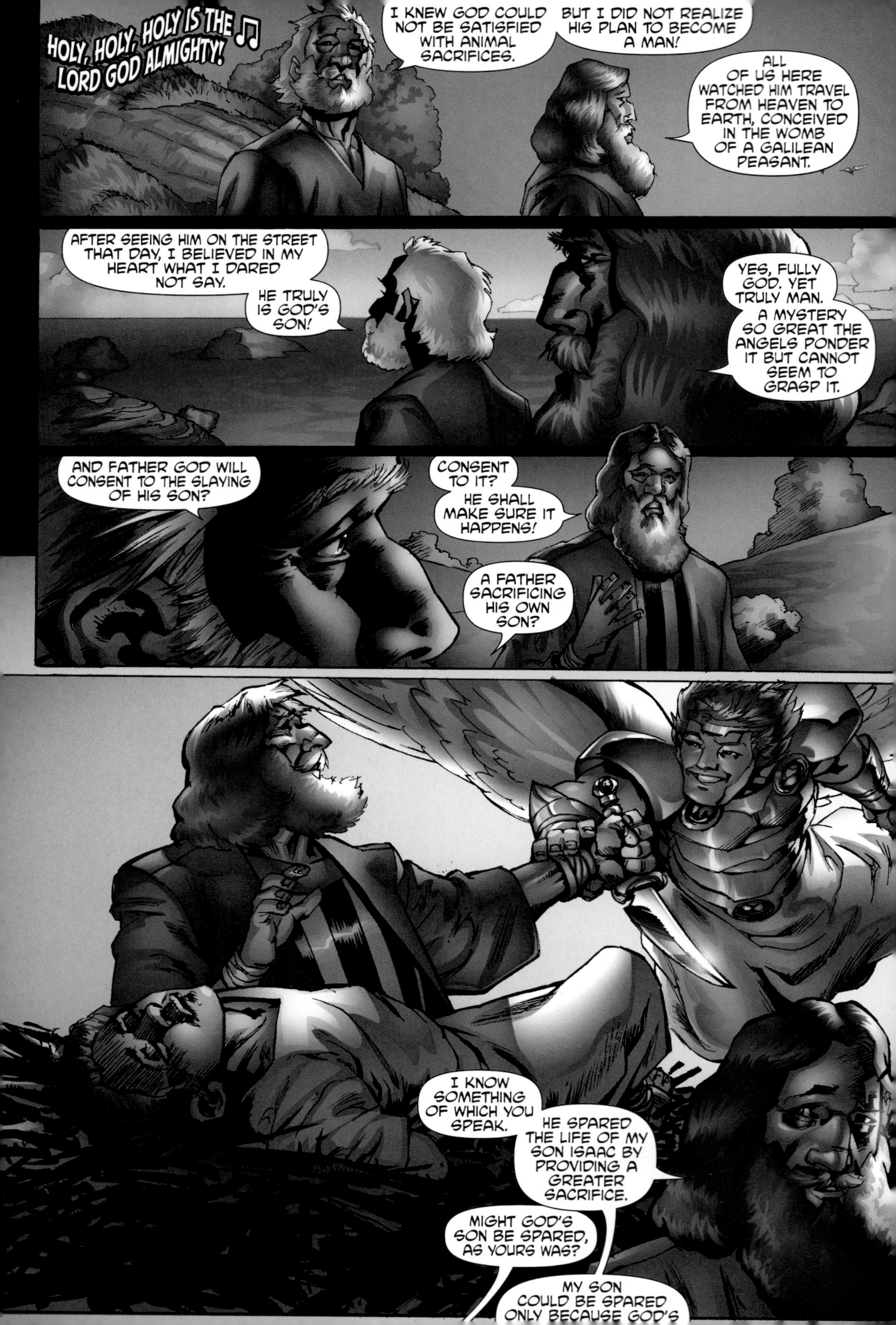
HOLY, HOLY, HOLY IS THE ♫ LORD GOD ALMIGHTY!
I KNEW GOD COULD NOT BE SATISFIED WITH ANIMAL SACRIFICES.
BUT I DID NOT REALIZE HIS PLAN TO BECOME A MAN!
ALL OF US HERE WATCHED HIM TRAVEL FROM HEAVEN TO EARTH, CONCEIVED IN THE WOMB OF A GALILEAN PEASANT.
AFTER SEEING HIM ON THE STREET THAT DAY, I BELIEVED IN MY HEART WHAT I DARED NOT SAY.
HE TRULY IS GOD'S SON!
YES, FULLY GOD. YET TRULY MAN.
A MYSTERY SO GREAT THE ANGELS PONDER IT BUT CANNOT SEEM TO GRASP IT.
AND FATHER GOD WILL CONSENT TO THE SLAYING OF HIS SON?
CONSENT TO IT?
HE SHALL MAKE SURE IT HAPPENS!
A FATHER SACRIFICING HIS OWN SON?
I KNOW SOMETHING OF WHICH YOU SPEAK.
HE SPARED THE LIFE OF MY SON ISAAC BY PROVIDING A GREATER SACRIFICE.
MIGHT GOD'S SON BE SPARED, AS YOURS WAS?
MY SON COULD BE SPARED ONLY BECAUSE GOD'S

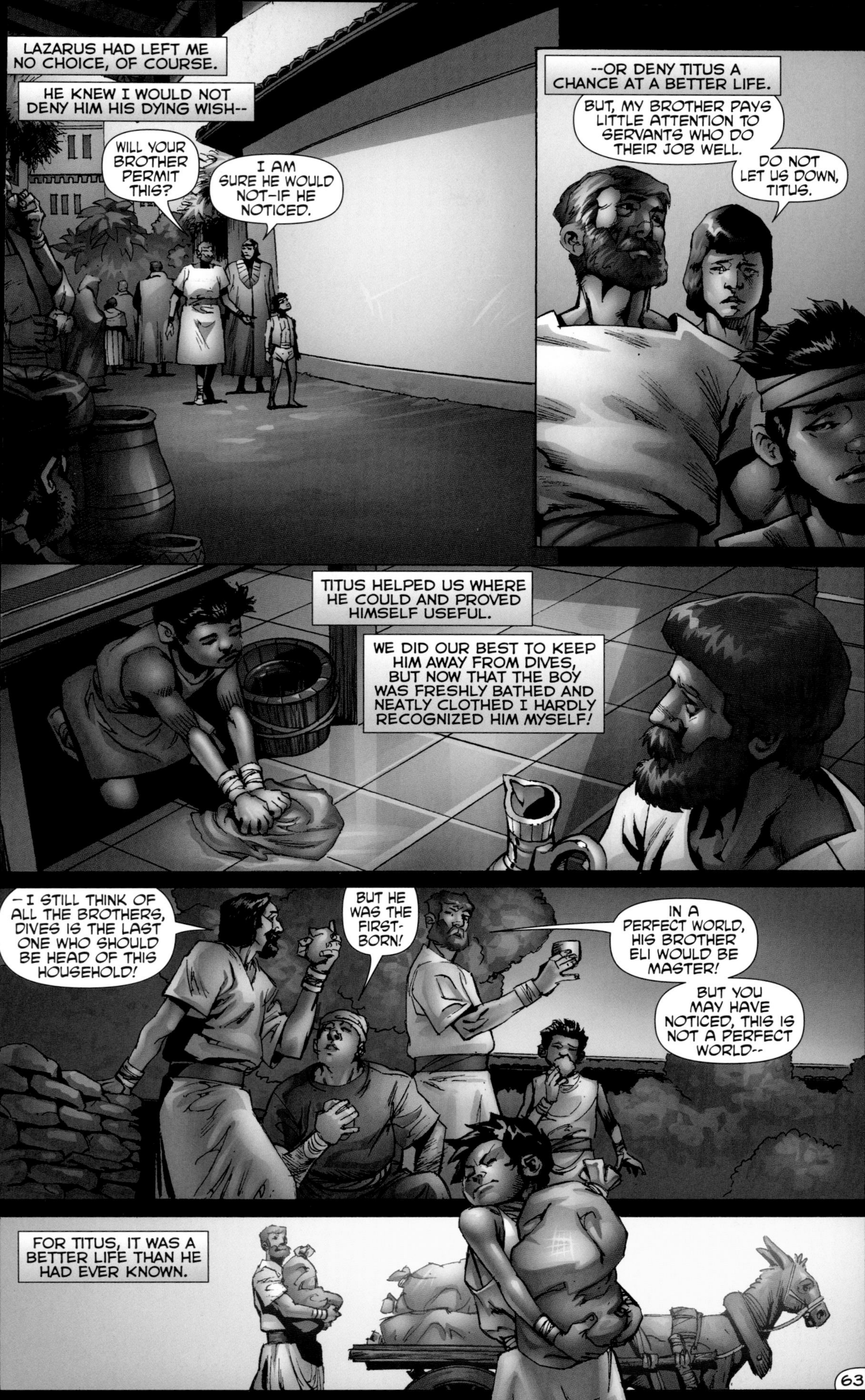

LAZARUS HAD LEFT ME NO CHOICE, OF COURSE.
HE KNEW I WOULD NOT DENY HIM HIS DYING WISH--
WILL YOUR BROTHER PERMIT THIS?
I AM SURE HE WOULD NOT-IF HE NOTICED.
--OR DENY TITUS A CHANCE AT A BETTER LIFE.
BUT, MY BROTHER PAYS LITTLE ATTENTION TO SERVANTS WHO DO THEIR JOB WELL.
DO NOT LET US DOWN, TITUS.
TITUS HELPED US WHERE HE COULD AND PROVED HIMSELF USEFUL.
WE DID OUR BEST TO KEEP HIM AWAY FROM DIVES, BUT NOW THAT THE BOY WAS FRESHLY BATHED AND NEATLY CLOTHED I HARDLY RECOGNIZED HIM MYSELF!
-I STILL THINK OF ALL THE BROTHERS, DIVES IS THE LAST ONE WHO SHOULD BE HEAD OF THIS HOUSEHOLD!
BUT HE WAS THE FIRST-BORN!
IN A PERFECT WORLD, HIS BROTHER ELI WOULD BE MASTER!
BUT YOU MAY HAVE NOTICED, THIS IS NOT A PERFECT WORLD--
FOR TITUS, IT WAS A BETTER LIFE THAN HE HAD EVER KNOWN.

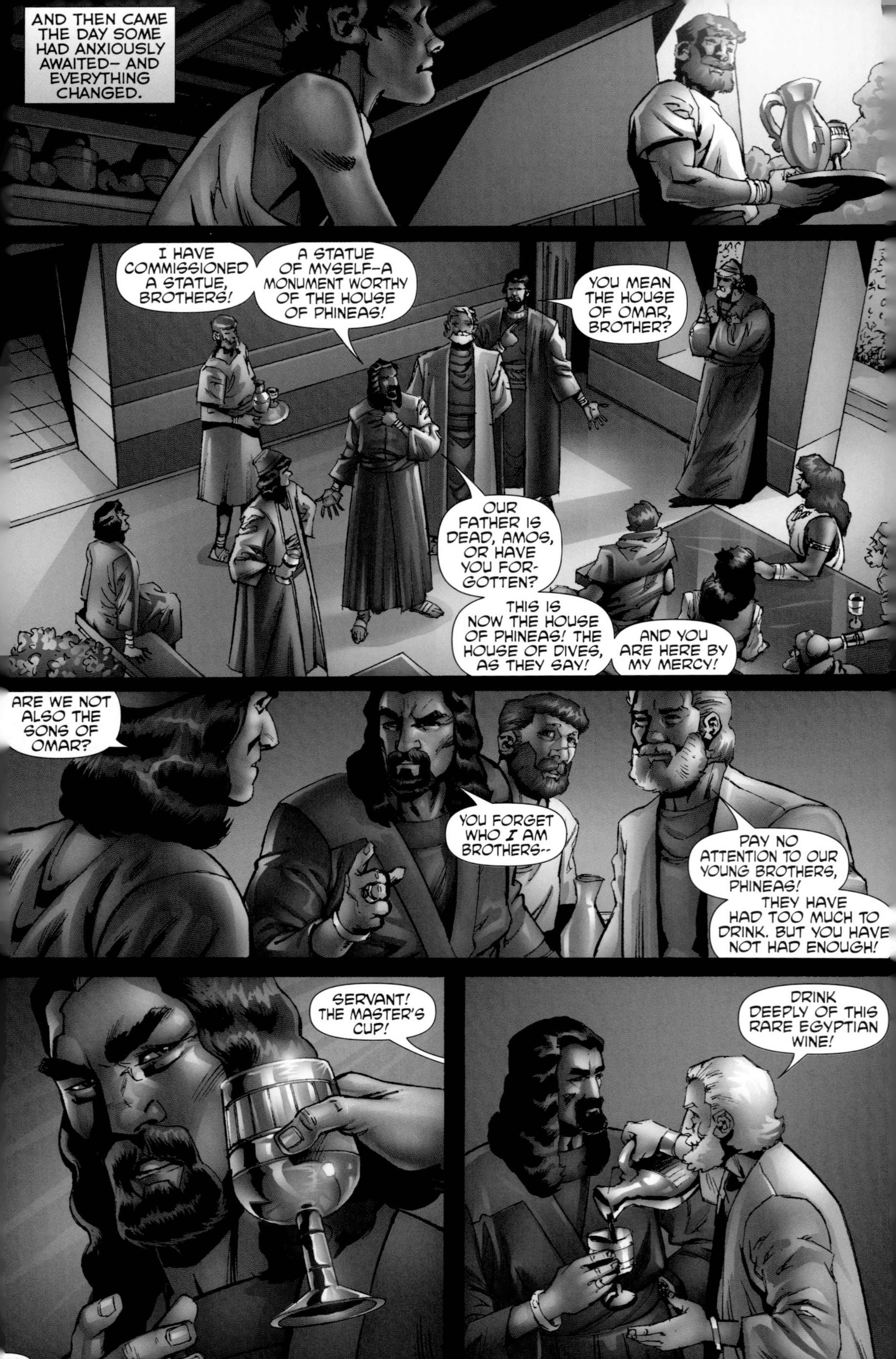
AND THEN CAME THE DAY SOME HAD ANXIOUSLY AWAITED-- AND EVERYTHING CHANGED.
I HAVE COMMISSIONED A STATUE, BROTHERS!
A STATUE OF MYSELF--A MONUMENT WORTHY OF THE HOUSE OF PHINEAS!
YOU MEAN THE HOUSE OF OMAR, BROTHER?
OUR FATHER IS DEAD, AMOS, OR HAVE YOU FOR-GOTTEN?
THIS IS NOW THE HOUSE OF PHINEAS! THE HOUSE OF DIVES, AS THEY SAY!
AND YOU ARE HERE BY MY MERCY!
ARE WE NOT ALSO THE SONS OF OMAR?
YOU FORGET WHO *I* AM BROTHERS--
PAY NO ATTENTION TO OUR YOUNG BROTHERS, PHINEAS!
THEY HAVE HAD TOO MUCH TO DRINK. BUT YOU HAVE NOT HAD ENOUGH!
SERVANT! THE MASTER'S CUP!
DRINK DEEPLY OF THIS RARE EGYPTIAN WINE!

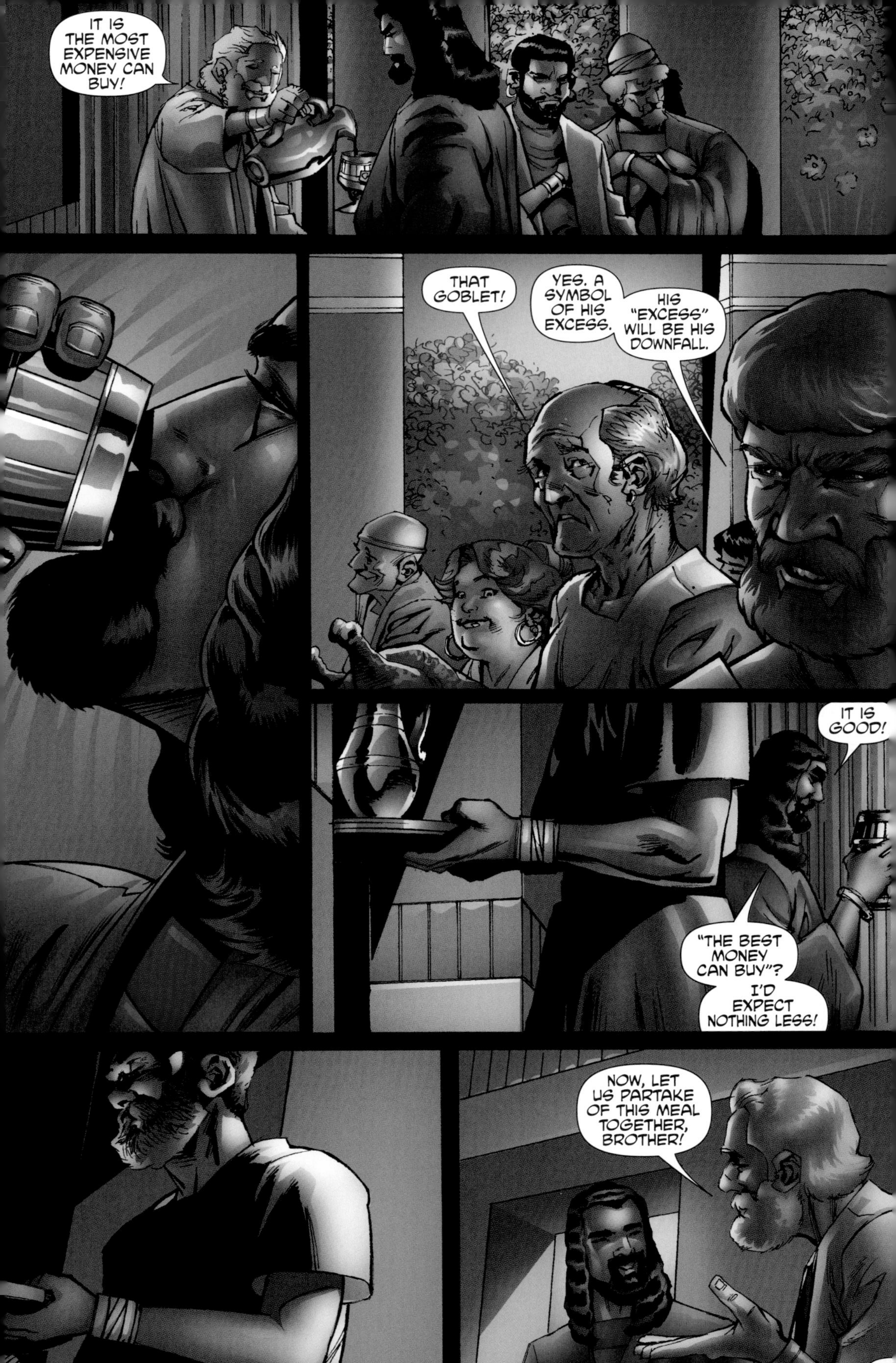

IT IS THE MOST EXPENSIVE MONEY CAN BUY!
THAT GOBLET!
YES. A SYMBOL OF HIS EXCESS.
HIS "EXCESS" WILL BE HIS DOWNFALL.
IT IS GOOD!
"THE BEST MONEY CAN BUY"?
I'D EXPECT NOTHING LESS!
NOW, LET US PARTAKE OF THIS MEAL TOGETHER, BROTHER!

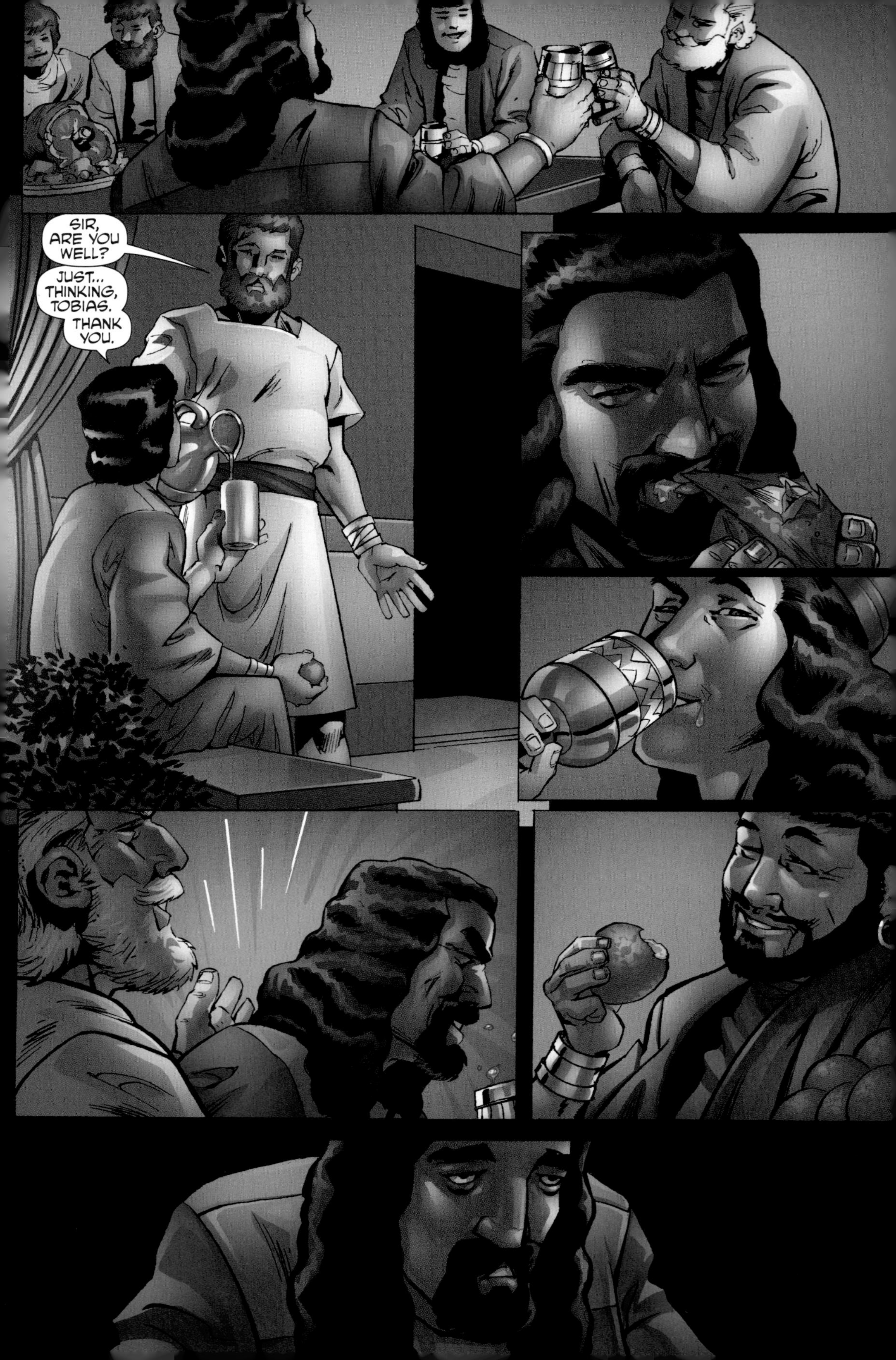
SIR, ARE YOU WELL?
JUST... THINKING, TOBIAS. THANK YOU.

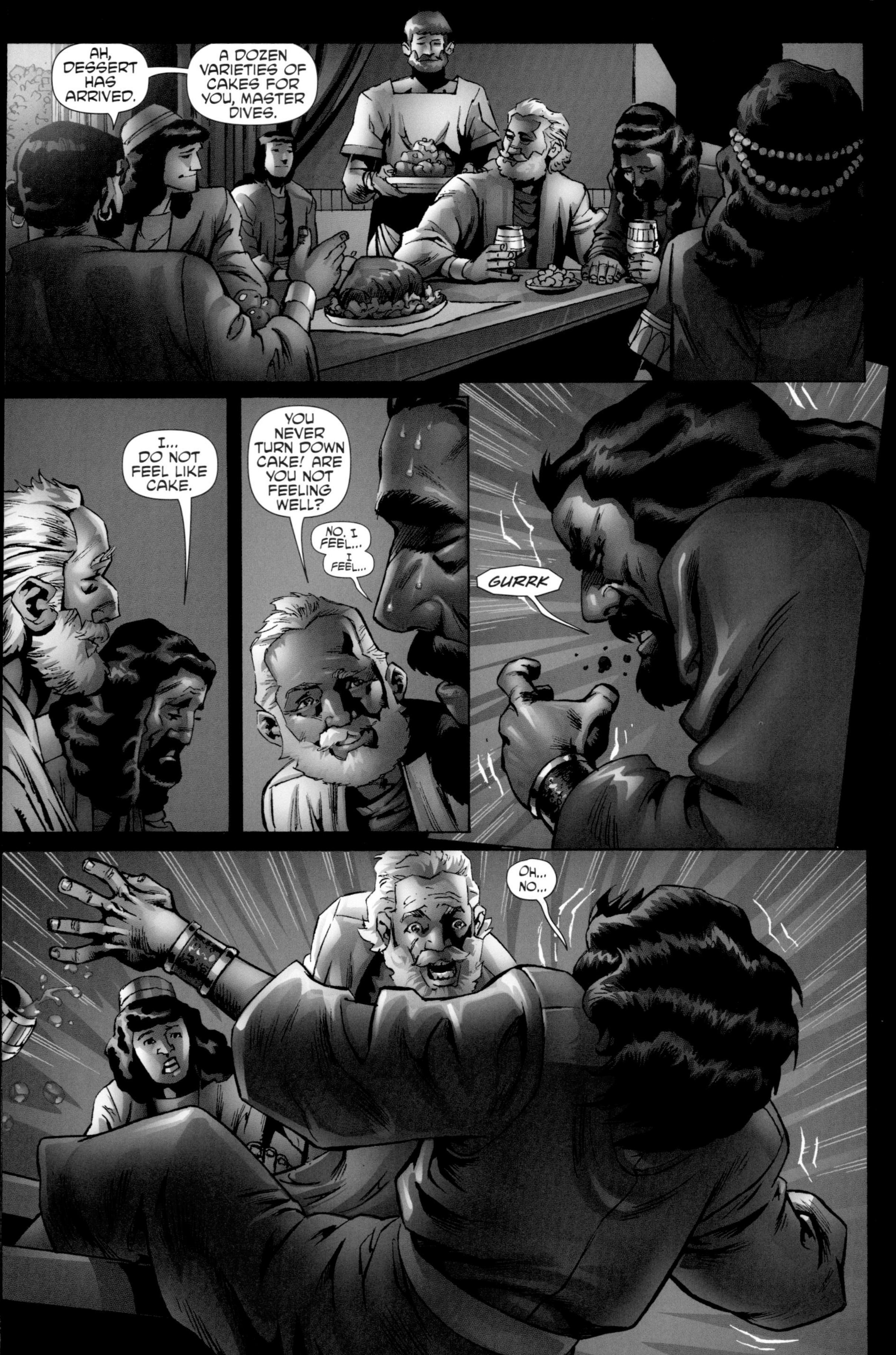
AH, DESSERT HAS ARRIVED.
A DOZEN VARIETIES OF CAKES FOR YOU, MASTER DIVES.
I... DO NOT FEEL LIKE CAKE.
YOU NEVER TURN DOWN CAKE! ARE YOU NOT FEELING WELL?
NO. I FEEL... I FEEL...
GURRK
OH... NO...

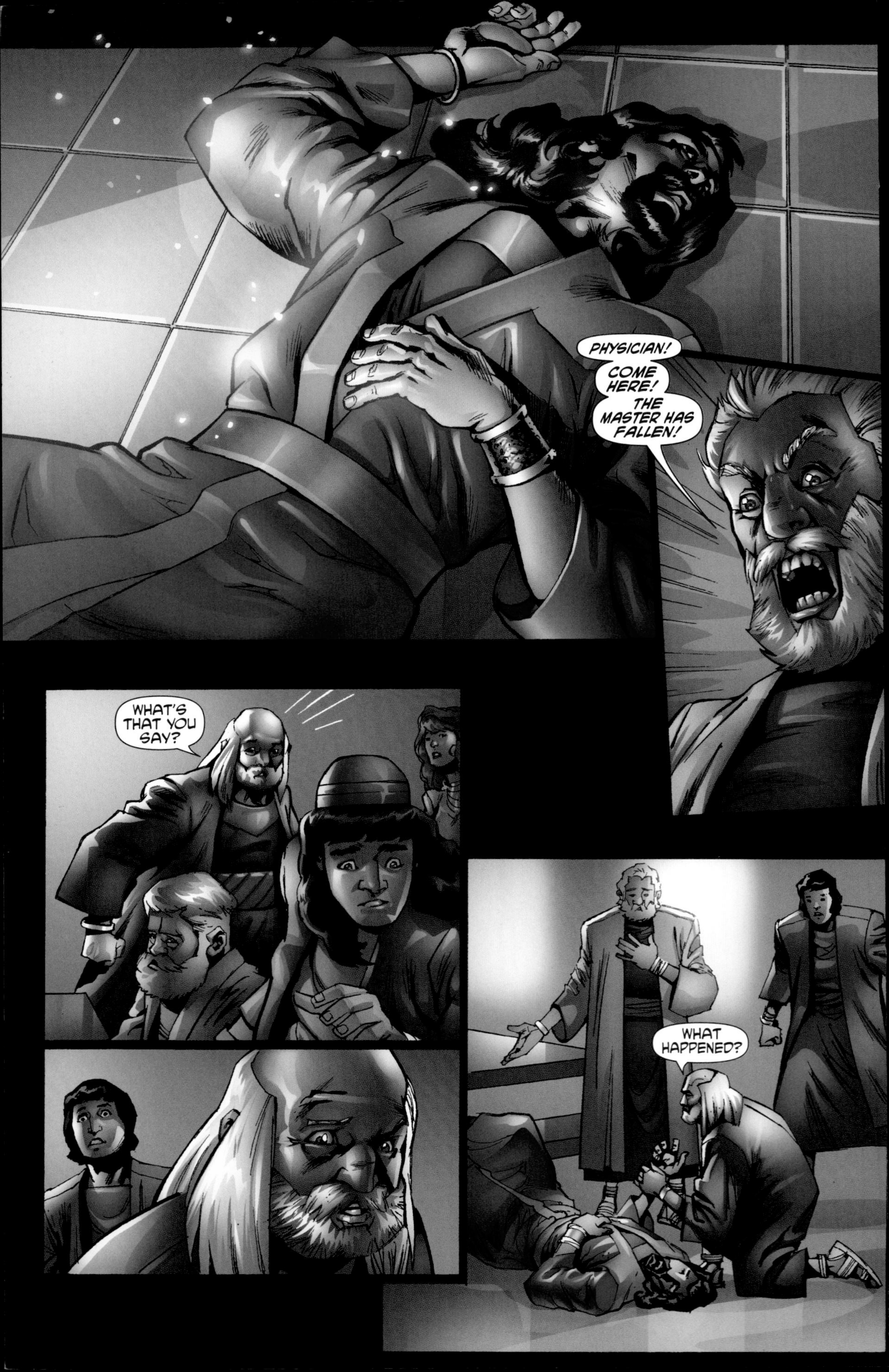
PHYSICIAN! COME HERE! THE MASTER HAS FALLEN!
WHAT'S THAT YOU SAY?
WHAT HAPPENED?

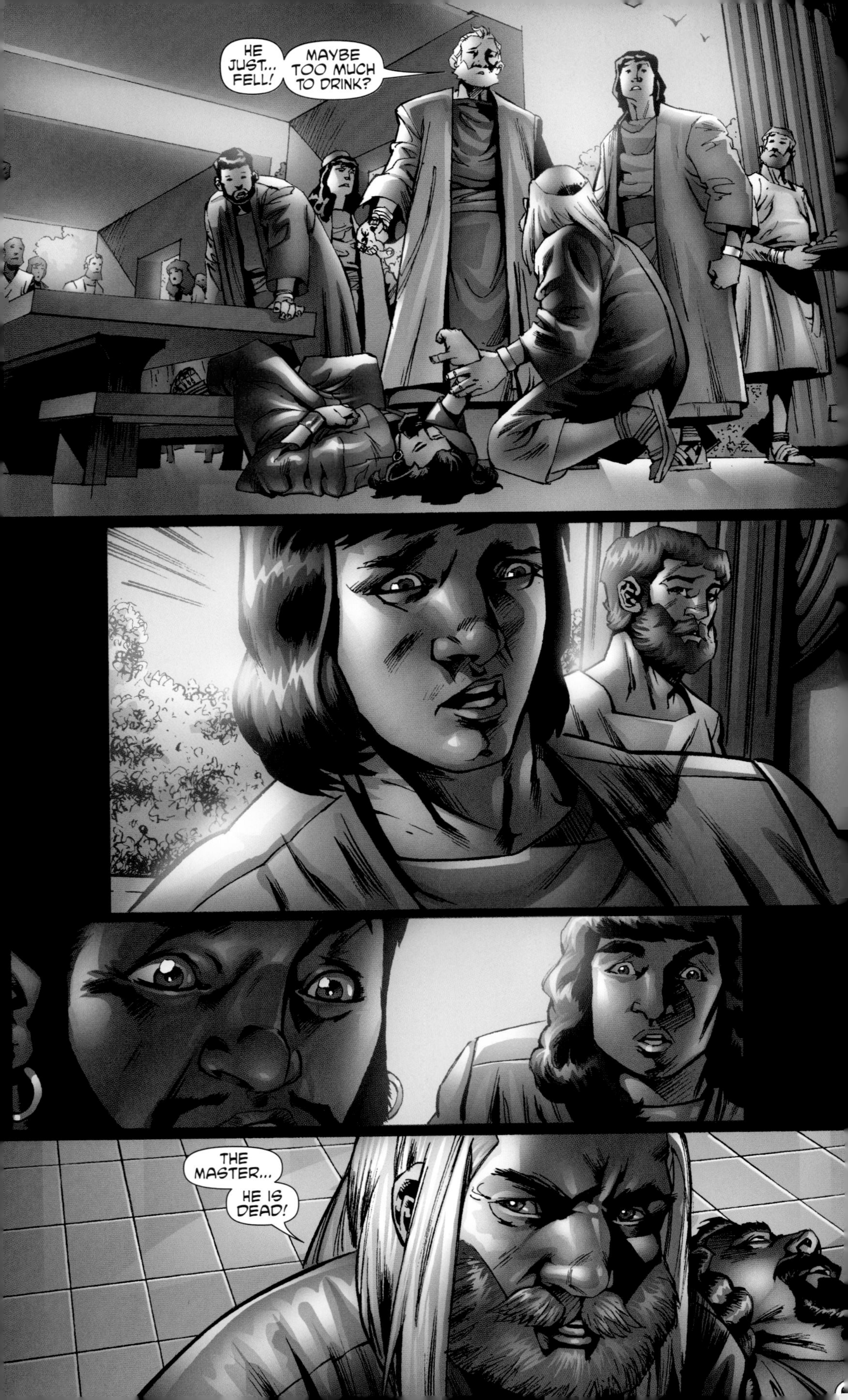
HE JUST... FELL!
MAYBE TOO MUCH TO DRINK?
THE MASTER... HE IS DEAD!

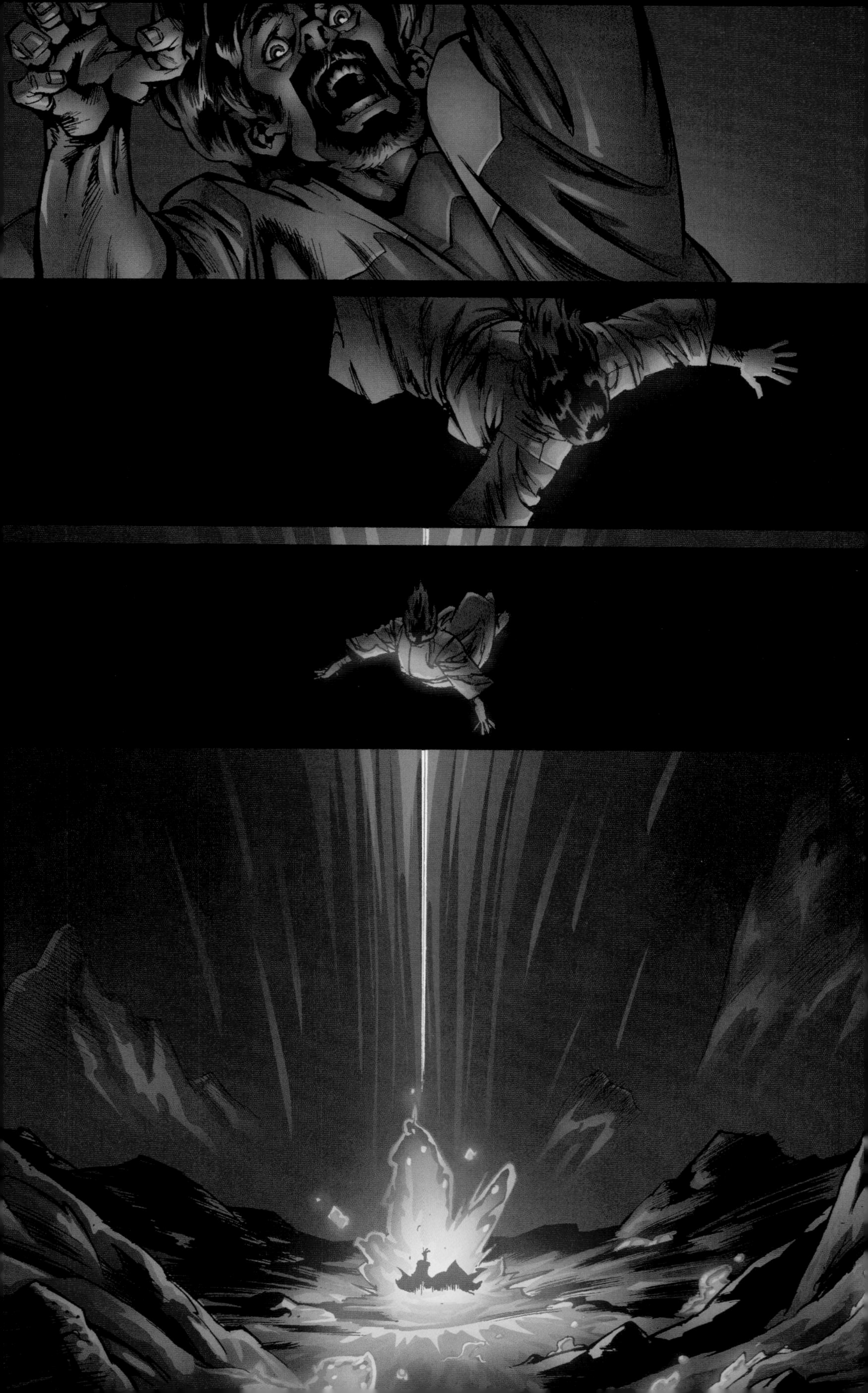

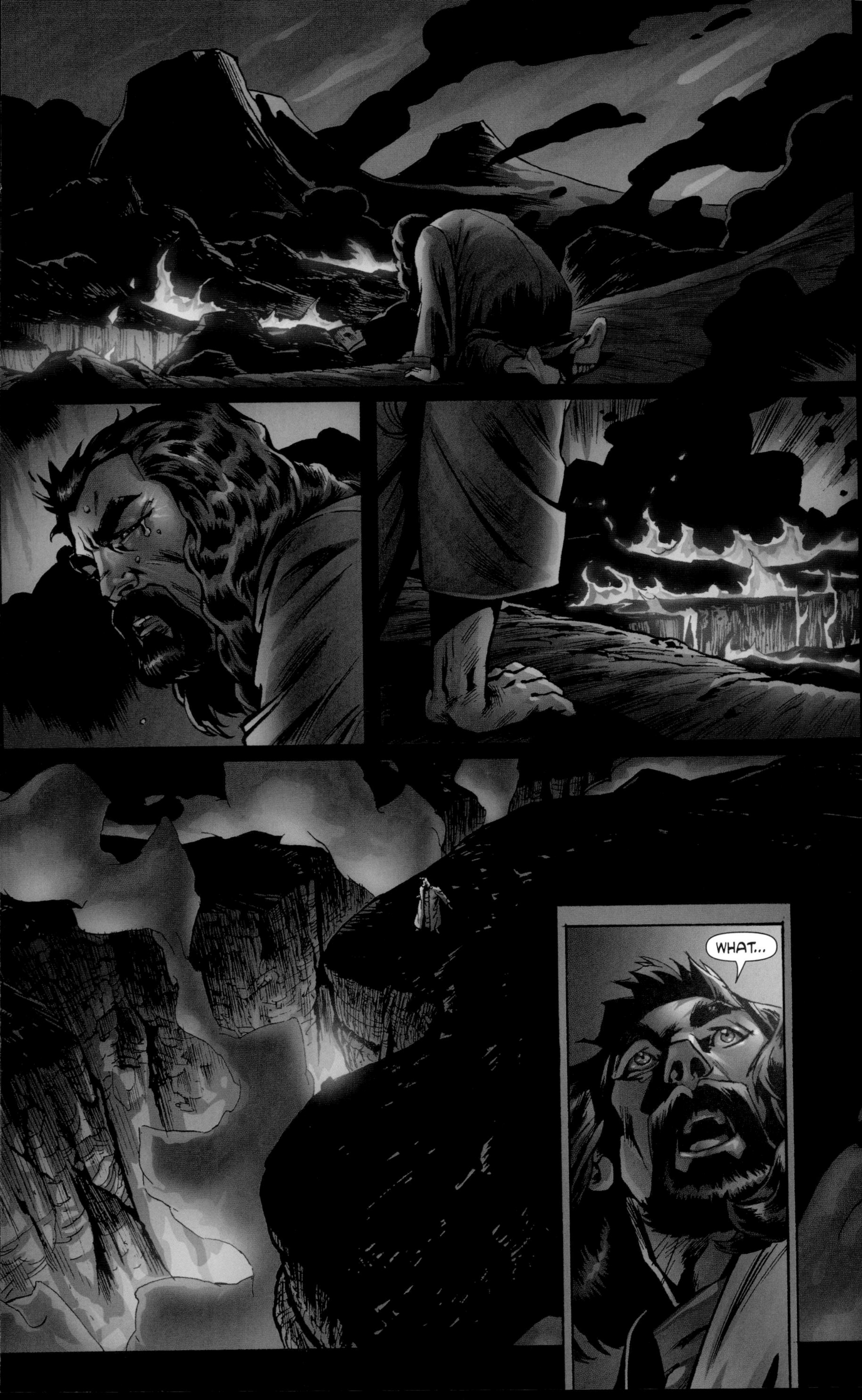
WHAT...

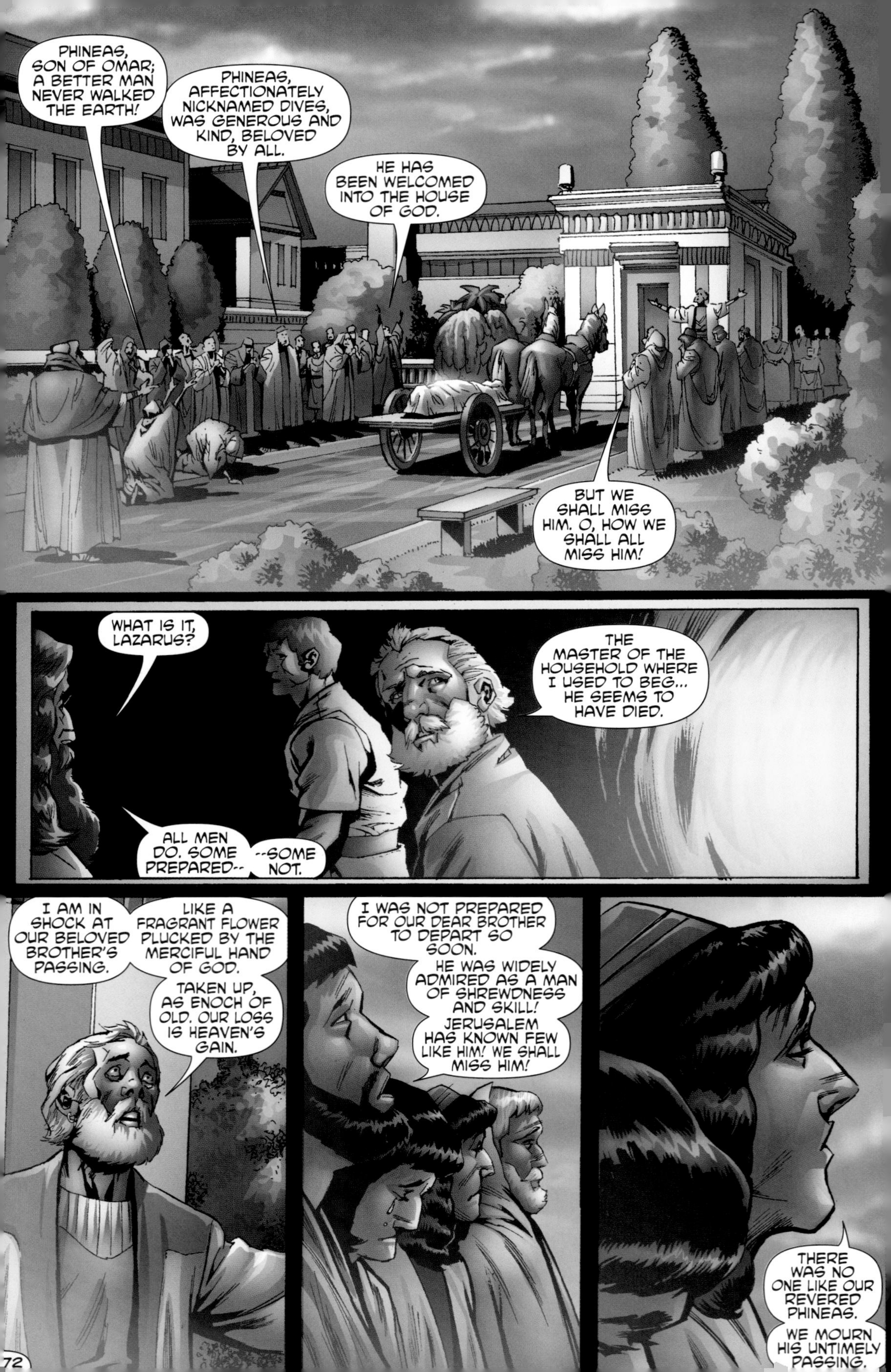
PHINEAS, SON OF OMAR; A BETTER MAN NEVER WALKED THE EARTH!
PHINEAS, AFFECTIONATELY NICKNAMED DIVES, WAS GENEROUS AND KIND, BELOVED BY ALL.
HE HAS BEEN WELCOMED INTO THE HOUSE OF GOD.
BUT WE SHALL MISS HIM. O, HOW WE SHALL ALL MISS HIM!
WHAT IS IT, LAZARUS?
THE MASTER OF THE HOUSEHOLD WHERE I USED TO BEG... HE SEEMS TO HAVE DIED.
ALL MEN DO. SOME PREPARED--
--SOME NOT.
I AM IN SHOCK AT OUR BELOVED BROTHER'S PASSING.
LIKE A FRAGRANT FLOWER PLUCKED BY THE MERCIFUL HAND OF GOD.
TAKEN UP, AS ENOCH OF OLD. OUR LOSS IS HEAVEN'S GAIN.
I WAS NOT PREPARED FOR OUR DEAR BROTHER TO DEPART SO SOON.
HE WAS WIDELY ADMIRED AS A MAN OF SHREWDNESS AND SKILL!
JERUSALEM HAS KNOWN FEW LIKE HIM! WE SHALL MISS HIM!
THERE WAS NO ONE LIKE OUR REVERED PHINEAS.
WE MOURN HIS UNTIMELY PASSING.

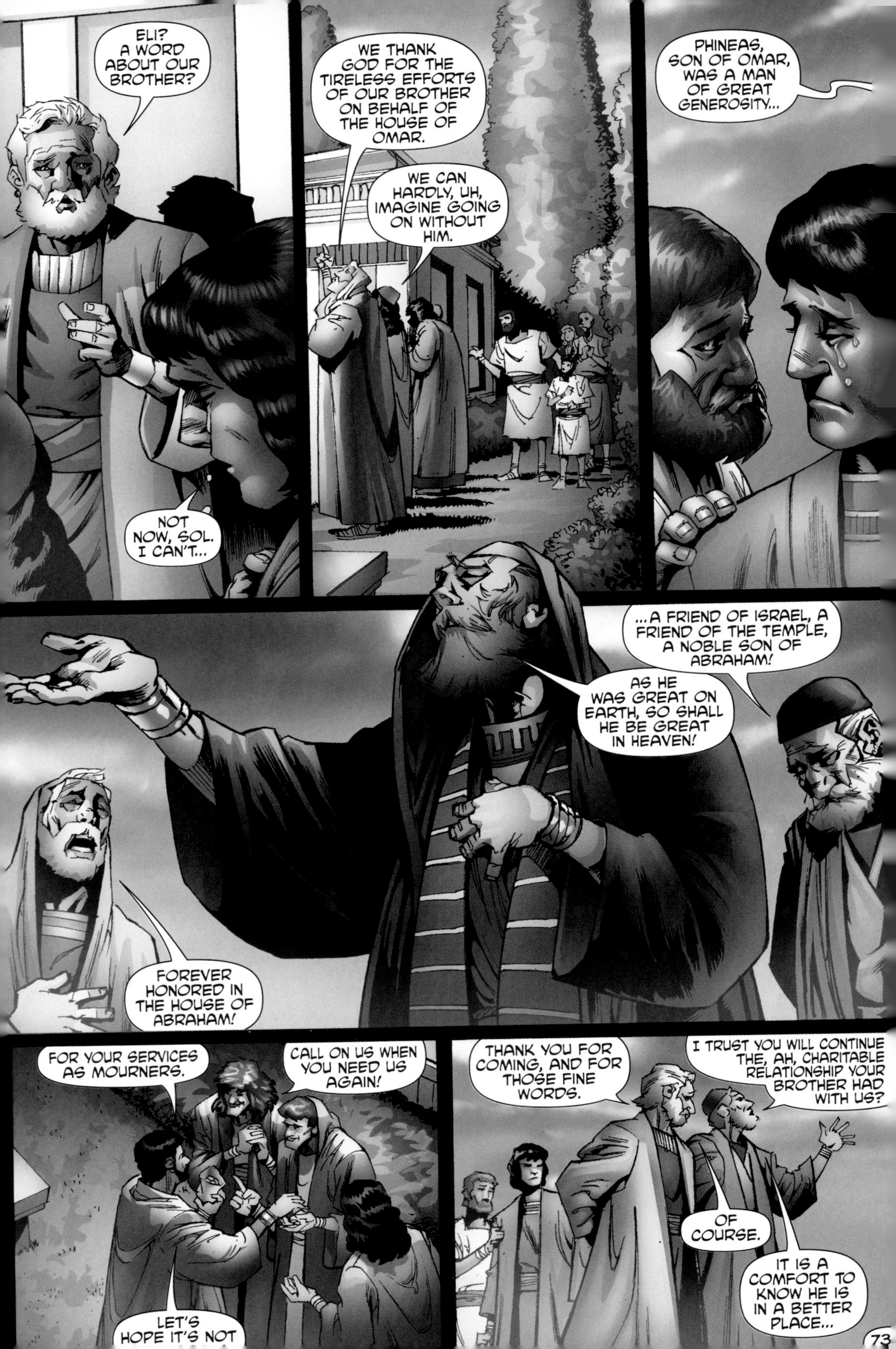
ELI? A WORD ABOUT OUR BROTHER?
NOT NOW, SOL. I CAN'T...
WE THANK GOD FOR THE TIRELESS EFFORTS OF OUR BROTHER ON BEHALF OF THE HOUSE OF OMAR.
WE CAN HARDLY, UH, IMAGINE GOING ON WITHOUT HIM.
PHINEAS, SON OF OMAR, WAS A MAN OF GREAT GENEROSITY...
...A FRIEND OF ISRAEL, A FRIEND OF THE TEMPLE, A NOBLE SON OF ABRAHAM!
AS HE WAS GREAT ON EARTH, SO SHALL HE BE GREAT IN HEAVEN!
FOREVER HONORED IN THE HOUSE OF ABRAHAM!
FOR YOUR SERVICES AS MOURNERS.
CALL ON US WHEN YOU NEED US AGAIN!
LET'S HOPE IT'S NOT
THANK YOU FOR COMING, AND FOR THOSE FINE WORDS.
I TRUST YOU WILL CONTINUE THE, AH, CHARITABLE RELATIONSHIP YOUR BROTHER HAD WITH US?
OF COURSE.
IT IS A COMFORT TO KNOW HE IS IN A BETTER PLACE...

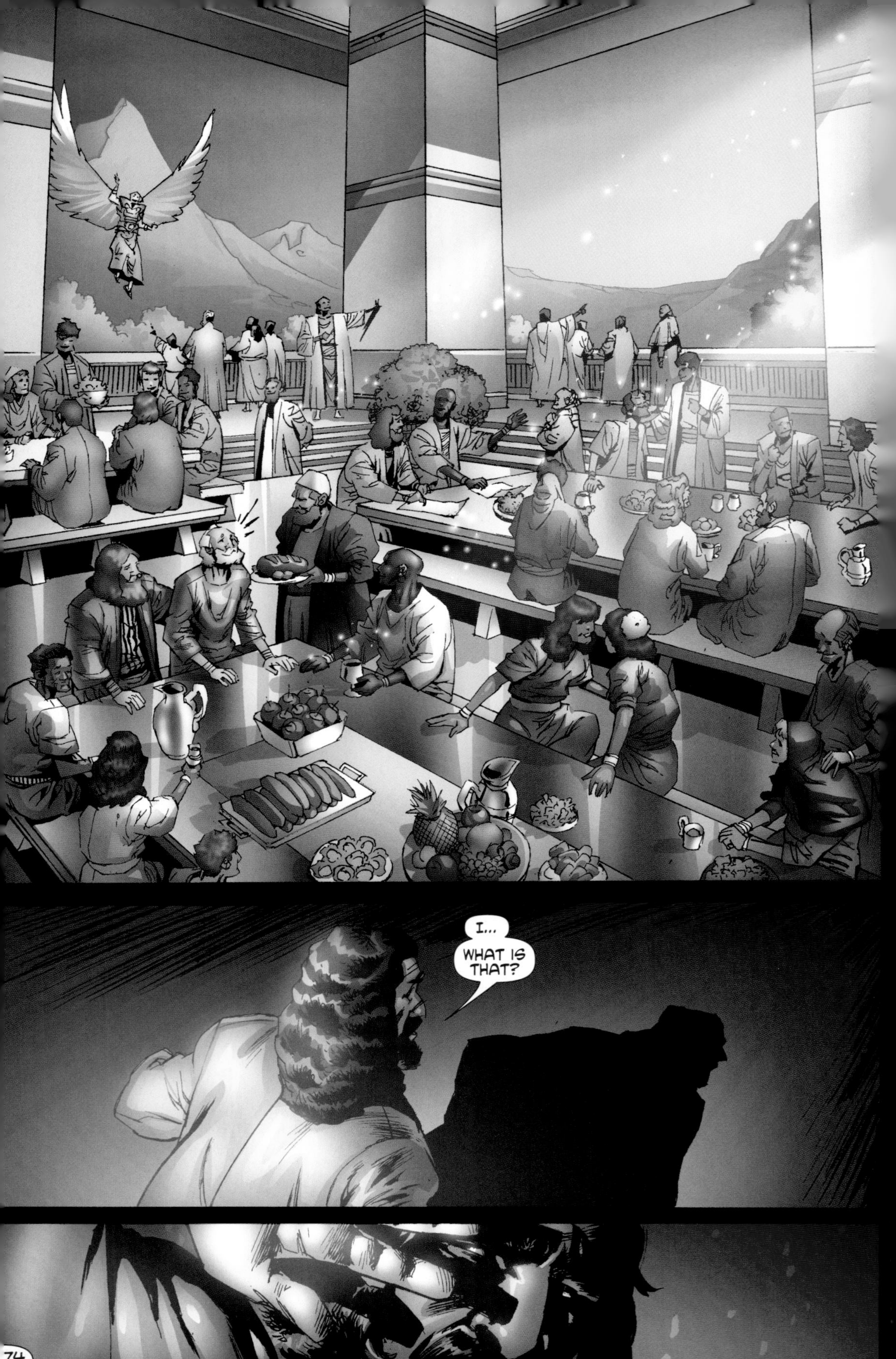
I... WHAT IS THAT?

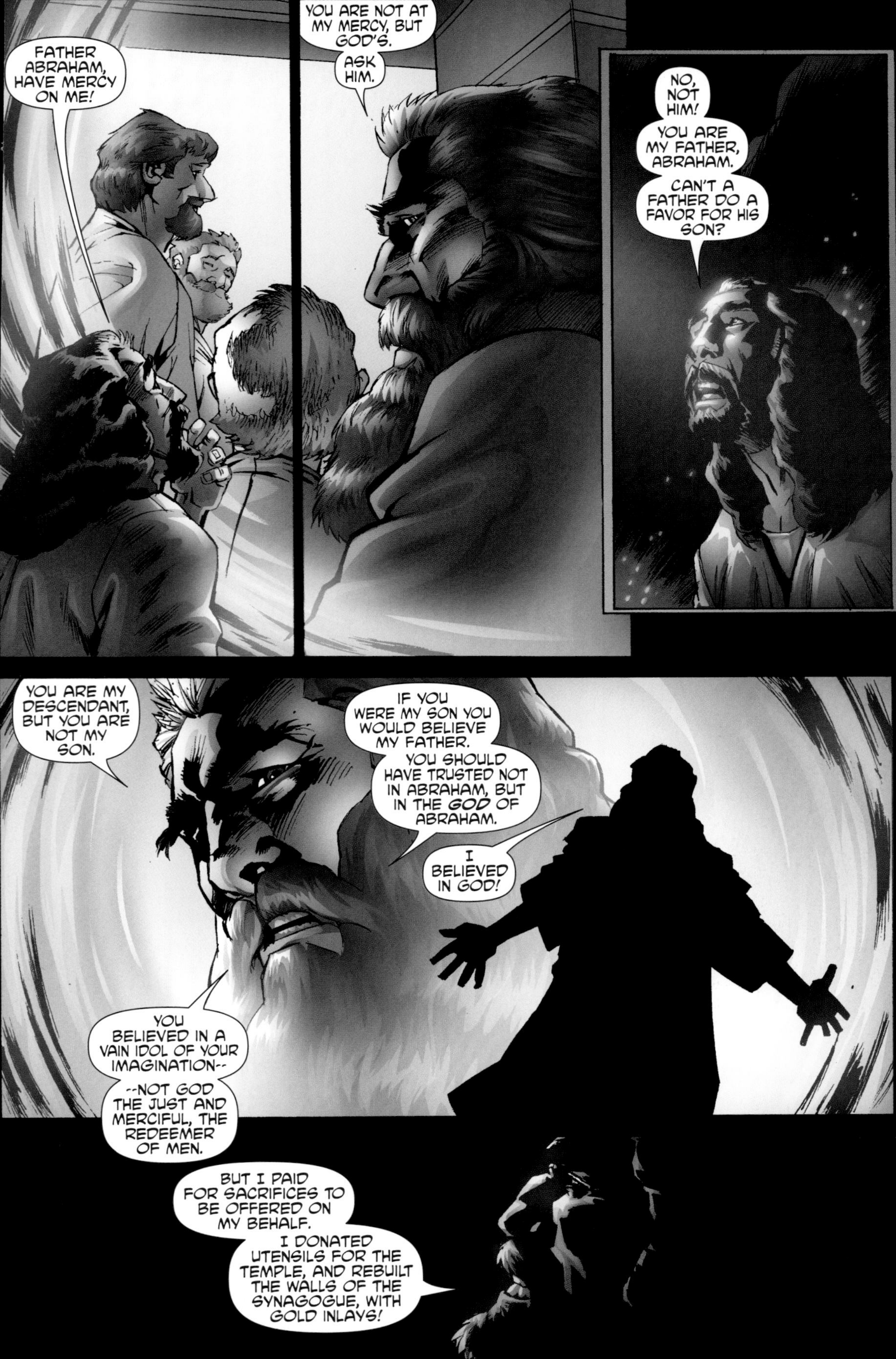
FATHER ABRAHAM, HAVE MERCY ON ME!
YOU ARE NOT AT MY MERCY, BUT GOD'S.
ASK HIM.
NO, NOT HIM!
YOU ARE MY FATHER, ABRAHAM.
CAN'T A FATHER DO A FAVOR FOR HIS SON?
YOU ARE MY DESCENDANT, BUT YOU ARE NOT MY SON.
IF YOU WERE MY SON YOU WOULD BELIEVE MY FATHER.
YOU SHOULD HAVE TRUSTED NOT IN ABRAHAM, BUT IN THE GOD OF ABRAHAM.
I BELIEVED IN GOD!
YOU BELIEVED IN A VAIN IDOL OF YOUR IMAGINATION--
--NOT GOD THE JUST AND MERCIFUL, THE REDEEMER OF MEN.
BUT I PAID FOR SACRIFICES TO BE OFFERED ON MY BEHALF.
I DONATED UTENSILS FOR THE TEMPLE, AND REBUILT THE WALLS OF THE SYNAGOGUE, WITH GOLD INLAYS!

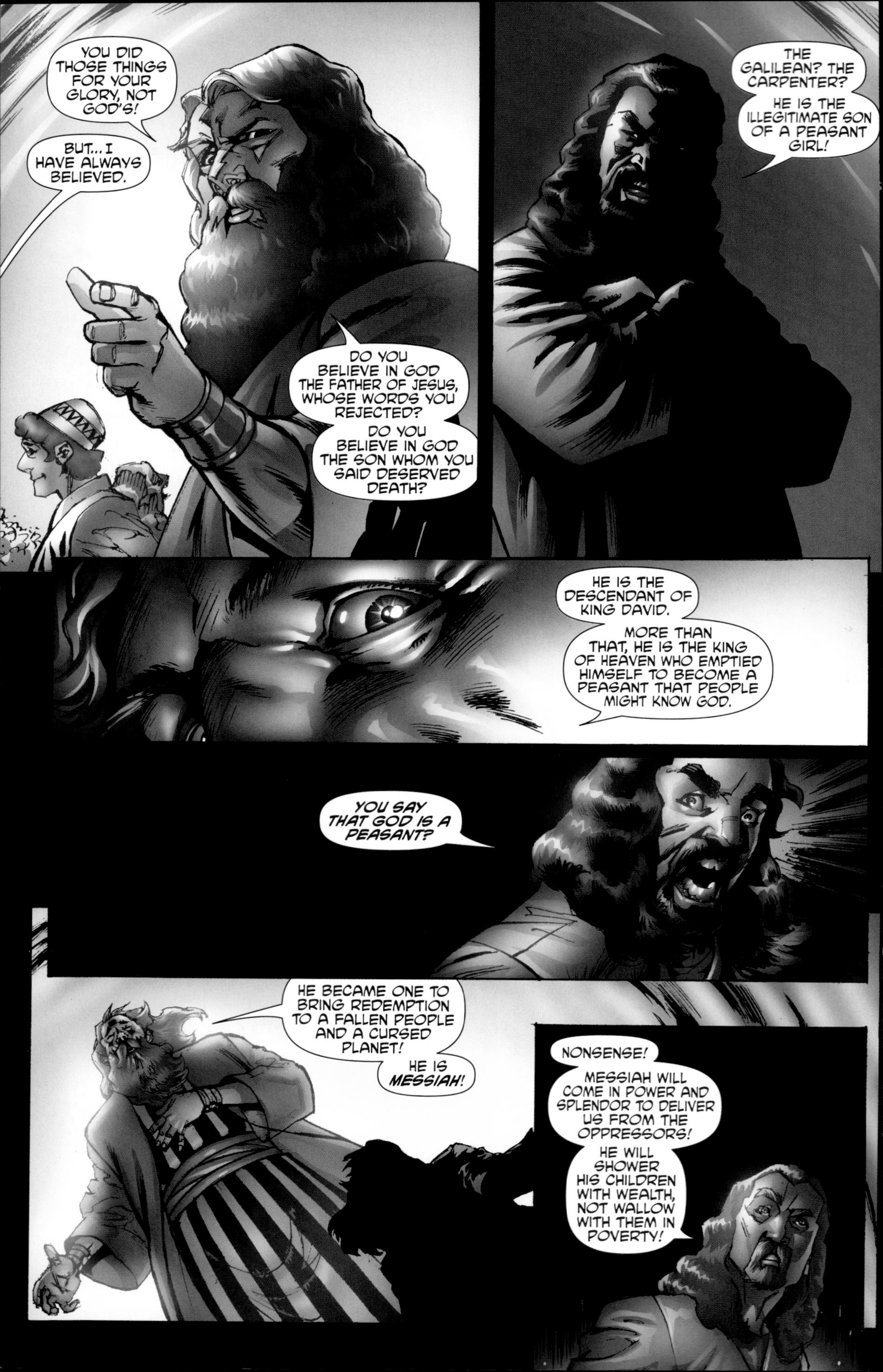
YOU DID THOSE THINGS FOR YOUR GLORY, NOT GOD'S!
BUT... I HAVE ALWAYS BELIEVED.
DO YOU BELIEVE IN GOD THE FATHER OF JESUS, WHOSE WORDS YOU REJECTED?
DO YOU BELIEVE IN GOD THE SON WHOM YOU SAID DESERVED DEATH?
THE GALILEAN? THE CARPENTER?
HE IS THE ILLEGITIMATE SON OF A PEASANT GIRL!
HE IS THE DESCENDANT OF KING DAVID.
MORE THAN THAT, HE IS THE KING OF HEAVEN WHO EMPTIED HIMSELF TO BECOME A PEASANT THAT PEOPLE MIGHT KNOW GOD.
YOU SAY THAT GOD IS A PEASANT?
HE BECAME ONE TO BRING REDEMPTION TO A FALLEN PEOPLE AND A CURSED PLANET!
HE IS MESSIAH!
NONSENSE!
MESSIAH WILL COME IN POWER AND SPLENDOR TO DELIVER US FROM THE OPPRESSORS!
HE WILL SHOWER HIS CHILDREN WITH WEALTH, NOT WALLOW WITH THEM IN POVERTY!

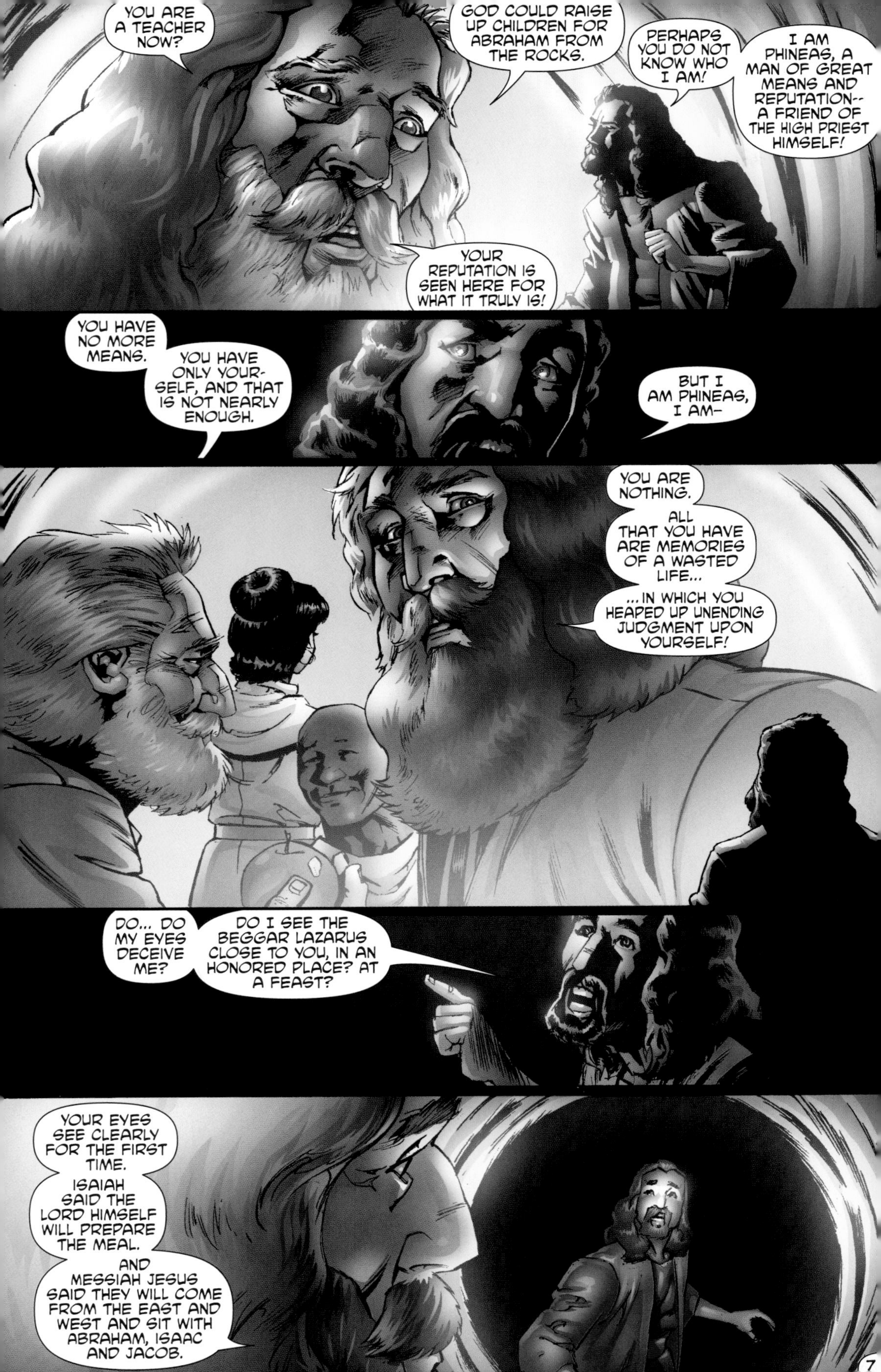
YOU ARE A TEACHER NOW?
GOD COULD RAISE UP CHILDREN FOR ABRAHAM FROM THE ROCKS.
PERHAPS YOU DO NOT KNOW WHO I AM!
I AM PHINEAS, A MAN OF GREAT MEANS AND REPUTATION-- A FRIEND OF THE HIGH PRIEST HIMSELF!
YOUR REPUTATION IS SEEN HERE FOR WHAT IT TRULY IS!
YOU HAVE NO MORE MEANS.
YOU HAVE ONLY YOURSELF, AND THAT IS NOT NEARLY ENOUGH.
BUT I AM PHINEAS, I AM—
YOU ARE NOTHING.
ALL THAT YOU HAVE ARE MEMORIES OF A WASTED LIFE...
...IN WHICH YOU HEAPED UP UNENDING JUDGMENT UPON YOURSELF!
DO... DO MY EYES DECEIVE ME?
DO I SEE THE BEGGAR LAZARUS CLOSE TO YOU, IN AN HONORED PLACE? AT A FEAST?
YOUR EYES SEE CLEARLY FOR THE FIRST TIME.
ISAIAH SAID THE LORD HIMSELF WILL PREPARE THE MEAL.
AND MESSIAH JESUS SAID THEY WILL COME FROM THE EAST AND WEST AND SIT WITH ABRAHAM, ISAAC AND JACOB.

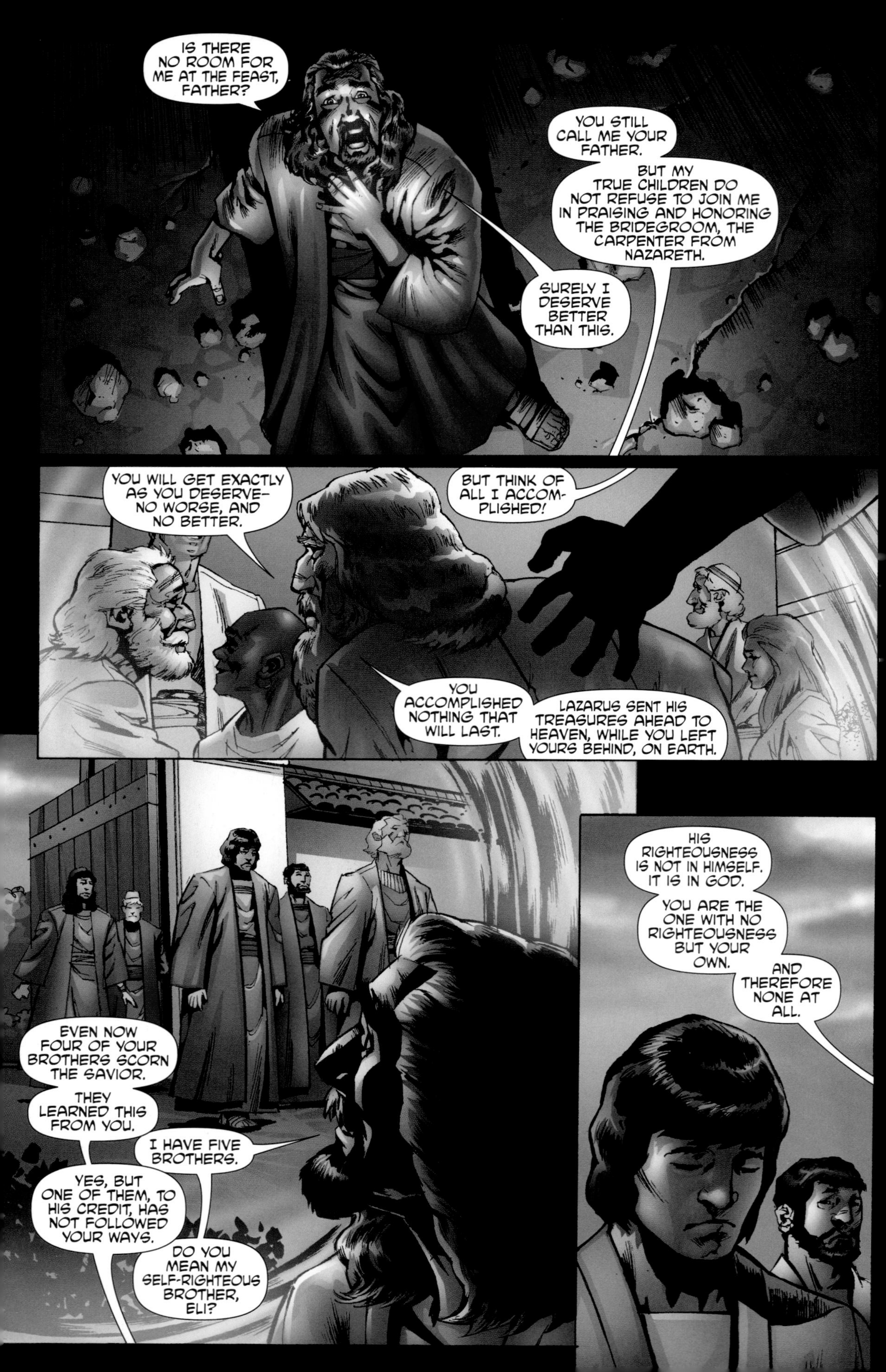
IS THERE NO ROOM FOR ME AT THE FEAST, FATHER?
YOU STILL CALL ME YOUR FATHER.
BUT MY TRUE CHILDREN DO NOT REFUSE TO JOIN ME IN PRAISING AND HONORING THE BRIDEGROOM, THE CARPENTER FROM NAZARETH.
SURELY I DESERVE BETTER THAN THIS.
YOU WILL GET EXACTLY AS YOU DESERVE— NO WORSE, AND NO BETTER.
BUT THINK OF ALL I ACCOMPLISHED!
YOU ACCOMPLISHED NOTHING THAT WILL LAST.
LAZARUS SENT HIS TREASURES AHEAD TO HEAVEN, WHILE YOU LEFT YOURS BEHIND, ON EARTH.
EVEN NOW FOUR OF YOUR BROTHERS SCORN THE SAVIOR.
THEY LEARNED THIS FROM YOU.
I HAVE FIVE BROTHERS.
YES, BUT ONE OF THEM, TO HIS CREDIT, HAS NOT FOLLOWED YOUR WAYS.
DO YOU MEAN MY SELF-RIGHTEOUS BROTHER, ELI?
HIS RIGHTEOUSNESS IS NOT IN HIMSELF. IT IS IN GOD.
YOU ARE THE ONE WITH NO RIGHTEOUSNESS BUT YOUR OWN.
AND THEREFORE NONE AT ALL.

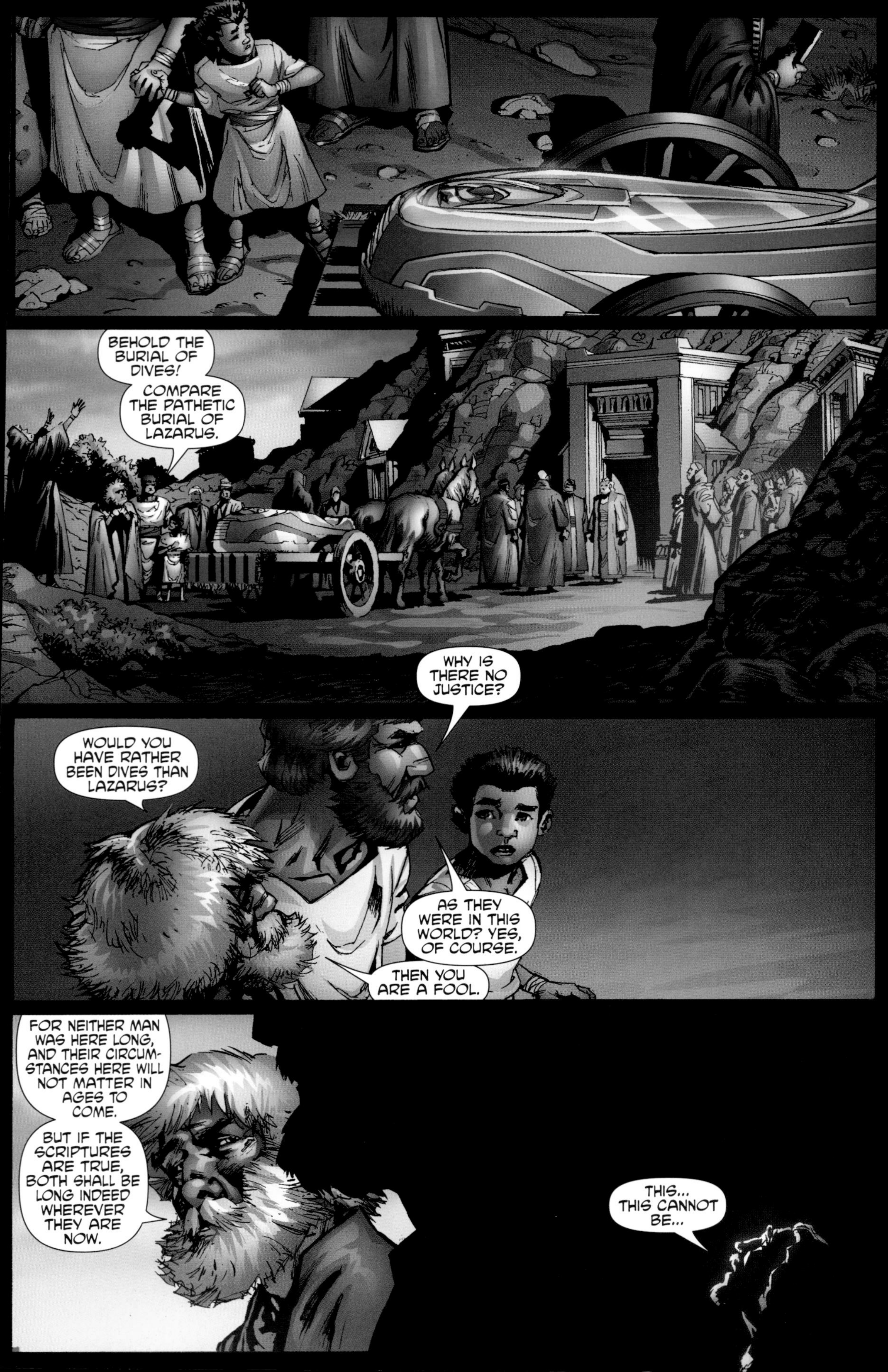
BEHOLD THE BURIAL OF DIVES!
COMPARE THE PATHETIC BURIAL OF LAZARUS.
WHY IS THERE NO JUSTICE?
WOULD YOU HAVE RATHER BEEN DIVES THAN LAZARUS?
AS THEY WERE IN THIS WORLD? YES, OF COURSE.
THEN YOU ARE A FOOL.
FOR NEITHER MAN WAS HERE LONG, AND THEIR CIRCUM-STANCES HERE WILL NOT MATTER IN AGES TO COME.
BUT IF THE SCRIPTURES ARE TRUE, BOTH SHALL BE LONG INDEED WHEREVER THEY ARE NOW.
THIS... THIS CANNOT BE...

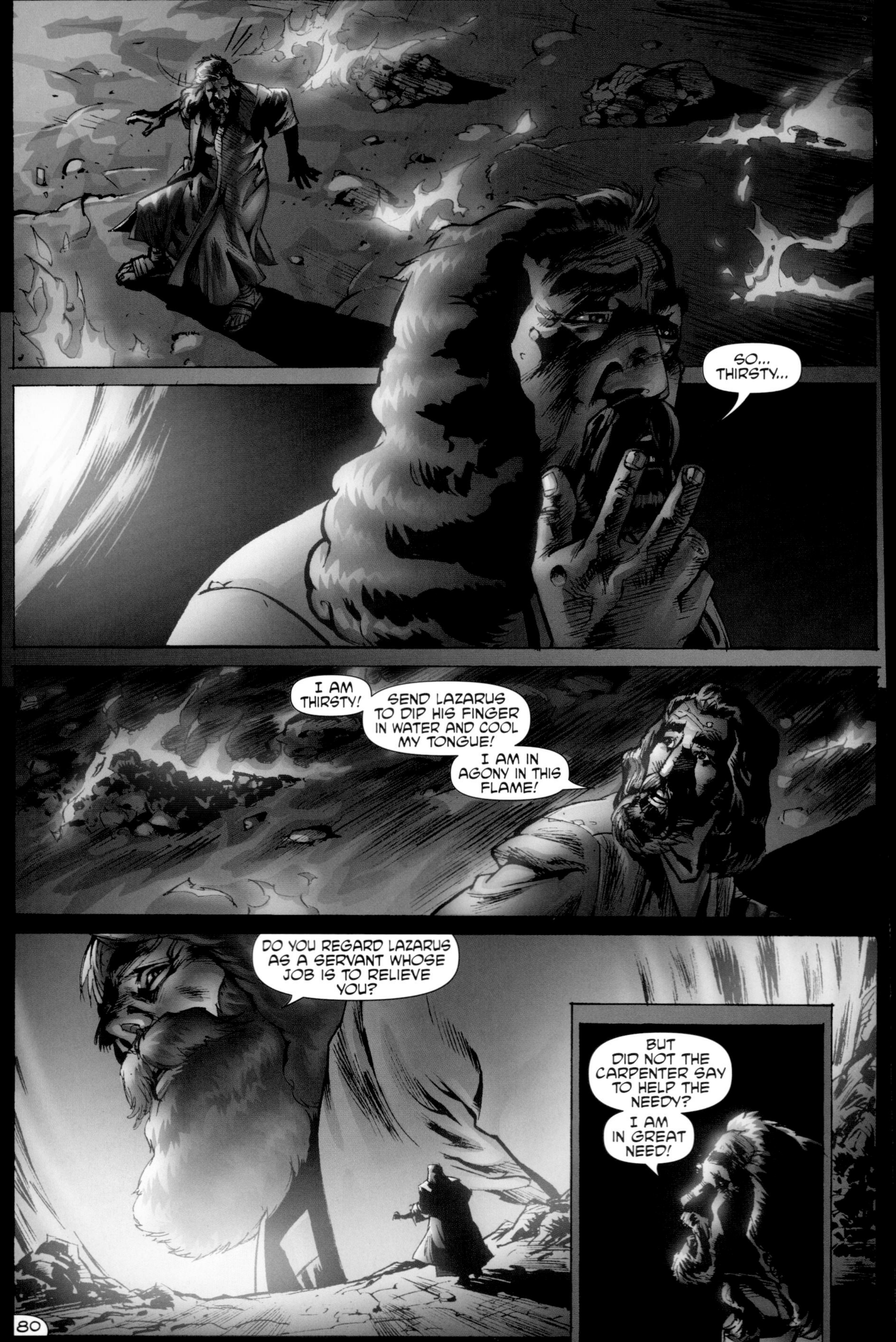
SO... THIRSTY...
I AM THIRSTY!
SEND LAZARUS TO DIP HIS FINGER IN WATER AND COOL MY TONGUE!
I AM IN AGONY IN THIS FLAME!
DO YOU REGARD LAZARUS AS A SERVANT WHOSE JOB IS TO RELIEVE YOU?
BUT DID NOT THE CARPENTER SAY TO HELP THE NEEDY?
I AM IN GREAT NEED!

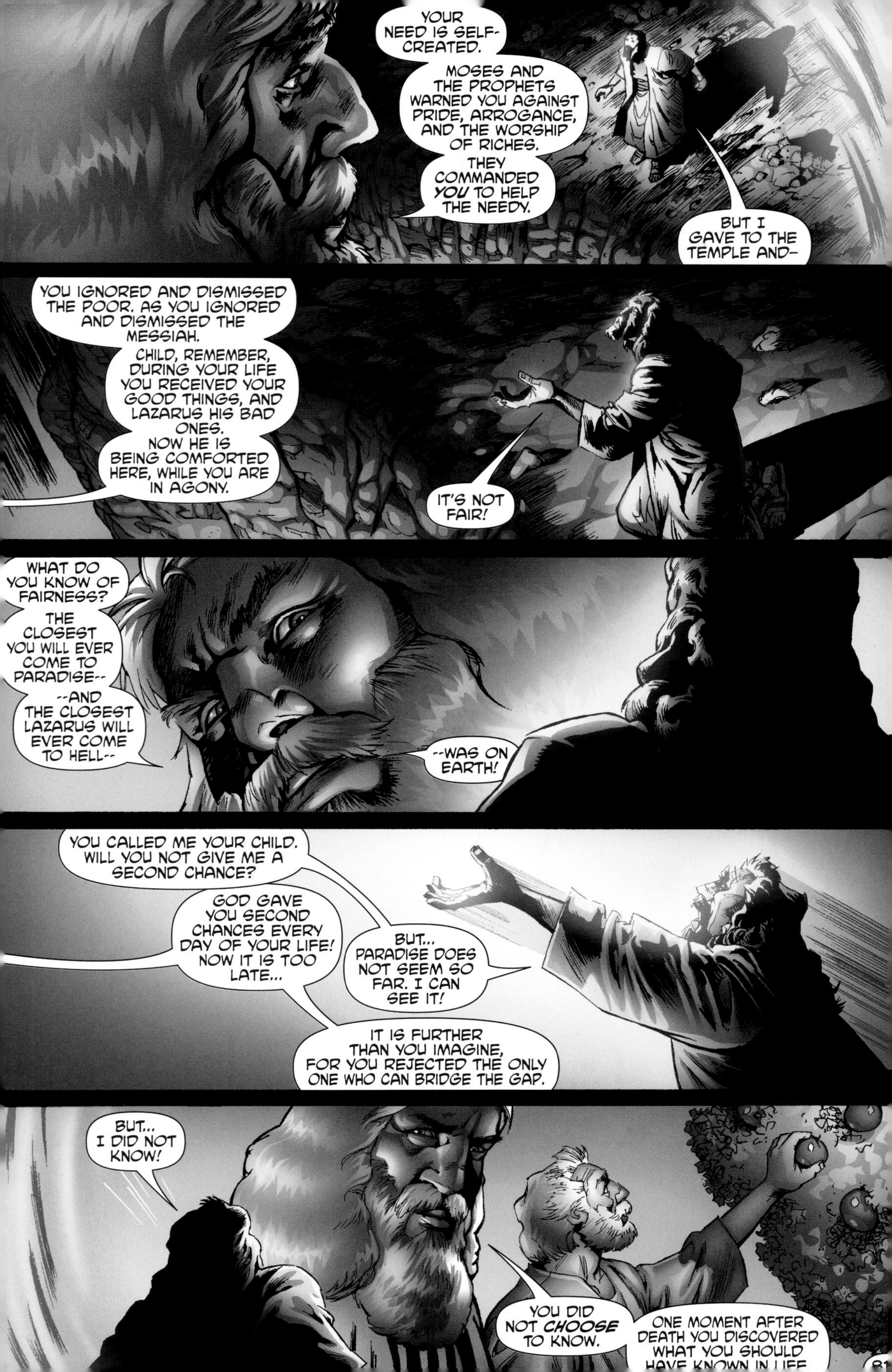
YOUR NEED IS SELF-CREATED.
MOSES AND THE PROPHETS WARNED YOU AGAINST PRIDE, ARROGANCE, AND THE WORSHIP OF RICHES.
THEY COMMANDED *YOU* TO HELP THE NEEDY.
BUT I GAVE TO THE TEMPLE AND-
YOU IGNORED AND DISMISSED THE POOR. AS YOU IGNORED AND DISMISSED THE MESSIAH.
CHILD, REMEMBER, DURING YOUR LIFE YOU RECEIVED YOUR GOOD THINGS, AND LAZARUS HIS BAD ONES.
NOW HE IS BEING COMFORTED HERE, WHILE YOU ARE IN AGONY.
IT'S NOT FAIR!
WHAT DO YOU KNOW OF FAIRNESS?
THE CLOSEST YOU WILL EVER COME TO PARADISE--
--AND THE CLOSEST LAZARUS WILL EVER COME TO HELL--
--WAS ON EARTH!
YOU CALLED ME YOUR CHILD. WILL YOU NOT GIVE ME A SECOND CHANCE?
GOD GAVE YOU SECOND CHANCES EVERY DAY OF YOUR LIFE! NOW IT IS TOO LATE...
BUT... PARADISE DOES NOT SEEM SO FAR. I CAN SEE IT!
IT IS FURTHER THAN YOU IMAGINE, FOR YOU REJECTED THE ONLY ONE WHO CAN BRIDGE THE GAP.
BUT... I DID NOT KNOW!
YOU DID NOT *CHOOSE* TO KNOW.
ONE MOMENT AFTER DEATH YOU DISCOVERED WHAT YOU SHOULD HAVE KNOWN IN LIFE

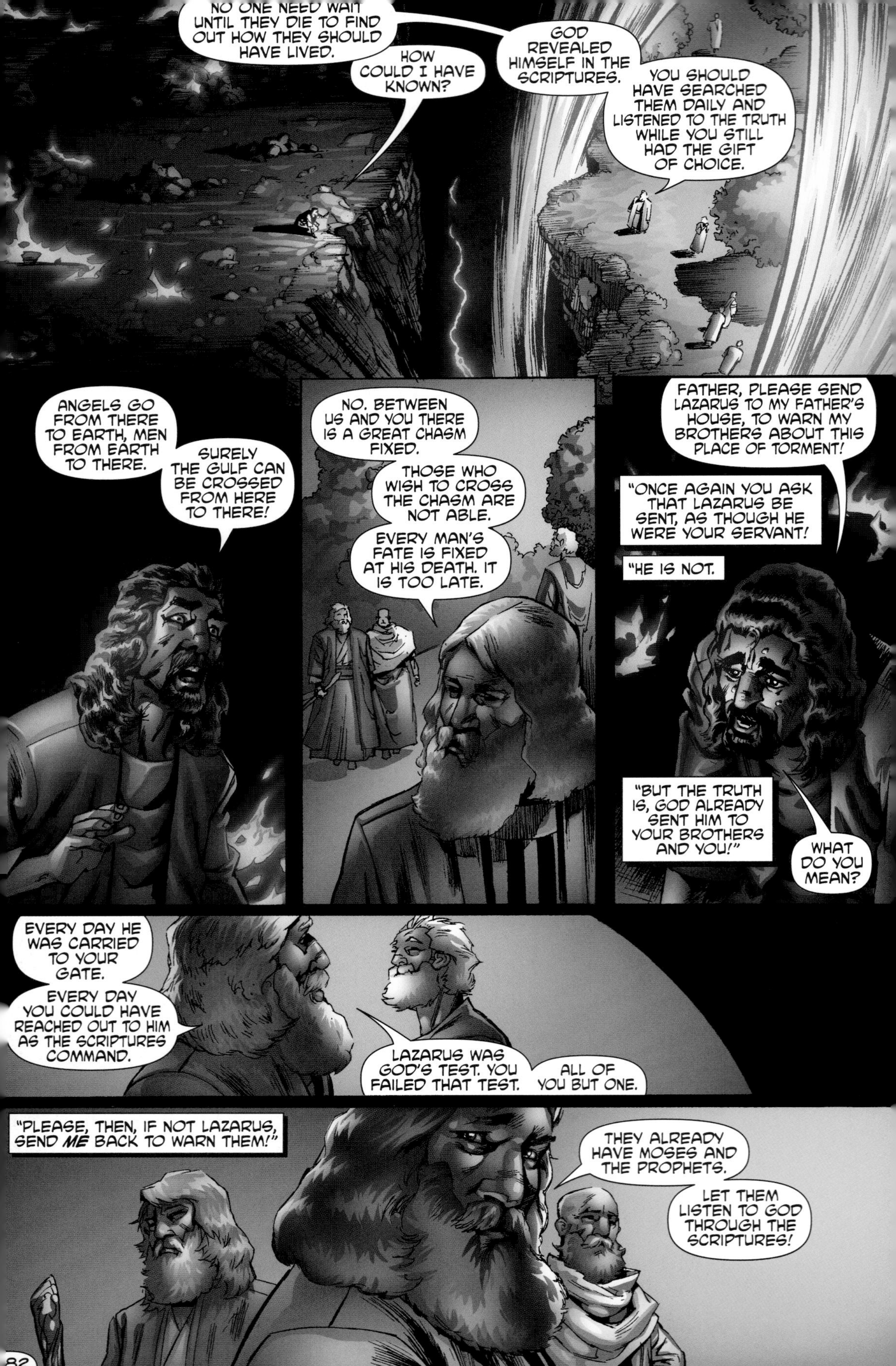
NO ONE NEED WAIT UNTIL THEY DIE TO FIND OUT HOW THEY SHOULD HAVE LIVED.
HOW COULD I HAVE KNOWN?
GOD REVEALED HIMSELF IN THE SCRIPTURES.
YOU SHOULD HAVE SEARCHED THEM DAILY AND LISTENED TO THE TRUTH WHILE YOU STILL HAD THE GIFT OF CHOICE.
ANGELS GO FROM THERE TO EARTH, MEN FROM EARTH TO THERE.
SURELY THE GULF CAN BE CROSSED FROM HERE TO THERE!
NO. BETWEEN US AND YOU THERE IS A GREAT CHASM FIXED.
THOSE WHO WISH TO CROSS THE CHASM ARE NOT ABLE.
EVERY MAN'S FATE IS FIXED AT HIS DEATH. IT IS TOO LATE.
FATHER, PLEASE SEND LAZARUS TO MY FATHER'S HOUSE, TO WARN MY BROTHERS ABOUT THIS PLACE OF TORMENT!
"ONCE AGAIN YOU ASK THAT LAZARUS BE SENT, AS THOUGH HE WERE YOUR SERVANT!
"HE IS NOT.
"BUT THE TRUTH IS, GOD ALREADY SENT HIM TO YOUR BROTHERS AND YOU!"
WHAT DO YOU MEAN?
EVERY DAY HE WAS CARRIED TO YOUR GATE.
EVERY DAY YOU COULD HAVE REACHED OUT TO HIM AS THE SCRIPTURES COMMAND.
LAZARUS WAS GOD'S TEST. YOU FAILED THAT TEST.
ALL OF YOU BUT ONE.
"PLEASE, THEN, IF NOT LAZARUS, SEND *ME* BACK TO WARN THEM!"
THEY ALREADY HAVE MOSES AND THE PROPHETS.
LET THEM LISTEN TO GOD THROUGH THE SCRIPTURES!

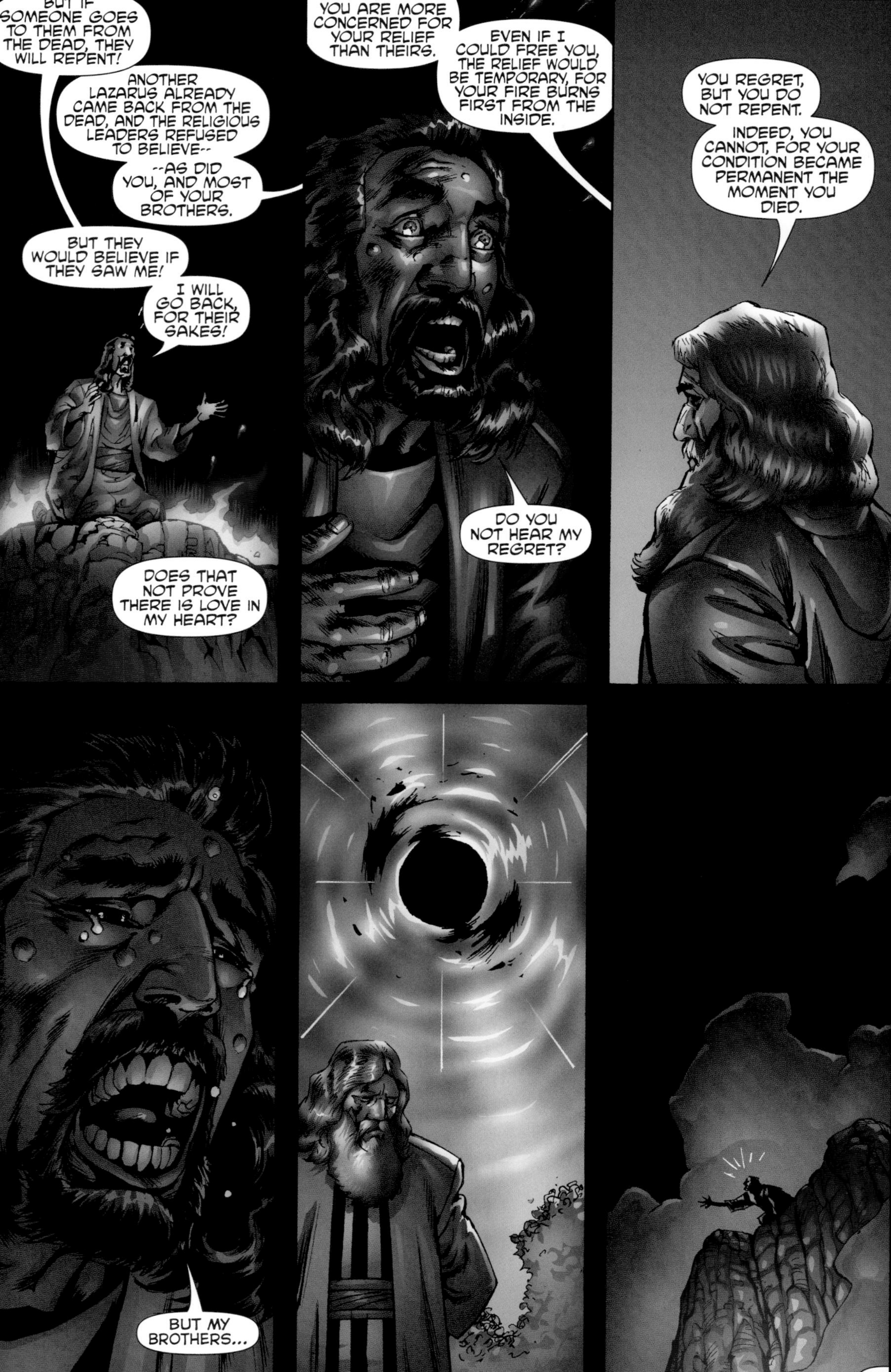
BUT IF SOMEONE GOES TO THEM FROM THE DEAD, THEY WILL REPENT!
ANOTHER LAZARUS ALREADY CAME BACK FROM THE DEAD, AND THE RELIGIOUS LEADERS REFUSED TO BELIEVE--
--AS DID YOU, AND MOST OF YOUR BROTHERS.
BUT THEY WOULD BELIEVE IF THEY SAW ME!
I WILL GO BACK, FOR THEIR SAKES!
DOES THAT NOT PROVE THERE IS LOVE IN MY HEART?
YOU ARE MORE CONCERNED FOR YOUR RELIEF THAN THEIRS.
EVEN IF I COULD FREE YOU, THE RELIEF WOULD BE TEMPORARY, FOR YOUR FIRE BURNS FIRST FROM THE INSIDE.
DO YOU NOT HEAR MY REGRET?
YOU REGRET, BUT YOU DO NOT REPENT.
INDEED, YOU CANNOT, FOR YOUR CONDITION BECAME PERMANENT THE MOMENT YOU DIED.
BUT MY BROTHERS...

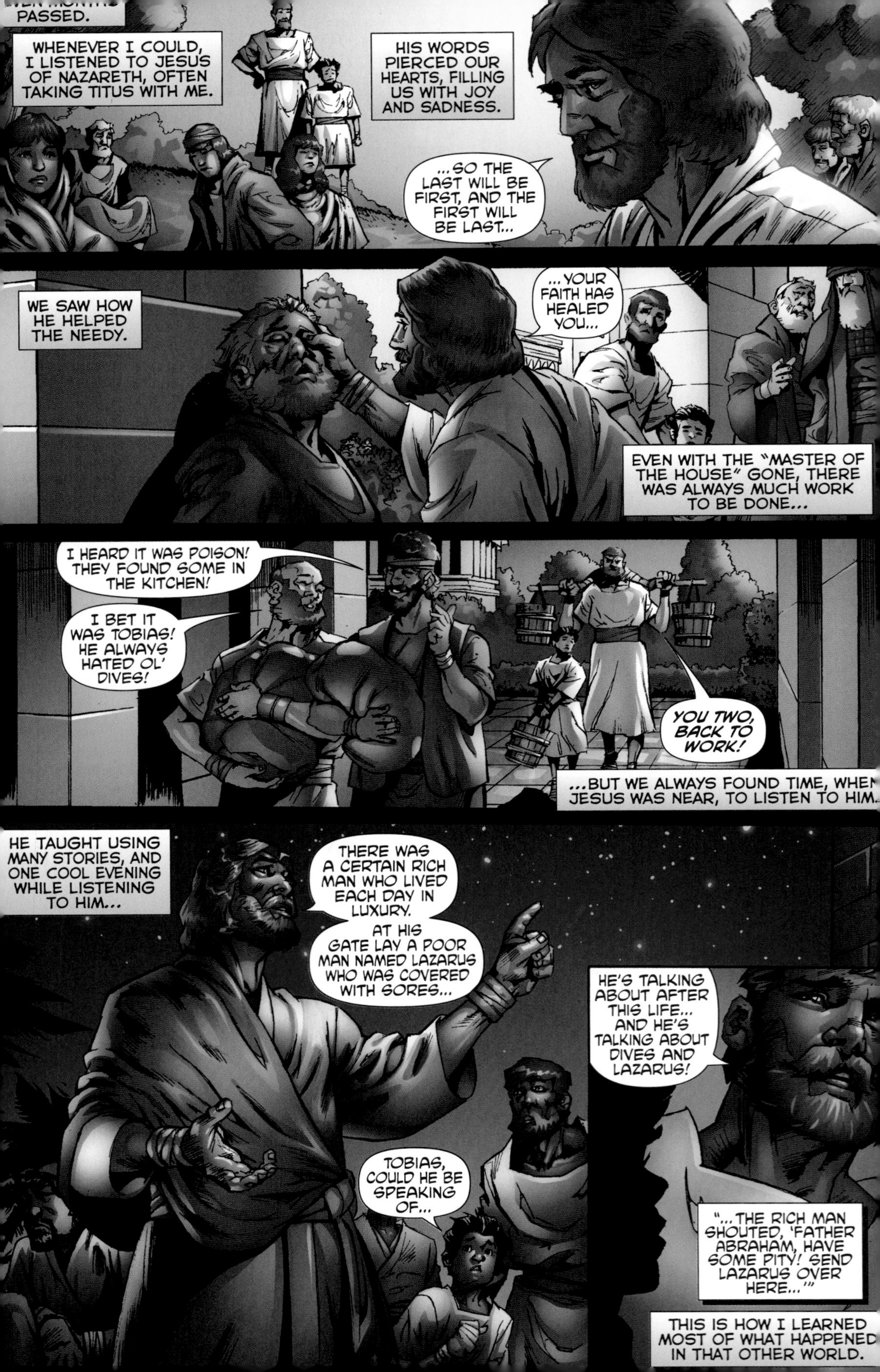
...PASSED.
WHENEVER I COULD, I LISTENED TO JESUS OF NAZARETH, OFTEN TAKING TITUS WITH ME.
HIS WORDS PIERCED OUR HEARTS, FILLING US WITH JOY AND SADNESS.
...SO THE LAST WILL BE FIRST, AND THE FIRST WILL BE LAST...
WE SAW HOW HE HELPED THE NEEDY.
...YOUR FAITH HAS HEALED YOU...
EVEN WITH THE "MASTER OF THE HOUSE" GONE, THERE WAS ALWAYS MUCH WORK TO BE DONE...
I HEARD IT WAS POISON! THEY FOUND SOME IN THE KITCHEN!
I BET IT WAS TOBIAS! HE ALWAYS HATED OL' DIVES!
YOU TWO, BACK TO WORK!
...BUT WE ALWAYS FOUND TIME, WHEN JESUS WAS NEAR, TO LISTEN TO HIM.
HE TAUGHT USING MANY STORIES, AND ONE COOL EVENING WHILE LISTENING TO HIM...
THERE WAS A CERTAIN RICH MAN WHO LIVED EACH DAY IN LUXURY.
AT HIS GATE LAY A POOR MAN NAMED LAZARUS WHO WAS COVERED WITH SORES...
TOBIAS, COULD HE BE SPEAKING OF...
HE'S TALKING ABOUT AFTER THIS LIFE... AND HE'S TALKING ABOUT DIVES AND LAZARUS!
"...THE RICH MAN SHOUTED, 'FATHER ABRAHAM, HAVE SOME PITY! SEND LAZARUS OVER HERE...'"
THIS IS HOW I LEARNED MOST OF WHAT HAPPENED IN THAT OTHER WORLD.

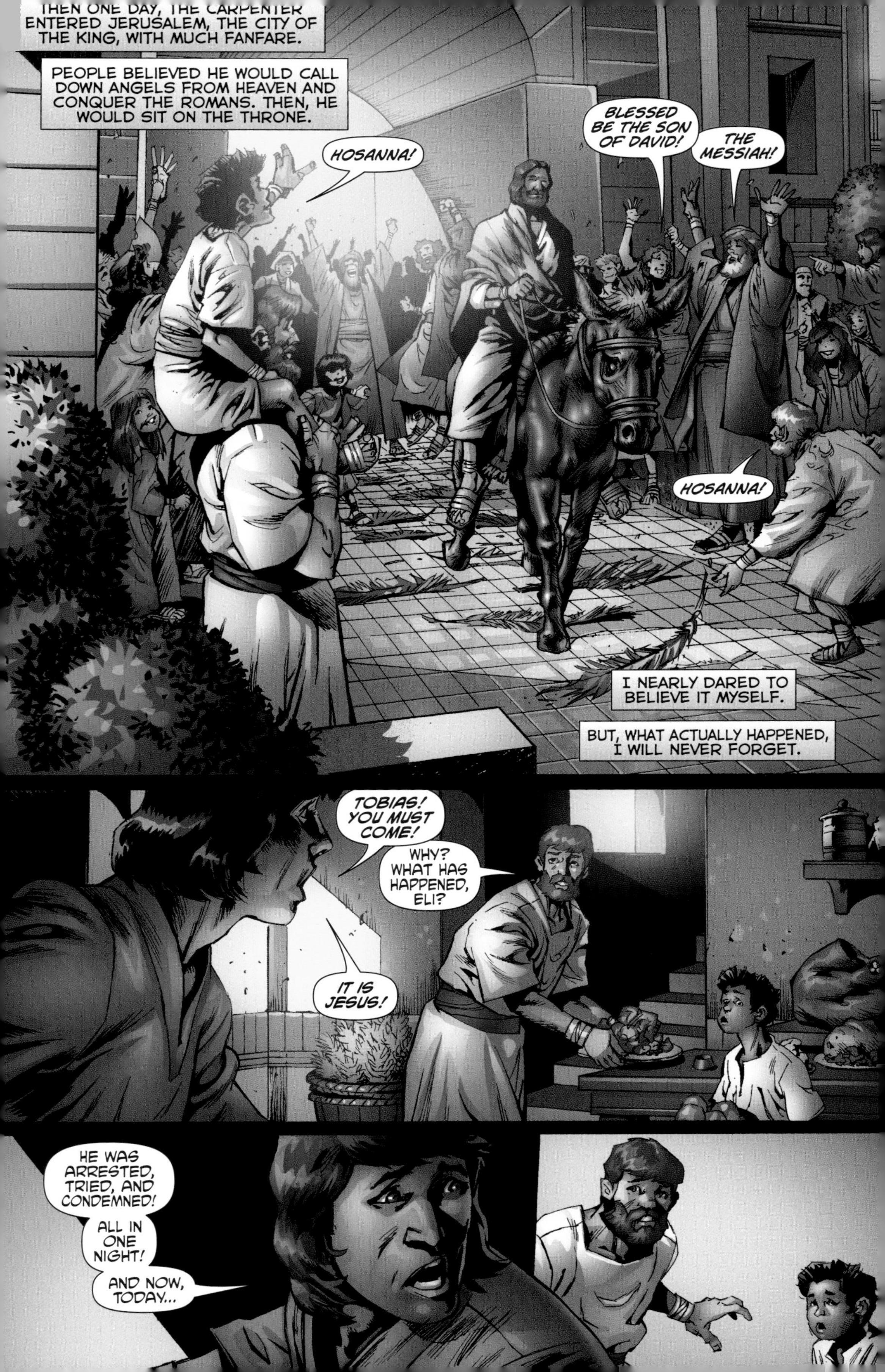
THEN ONE DAY, THE CARPENTER ENTERED JERUSALEM, THE CITY OF THE KING, WITH MUCH FANFARE.
PEOPLE BELIEVED HE WOULD CALL DOWN ANGELS FROM HEAVEN AND CONQUER THE ROMANS. THEN, HE WOULD SIT ON THE THRONE.
HOSANNA!
BLESSED BE THE SON OF DAVID!
THE MESSIAH!
HOSANNA!
I NEARLY DARED TO BELIEVE IT MYSELF.
BUT, WHAT ACTUALLY HAPPENED, I WILL NEVER FORGET.
TOBIAS! YOU MUST COME!
WHY? WHAT HAS HAPPENED, ELI?
IT IS JESUS!
HE WAS ARRESTED, TRIED, AND CONDEMNED!
ALL IN ONE NIGHT!
AND NOW, TODAY...

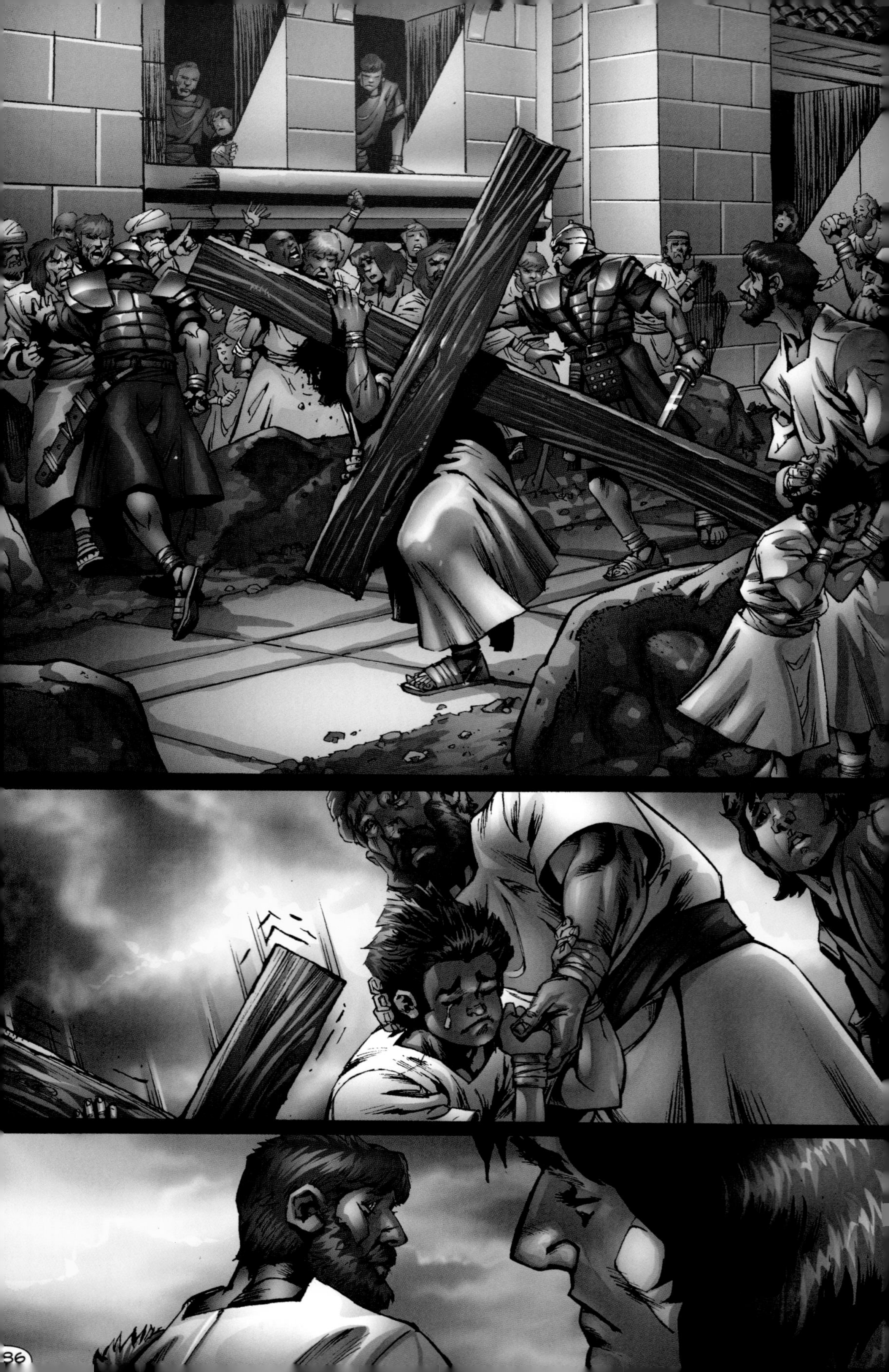

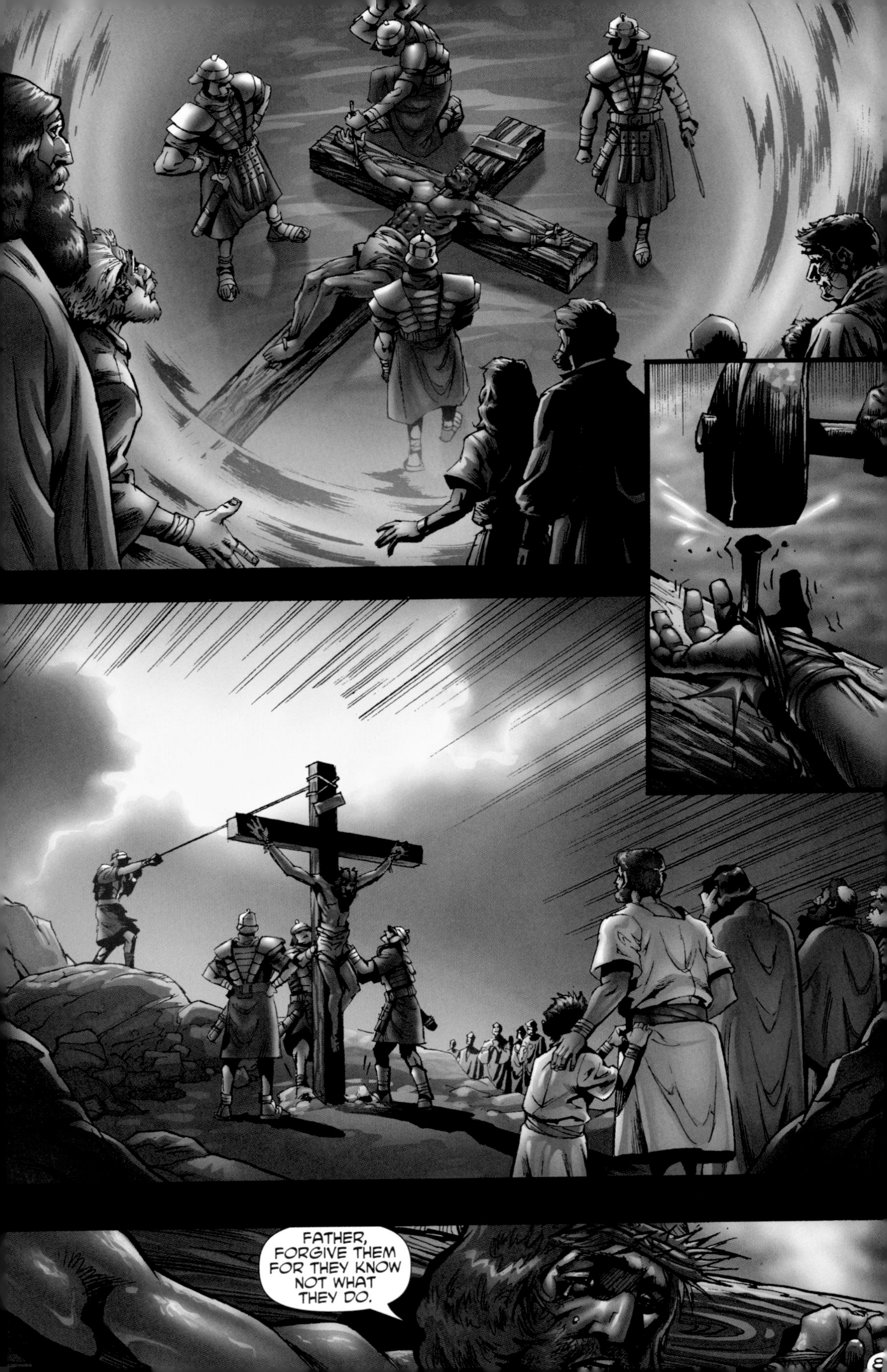
FATHER, FORGIVE THEM FOR THEY KNOW NOT WHAT THEY DO.

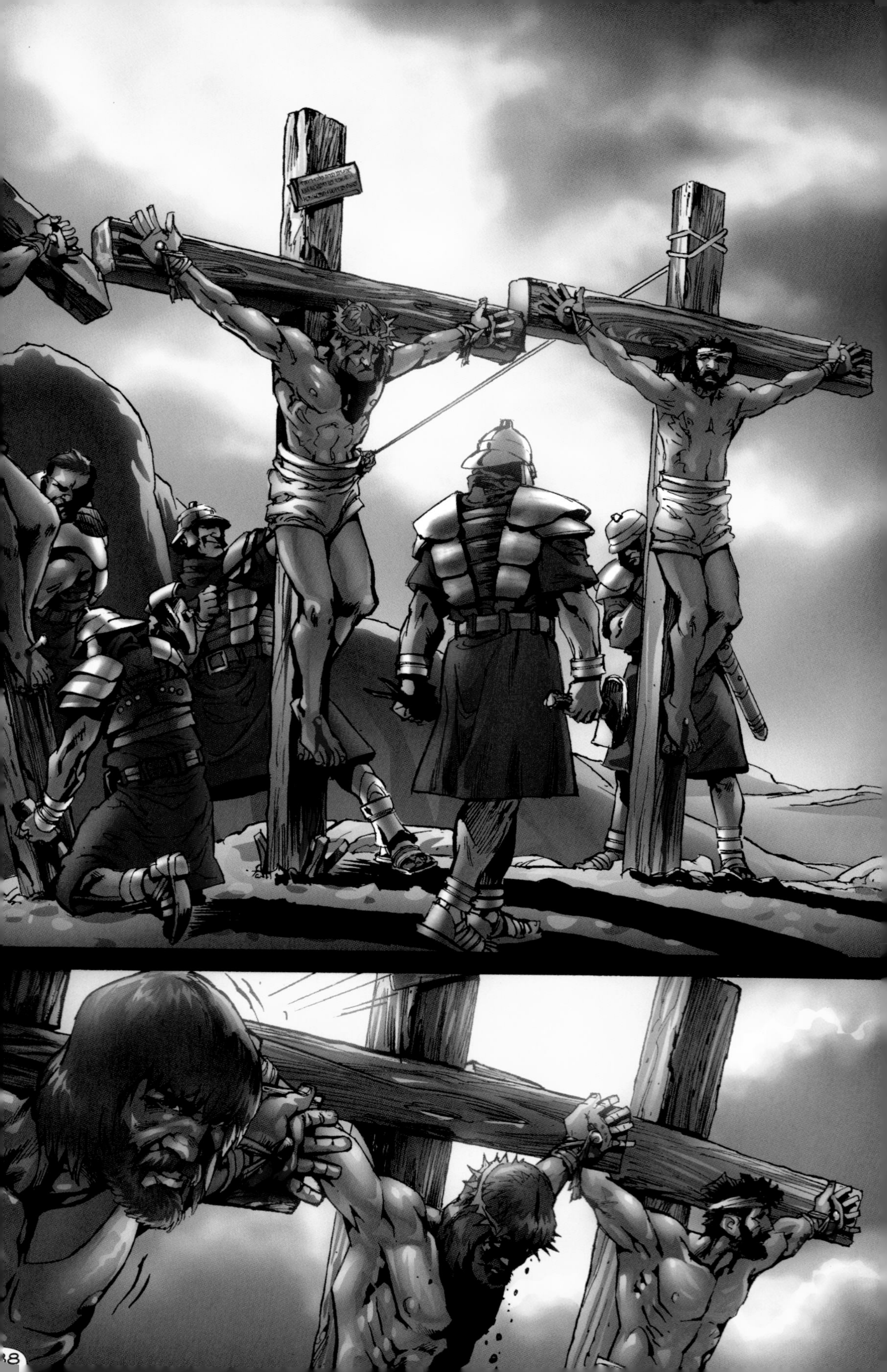

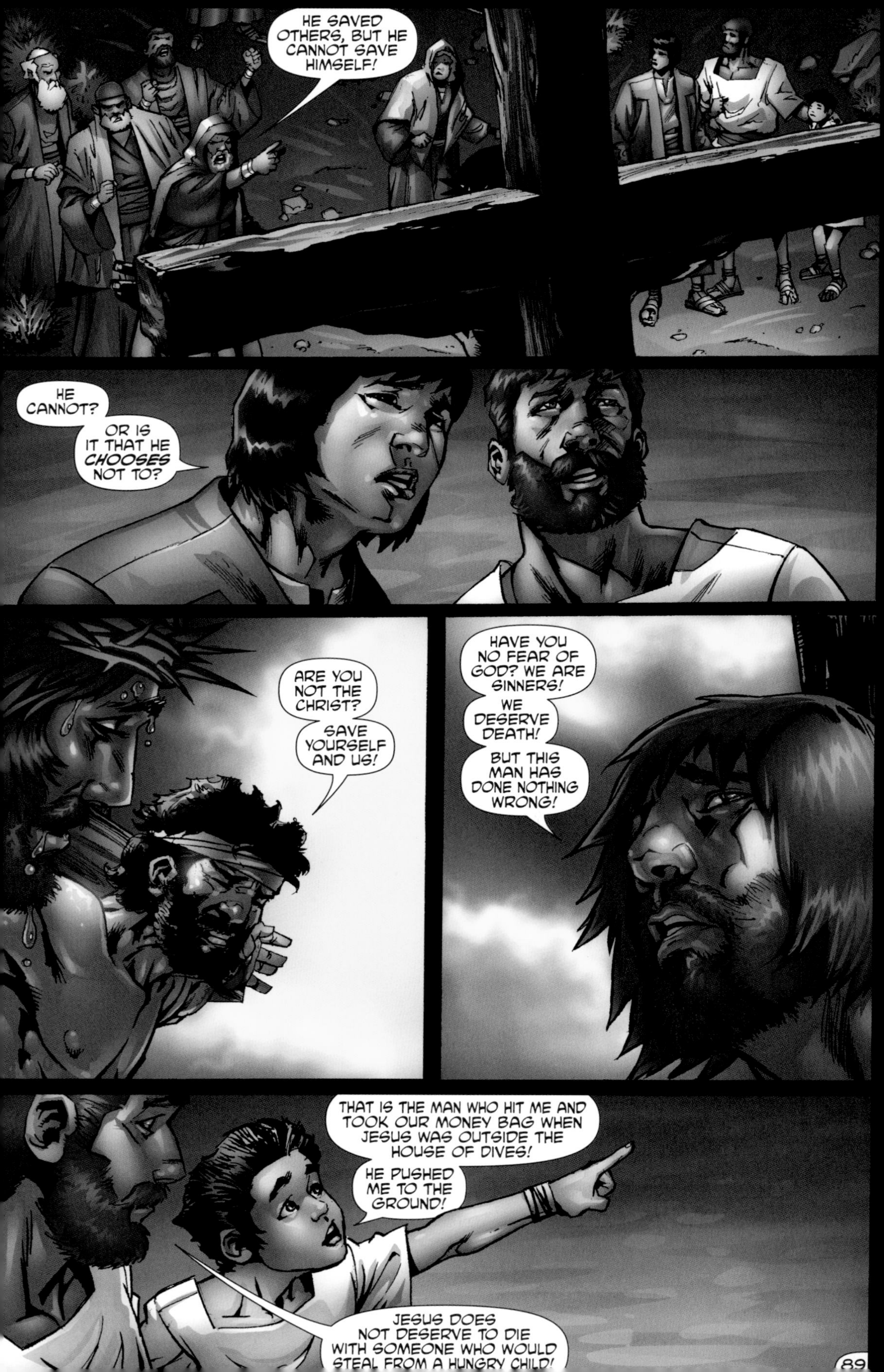
HE SAVED OTHERS, BUT HE CANNOT SAVE HIMSELF!
HE CANNOT?
OR IS IT THAT HE *CHOOSES* NOT TO?
ARE YOU NOT THE CHRIST?
SAVE YOURSELF AND US!
HAVE YOU NO FEAR OF GOD? WE ARE SINNERS!
WE DESERVE DEATH!
BUT THIS MAN HAS DONE NOTHING WRONG!
THAT IS THE MAN WHO HIT ME AND TOOK OUR MONEY BAG WHEN JESUS WAS OUTSIDE THE HOUSE OF DIVES!
HE PUSHED ME TO THE GROUND!
JESUS DOES NOT DESERVE TO DIE WITH SOMEONE WHO WOULD STEAL FROM A HUNGRY CHILD!

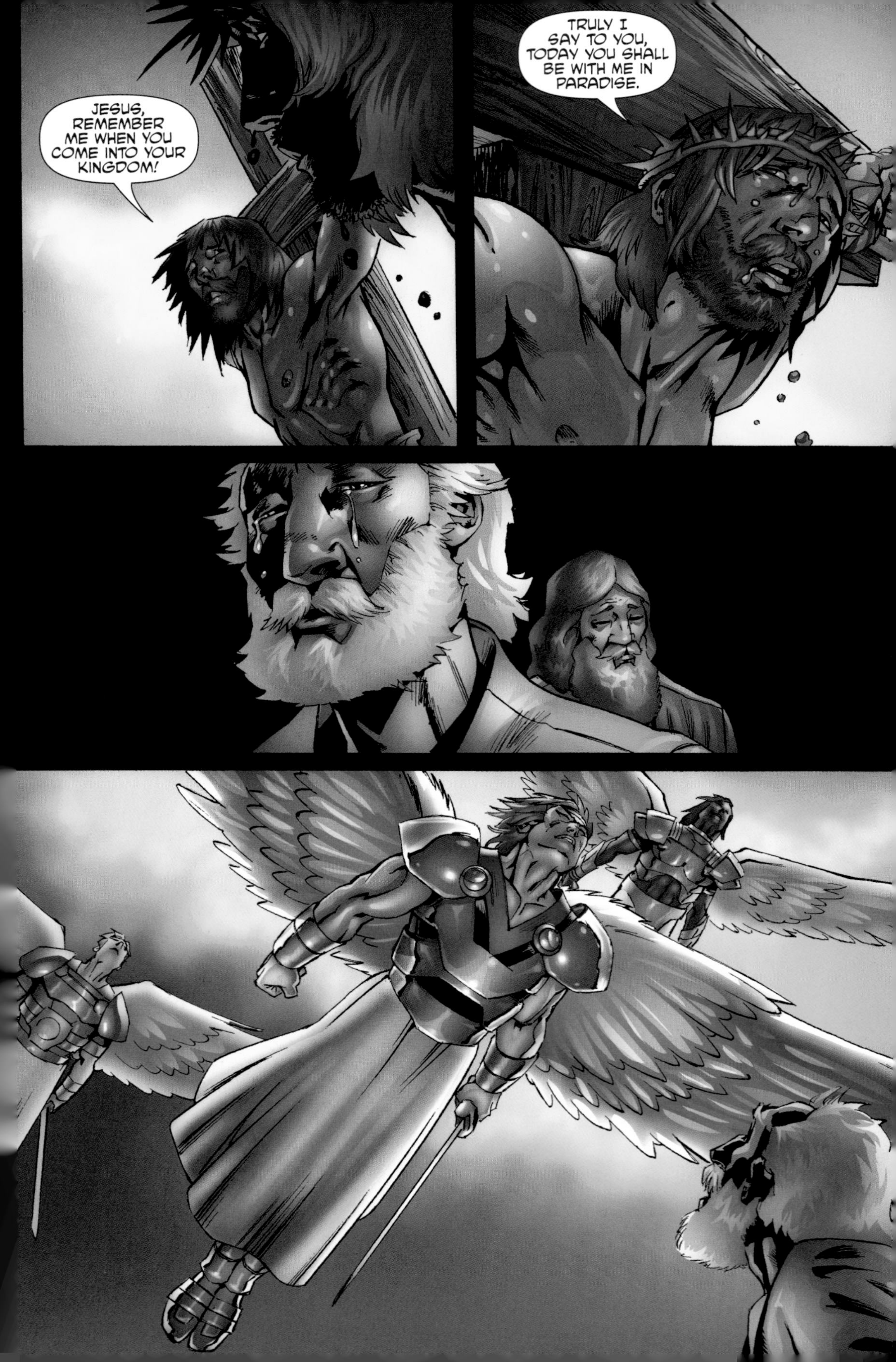
JESUS, REMEMBER ME WHEN YOU COME INTO YOUR KINGDOM!
TRULY I SAY TO YOU, TODAY YOU SHALL BE WITH ME IN PARADISE.

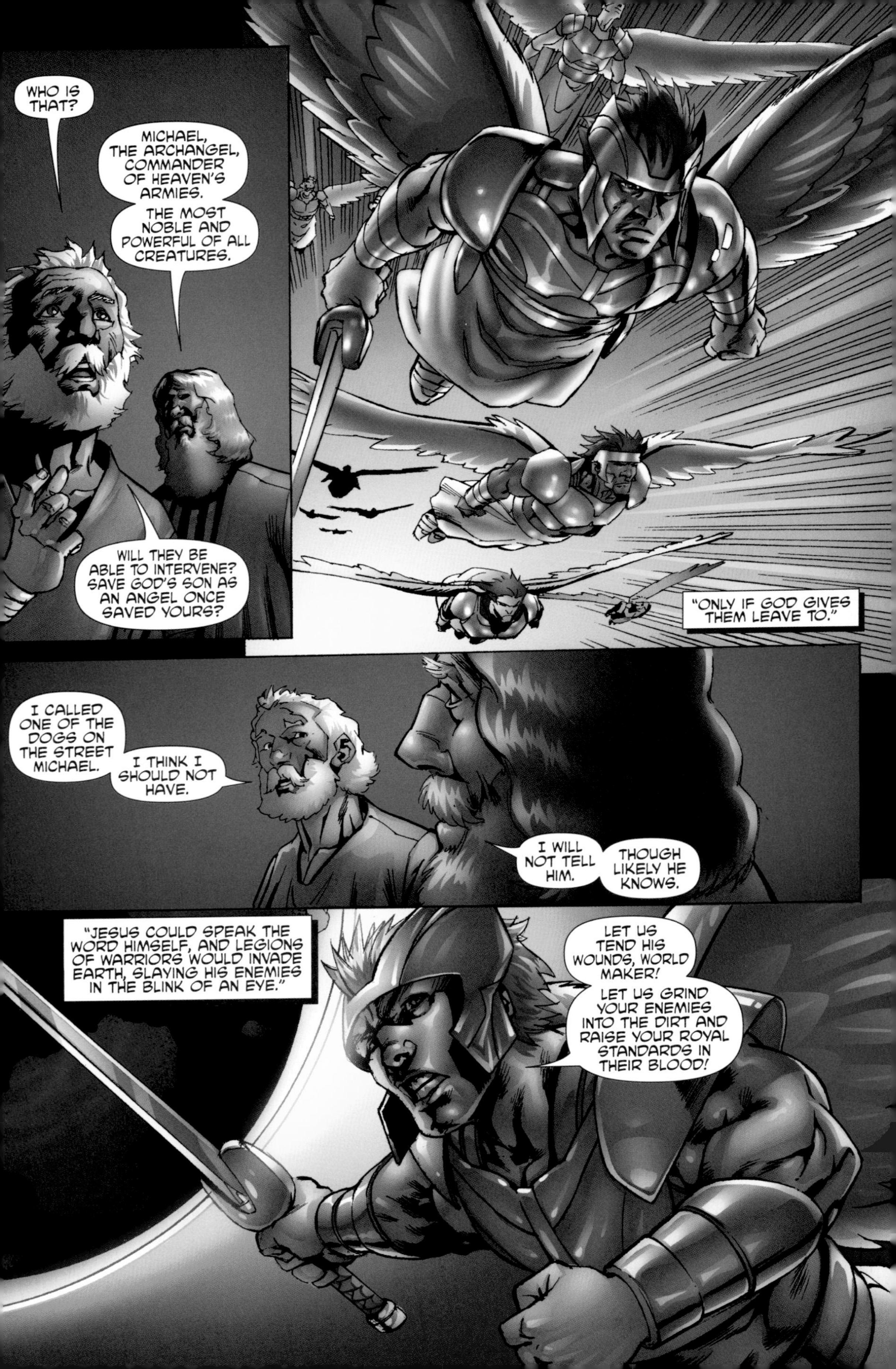
WHO IS THAT?
MICHAEL, THE ARCHANGEL, COMMANDER OF HEAVEN'S ARMIES.
THE MOST NOBLE AND POWERFUL OF ALL CREATURES.
WILL THEY BE ABLE TO INTERVENE? SAVE GOD'S SON AS AN ANGEL ONCE SAVED YOURS?
"ONLY IF GOD GIVES THEM LEAVE TO."
I CALLED ONE OF THE DOGS ON THE STREET MICHAEL.
I THINK I SHOULD NOT HAVE.
I WILL NOT TELL HIM.
THOUGH LIKELY HE KNOWS.
"JESUS COULD SPEAK THE WORD HIMSELF, AND LEGIONS OF WARRIORS WOULD INVADE EARTH, SLAYING HIS ENEMIES IN THE BLINK OF AN EYE."
LET US TEND HIS WOUNDS, WORLD MAKER!
LET US GRIND YOUR ENEMIES INTO THE DIRT AND RAISE YOUR ROYAL STANDARDS IN THEIR BLOOD!

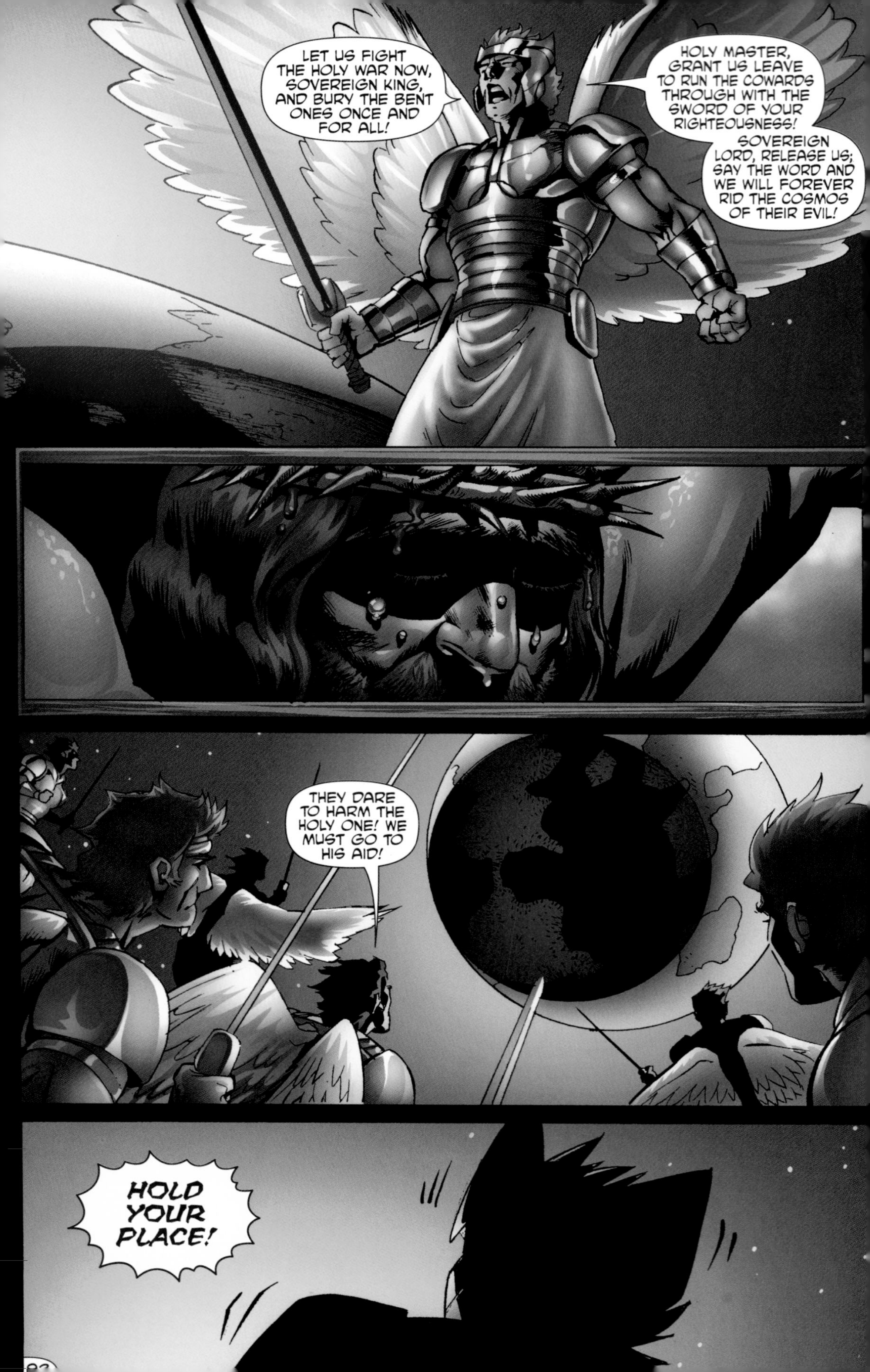
LET US FIGHT THE HOLY WAR NOW, SOVEREIGN KING, AND BURY THE BENT ONES ONCE AND FOR ALL!
HOLY MASTER, GRANT US LEAVE TO RUN THE COWARDS THROUGH WITH THE SWORD OF YOUR RIGHTEOUSNESS!
SOVEREIGN LORD, RELEASE US; SAY THE WORD AND WE WILL FOREVER RID THE COSMOS OF THEIR EVIL!
THEY DARE TO HARM THE HOLY ONE! WE MUST GO TO HIS AID!
HOLD YOUR PLACE!

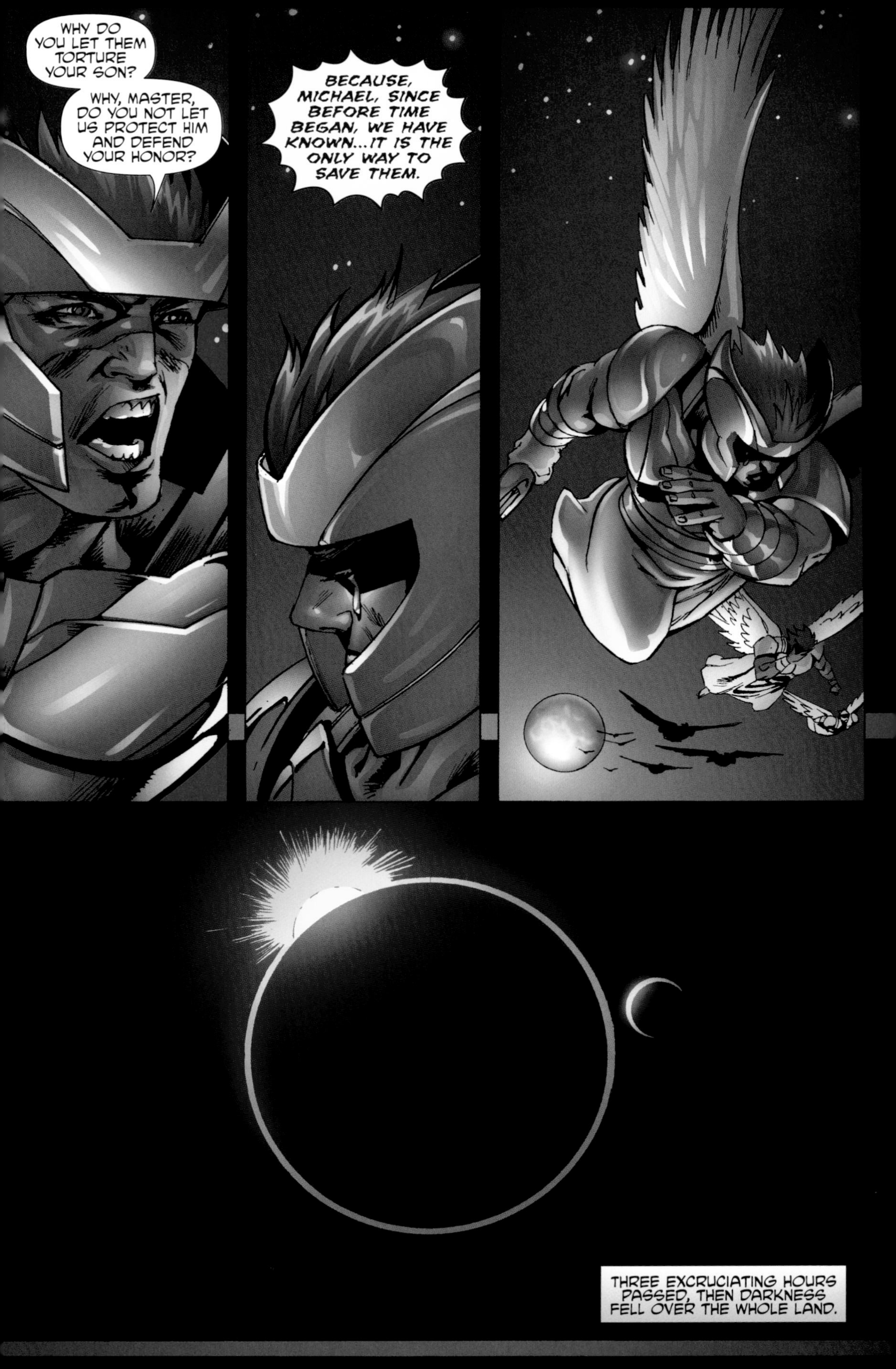
WHY DO YOU LET THEM TORTURE YOUR SON?
WHY, MASTER, DO YOU NOT LET US PROTECT HIM AND DEFEND YOUR HONOR?
BECAUSE, MICHAEL, SINCE BEFORE TIME BEGAN, WE HAVE KNOWN...IT IS THE ONLY WAY TO SAVE THEM.
THREE EXCRUCIATING HOURS PASSED, THEN DARKNESS FELL OVER THE WHOLE LAND.

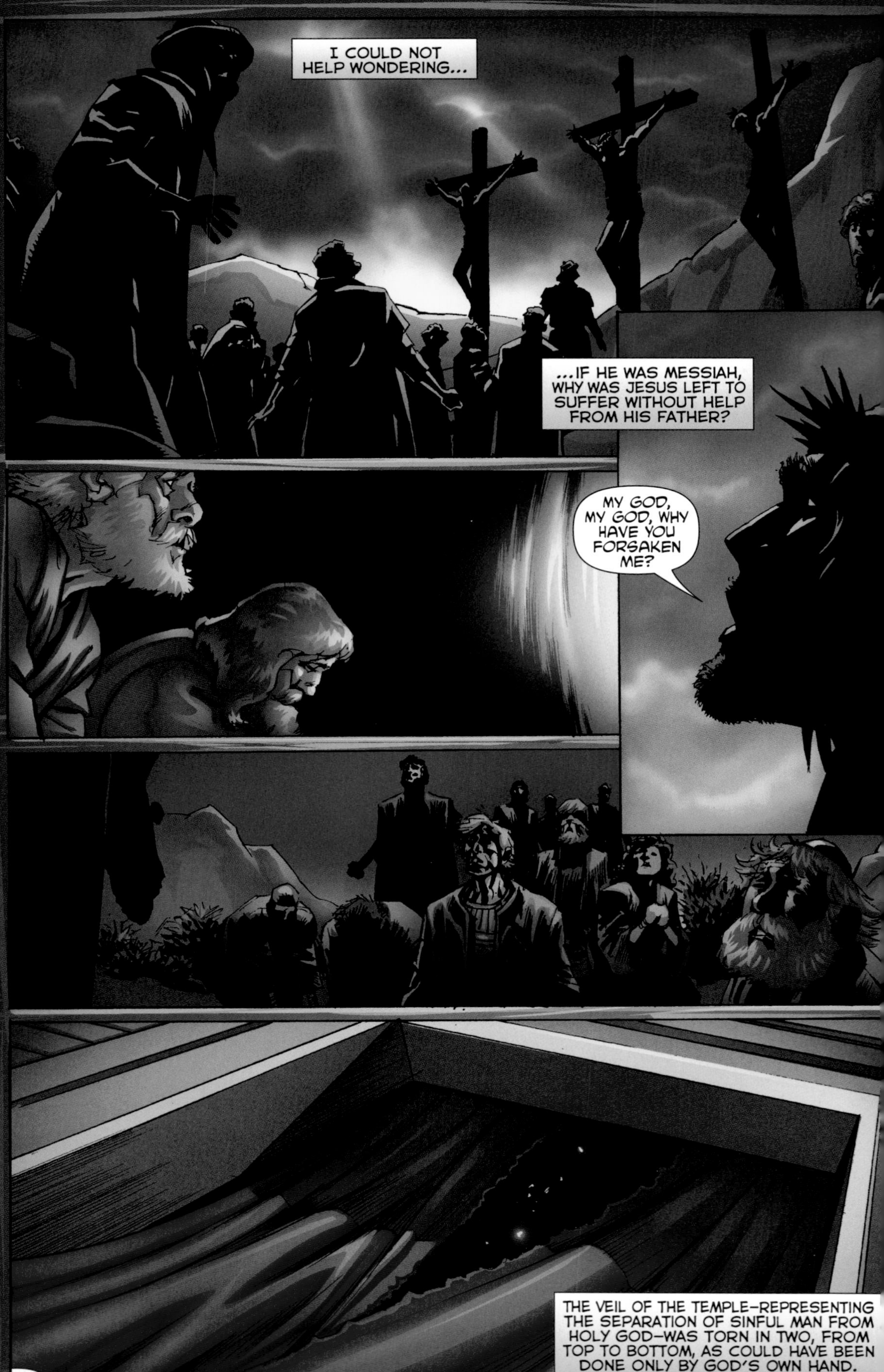
I COULD NOT HELP WONDERING...
...IF HE WAS MESSIAH, WHY WAS JESUS LEFT TO SUFFER WITHOUT HELP FROM HIS FATHER?
MY GOD, MY GOD, WHY HAVE YOU FORSAKEN ME?
THE VEIL OF THE TEMPLE—REPRESENTING THE SEPARATION OF SINFUL MAN FROM HOLY GOD—WAS TORN IN TWO, FROM TOP TO BOTTOM, AS COULD HAVE BEEN DONE ONLY BY GOD'S OWN HAND.

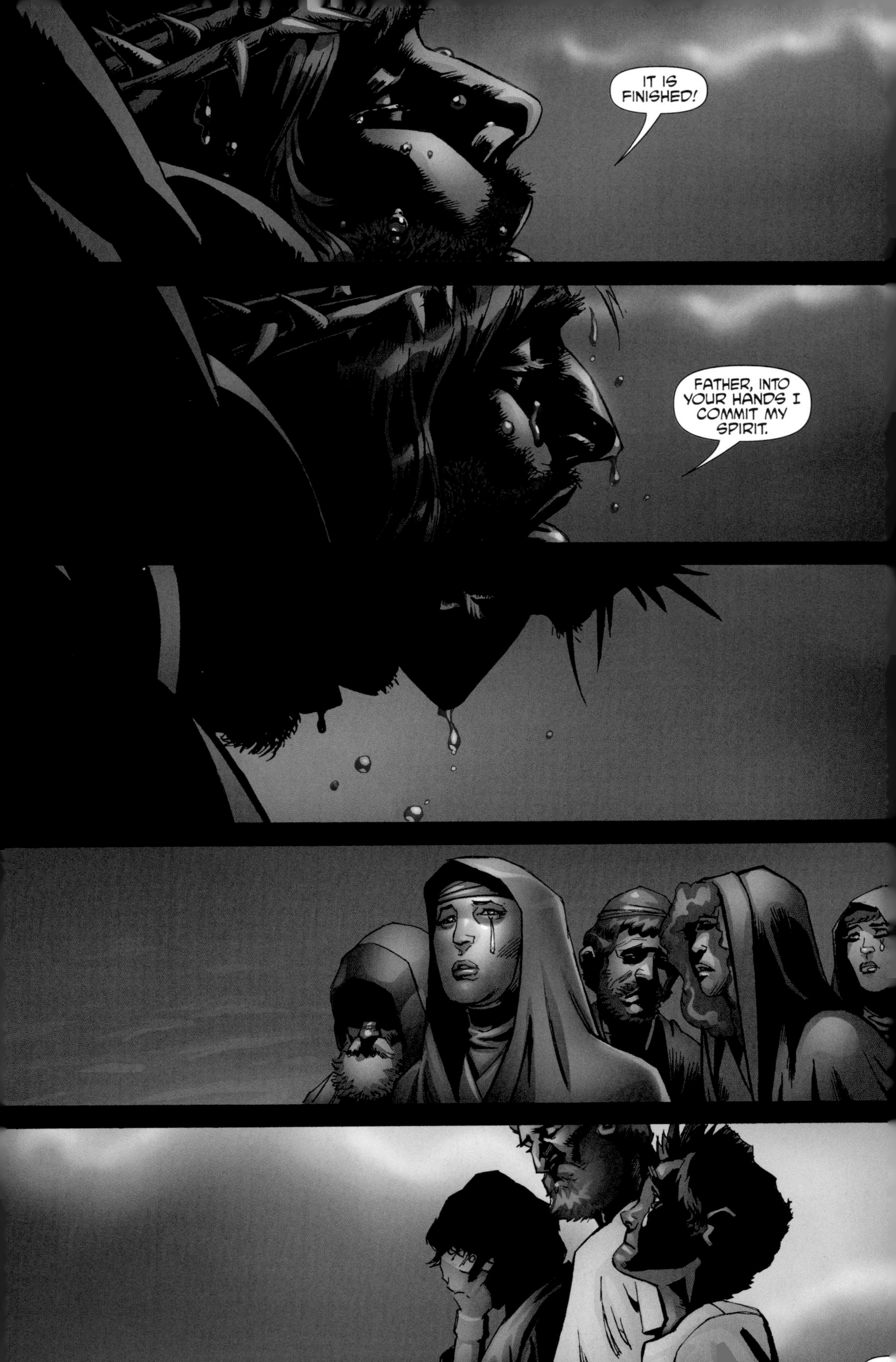
IT IS FINISHED!
FATHER, INTO YOUR HANDS I COMMIT MY SPIRIT.

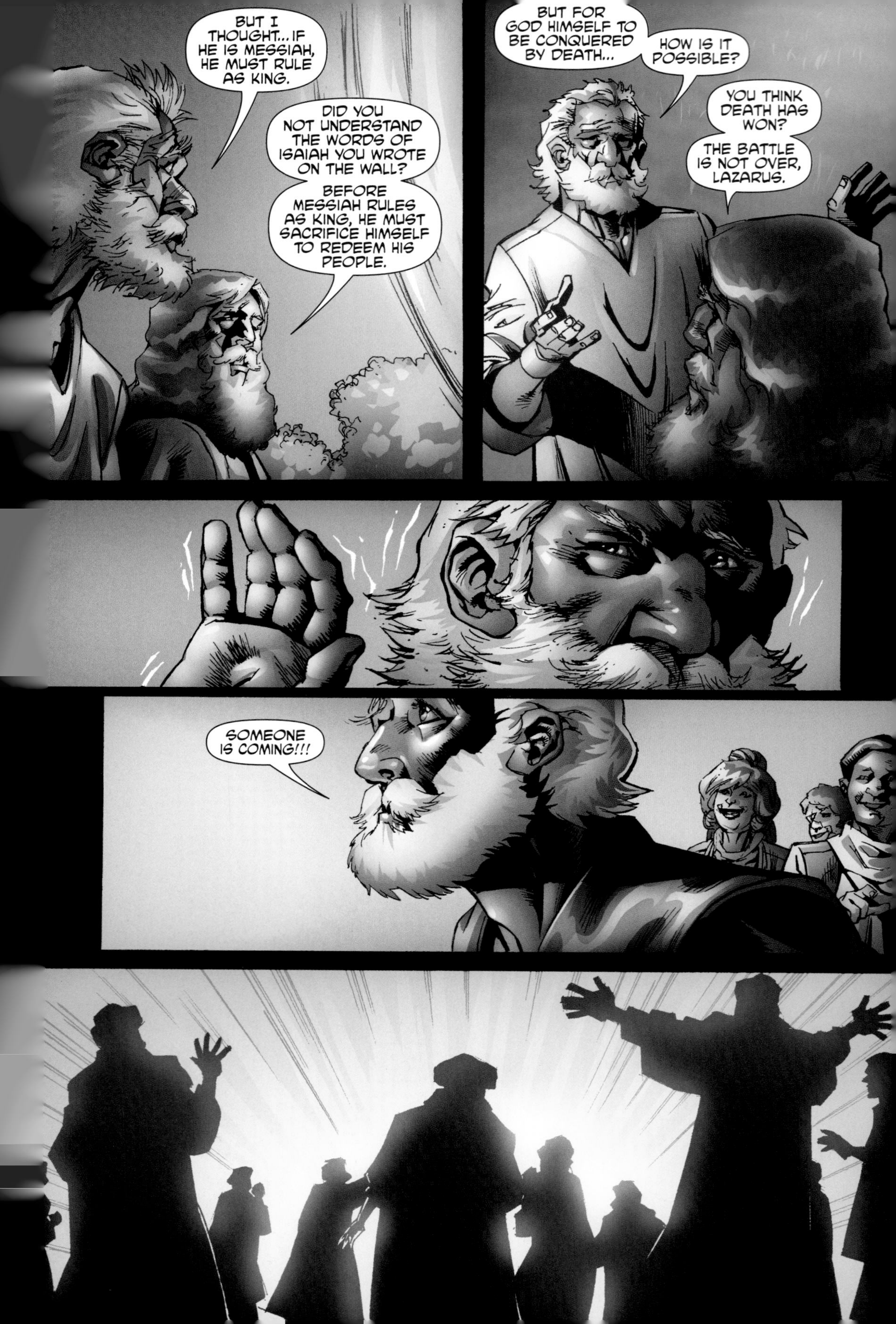
BUT I THOUGHT... IF HE IS MESSIAH, HE MUST RULE AS KING.
DID YOU NOT UNDERSTAND THE WORDS OF ISAIAH YOU WROTE ON THE WALL?
BEFORE MESSIAH RULES AS KING, HE MUST SACRIFICE HIMSELF TO REDEEM HIS PEOPLE.
BUT FOR GOD HIMSELF TO BE CONQUERED BY DEATH...
HOW IS IT POSSIBLE?
YOU THINK DEATH HAS WON?
THE BATTLE IS NOT OVER, LAZARUS.
SOMEONE IS COMING!!!

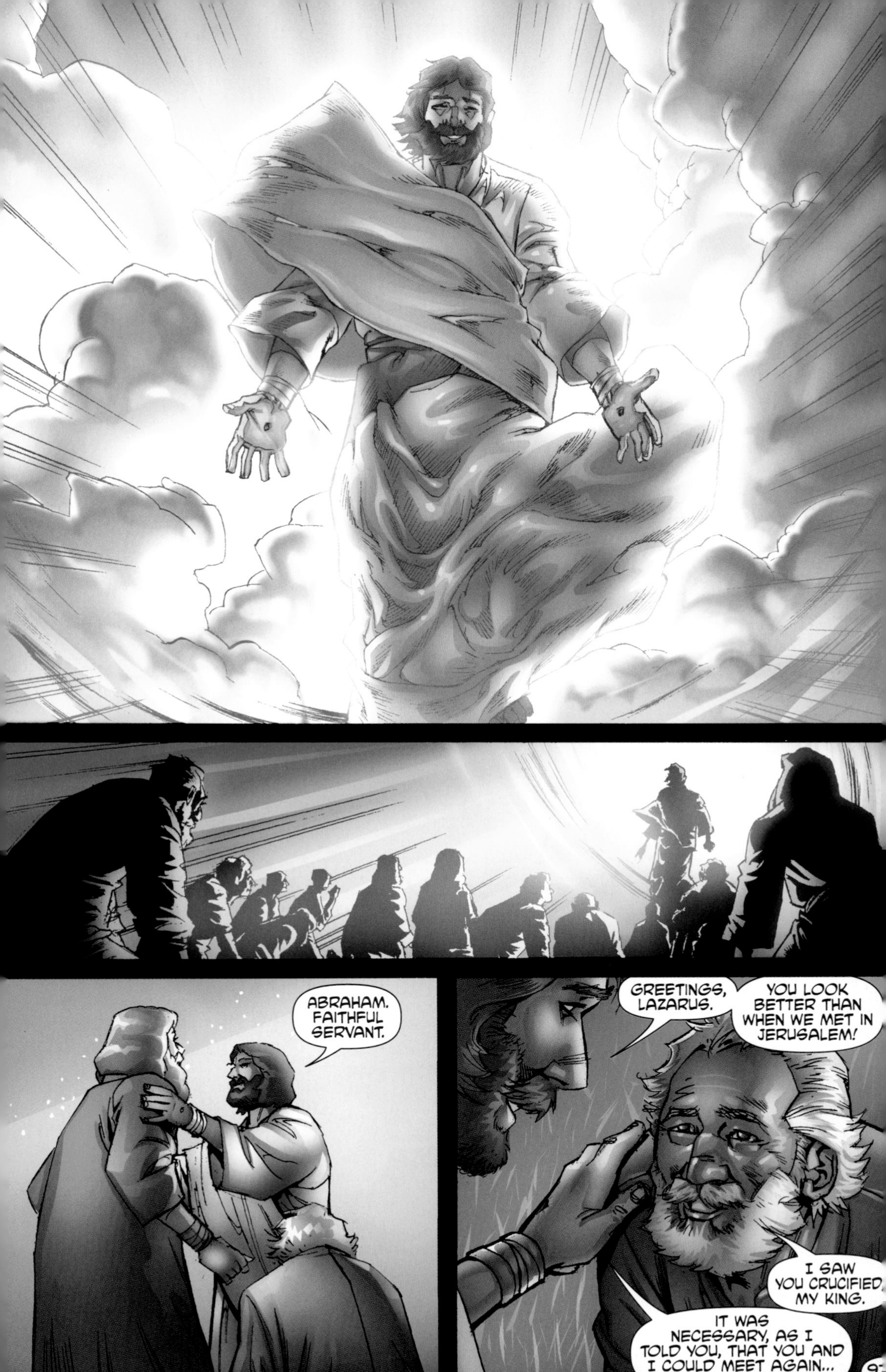
ABRAHAM. FAITHFUL SERVANT.
GREETINGS, LAZARUS.
YOU LOOK BETTER THAN WHEN WE MET IN JERUSALEM!
I SAW YOU CRUCIFIED, MY KING.
IT WAS NECESSARY, AS I TOLD YOU, THAT YOU AND I COULD MEET AGAIN...

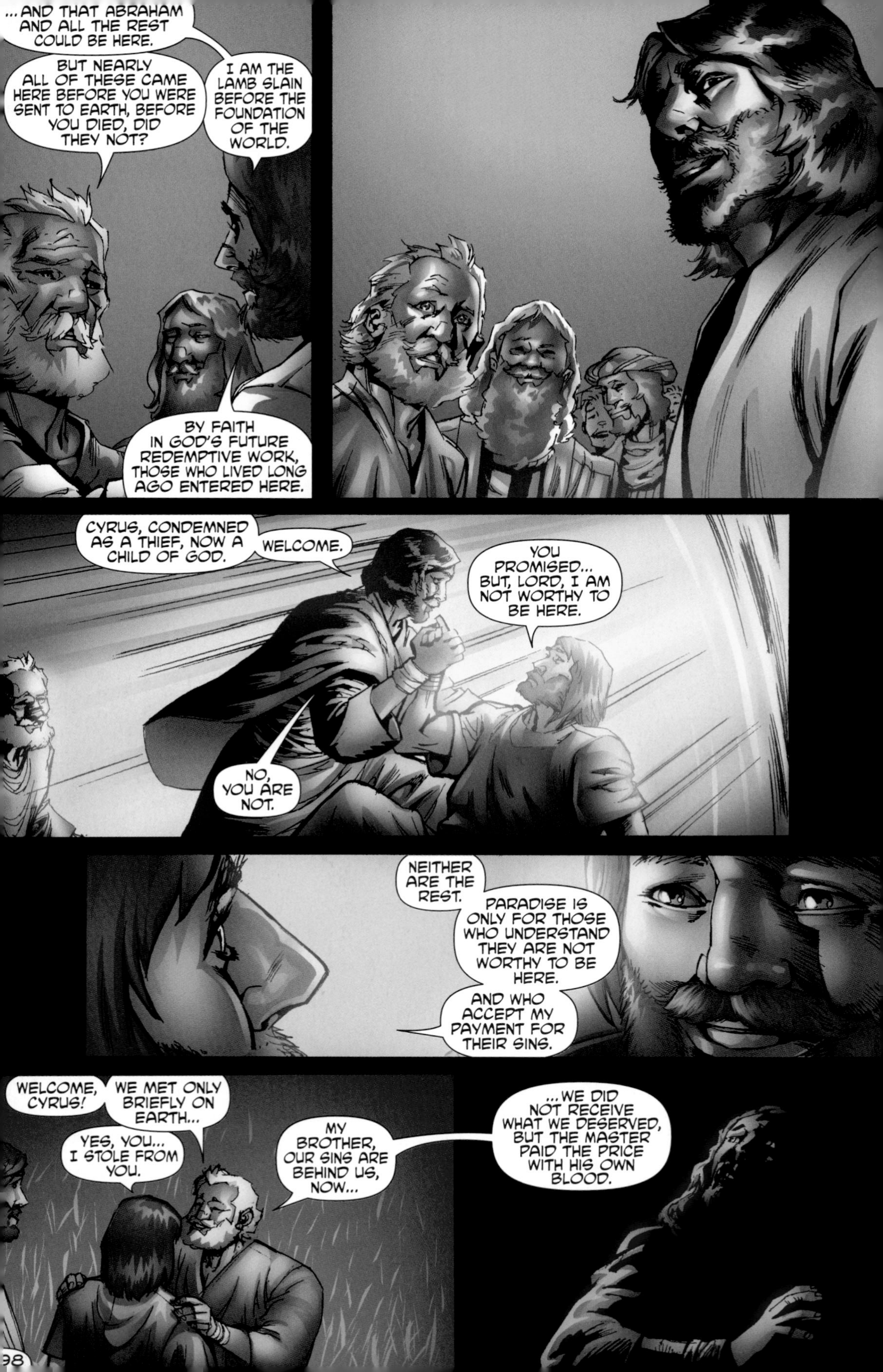
...AND THAT ABRAHAM AND ALL THE REST COULD BE HERE.
BUT NEARLY ALL OF THESE CAME HERE BEFORE YOU WERE SENT TO EARTH, BEFORE YOU DIED, DID THEY NOT?
I AM THE LAMB SLAIN BEFORE THE FOUNDATION OF THE WORLD.
BY FAITH IN GOD'S FUTURE REDEMPTIVE WORK, THOSE WHO LIVED LONG AGO ENTERED HERE.
CYRUS, CONDEMNED AS A THIEF, NOW A CHILD OF GOD.
WELCOME.
YOU PROMISED... BUT, LORD, I AM NOT WORTHY TO BE HERE.
NO, YOU ARE NOT.
NEITHER ARE THE REST.
PARADISE IS ONLY FOR THOSE WHO UNDERSTAND THEY ARE NOT WORTHY TO BE HERE.
AND WHO ACCEPT MY PAYMENT FOR THEIR SINS.
WELCOME, CYRUS!
WE MET ONLY BRIEFLY ON EARTH...
YES, YOU... I STOLE FROM YOU.
MY BROTHER, OUR SINS ARE BEHIND US, NOW...
...WE DID NOT RECEIVE WHAT WE DESERVED, BUT THE MASTER PAID THE PRICE WITH HIS OWN BLOOD.

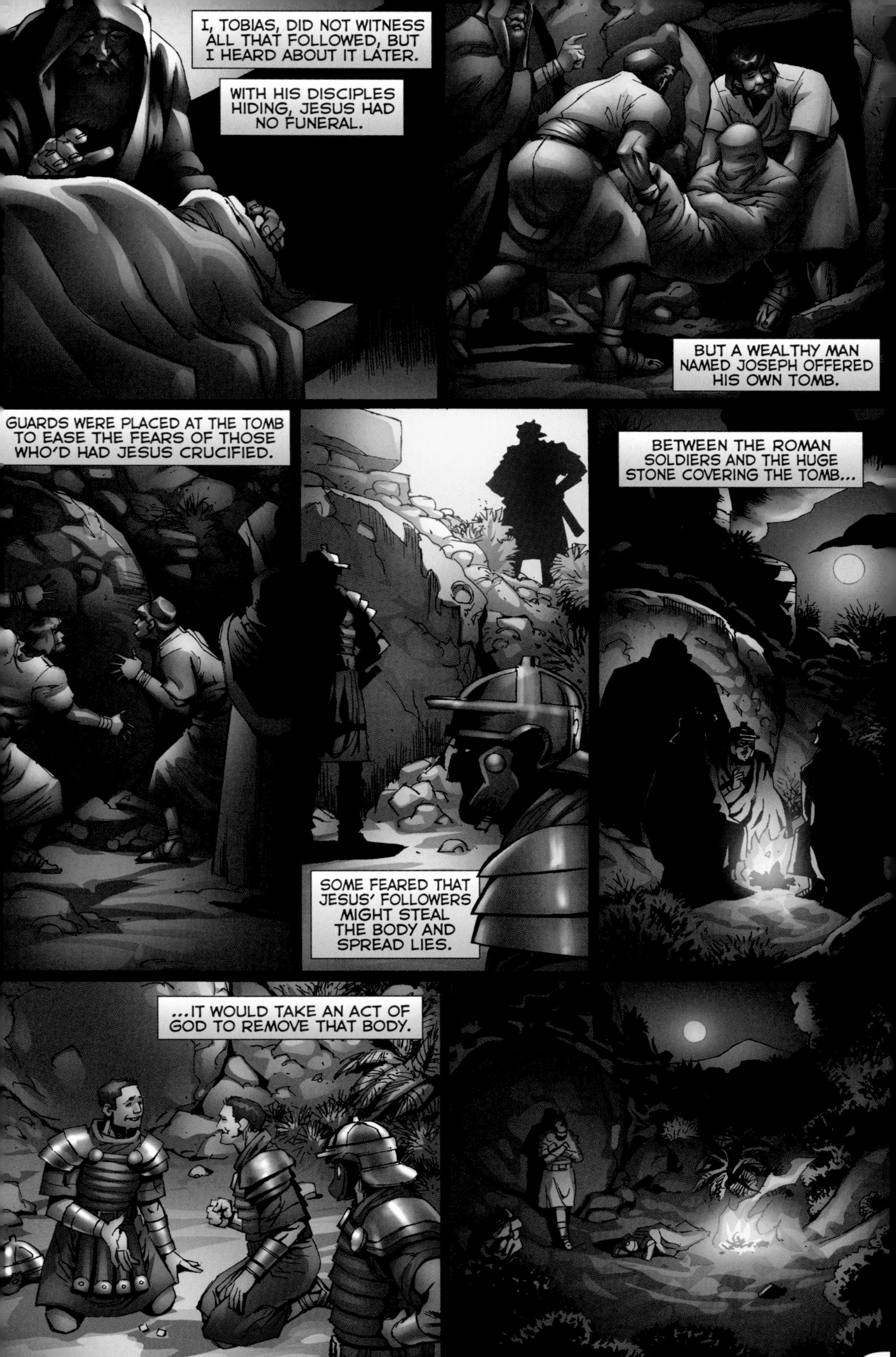
I, TOBIAS, DID NOT WITNESS ALL THAT FOLLOWED, BUT I HEARD ABOUT IT LATER.
WITH HIS DISCIPLES HIDING, JESUS HAD NO FUNERAL.
BUT A WEALTHY MAN NAMED JOSEPH OFFERED HIS OWN TOMB.
GUARDS WERE PLACED AT THE TOMB TO EASE THE FEARS OF THOSE WHO'D HAD JESUS CRUCIFIED.
SOME FEARED THAT JESUS' FOLLOWERS MIGHT STEAL THE BODY AND SPREAD LIES.
BETWEEN THE ROMAN SOLDIERS AND THE HUGE STONE COVERING THE TOMB...
...IT WOULD TAKE AN ACT OF GOD TO REMOVE THAT BODY.

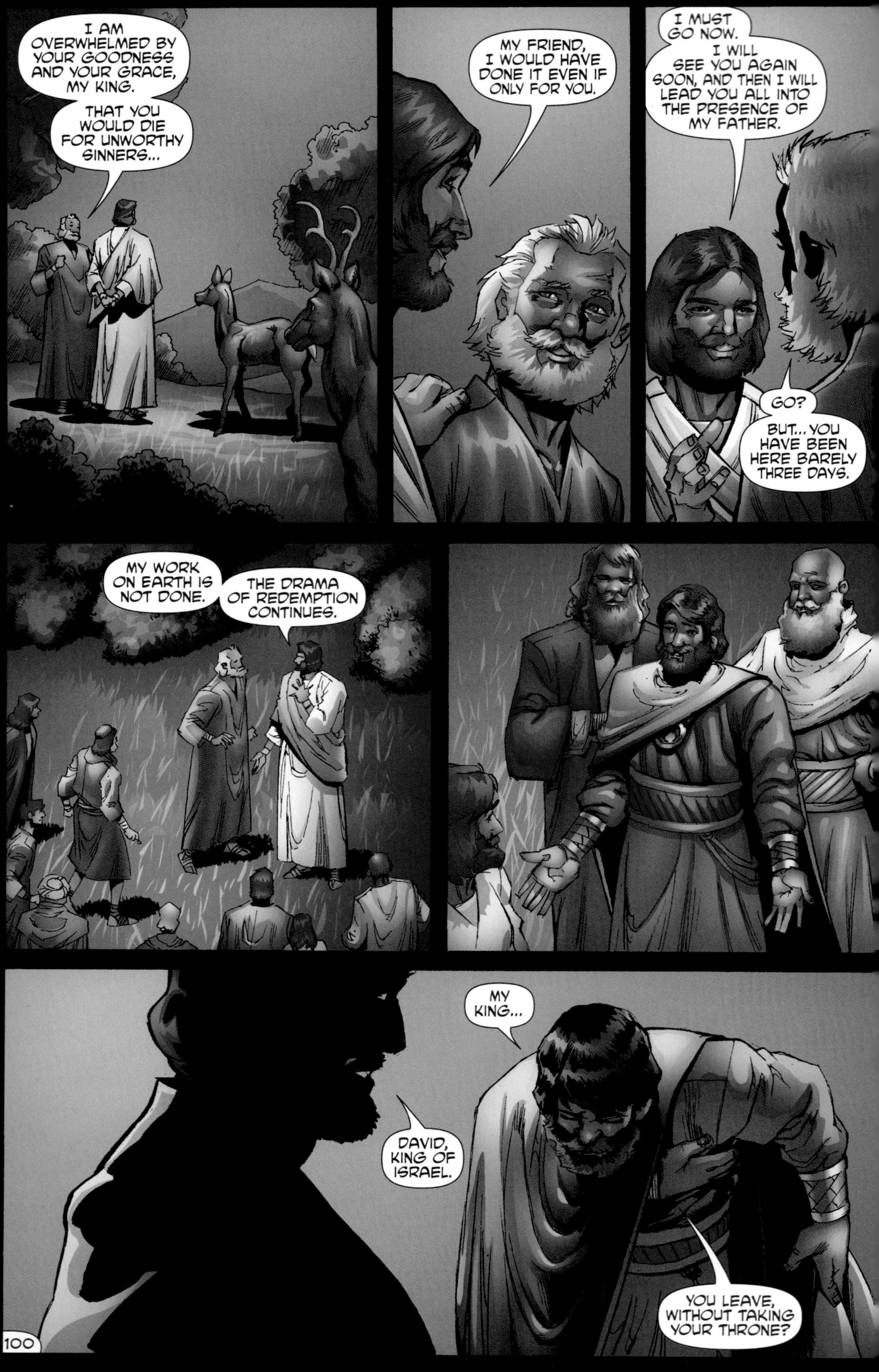
I AM OVERWHELMED BY YOUR GOODNESS AND YOUR GRACE, MY KING.
THAT YOU WOULD DIE FOR UNWORTHY SINNERS...
MY FRIEND, I WOULD HAVE DONE IT EVEN IF ONLY FOR YOU.
I MUST GO NOW.
I WILL SEE YOU AGAIN SOON, AND THEN I WILL LEAD YOU ALL INTO THE PRESENCE OF MY FATHER.
GO?
BUT... YOU HAVE BEEN HERE BARELY THREE DAYS.
MY WORK ON EARTH IS NOT DONE.
THE DRAMA OF REDEMPTION CONTINUES.
MY KING...
DAVID, KING OF ISRAEL.
YOU LEAVE, WITHOUT TAKING YOUR THRONE?

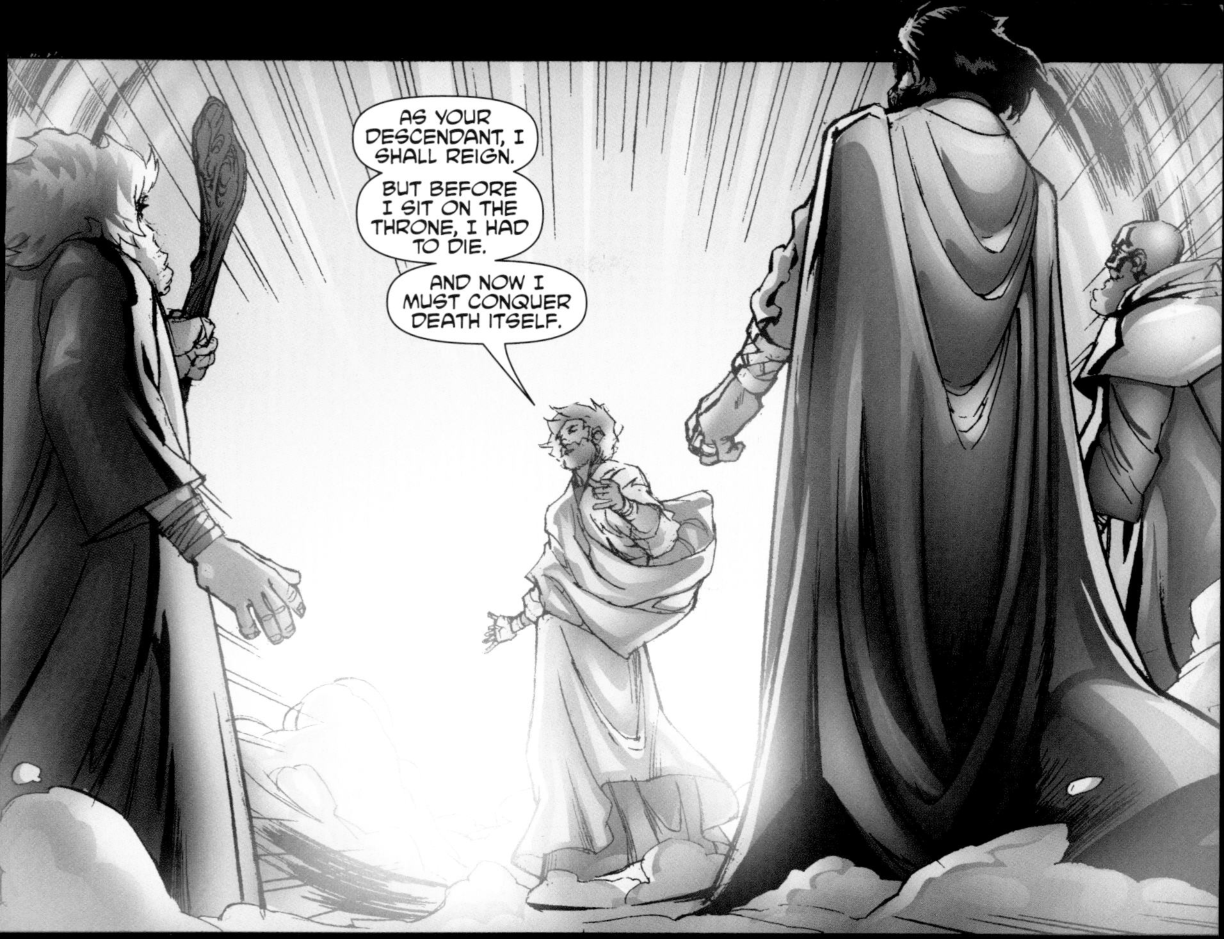
AS YOUR DESCENDANT, I SHALL REIGN.
BUT BEFORE I SIT ON THE THRONE, I HAD TO DIE.
AND NOW I MUST CONQUER DEATH ITSELF.

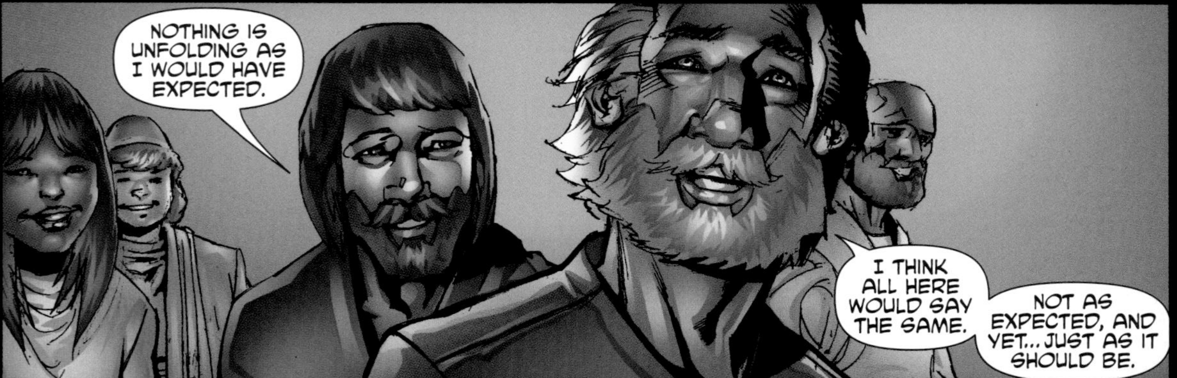
NOTHING IS UNFOLDING AS I WOULD HAVE EXPECTED.
I THINK ALL HERE WOULD SAY THE SAME.
NOT AS EXPECTED, AND YET... JUST AS IT SHOULD BE.

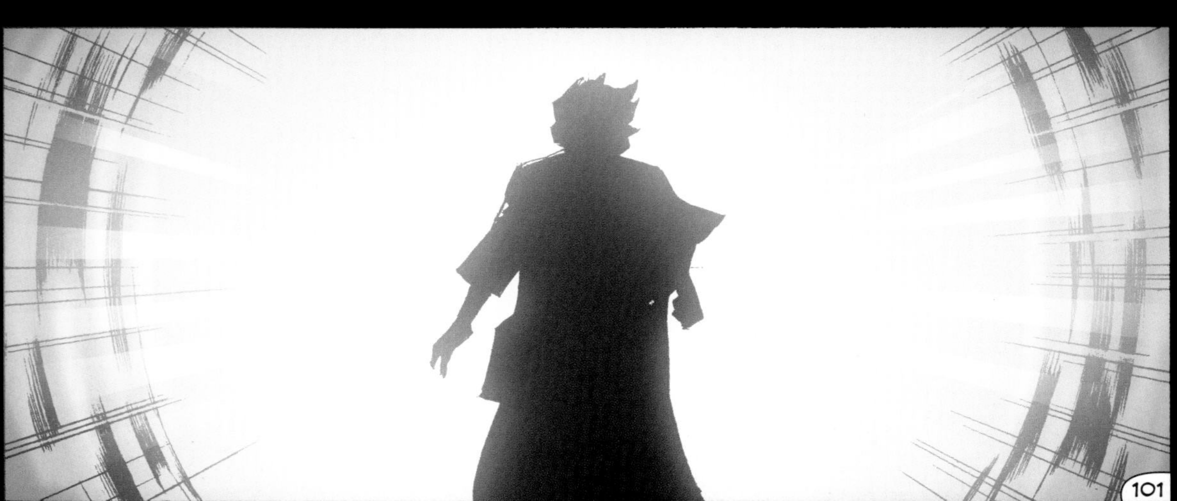

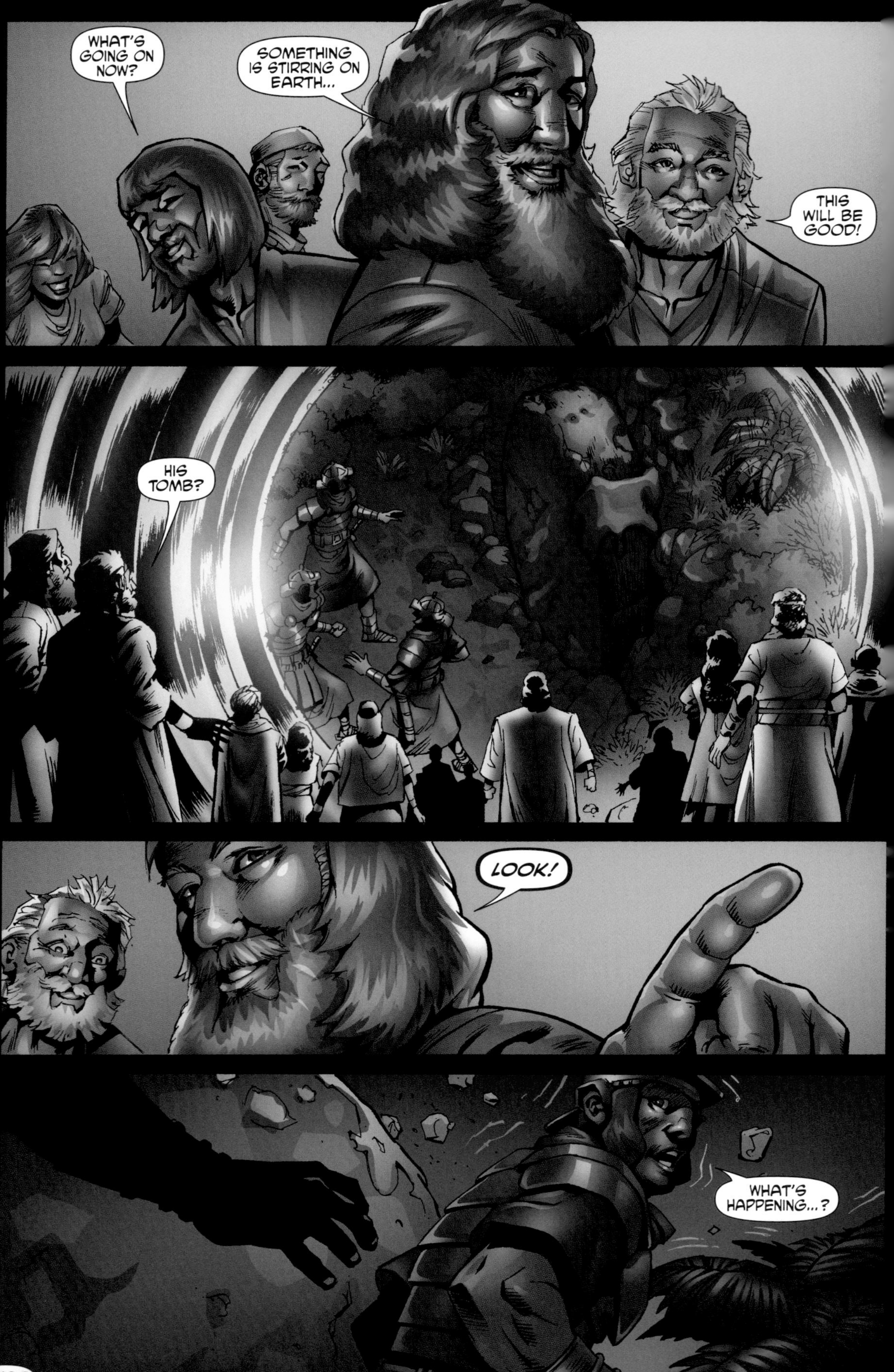
WHAT'S GOING ON NOW?
SOMETHING IS STIRRING ON EARTH...
THIS WILL BE GOOD!
HIS TOMB?
LOOK!
WHAT'S HAPPENING...?

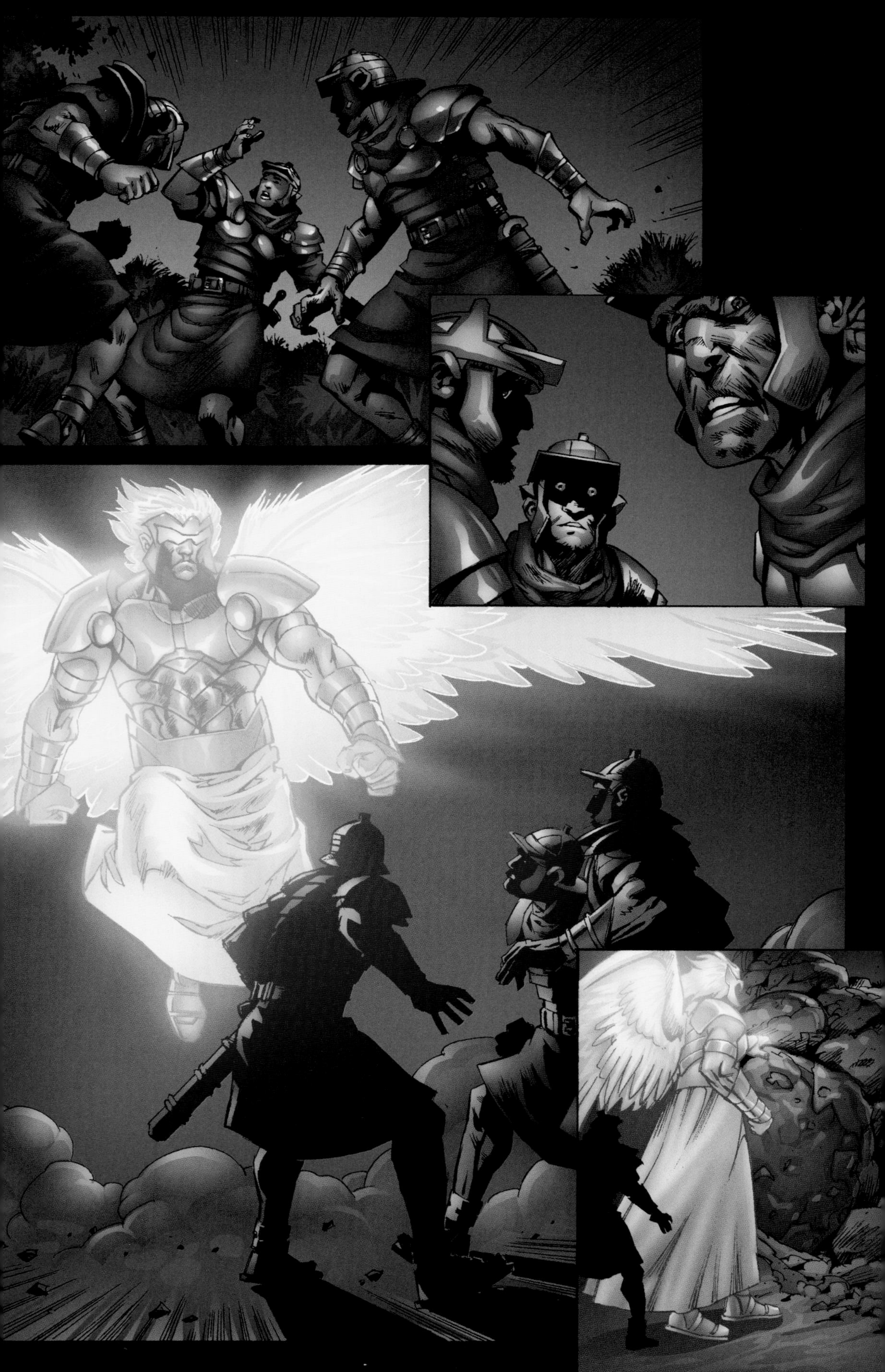

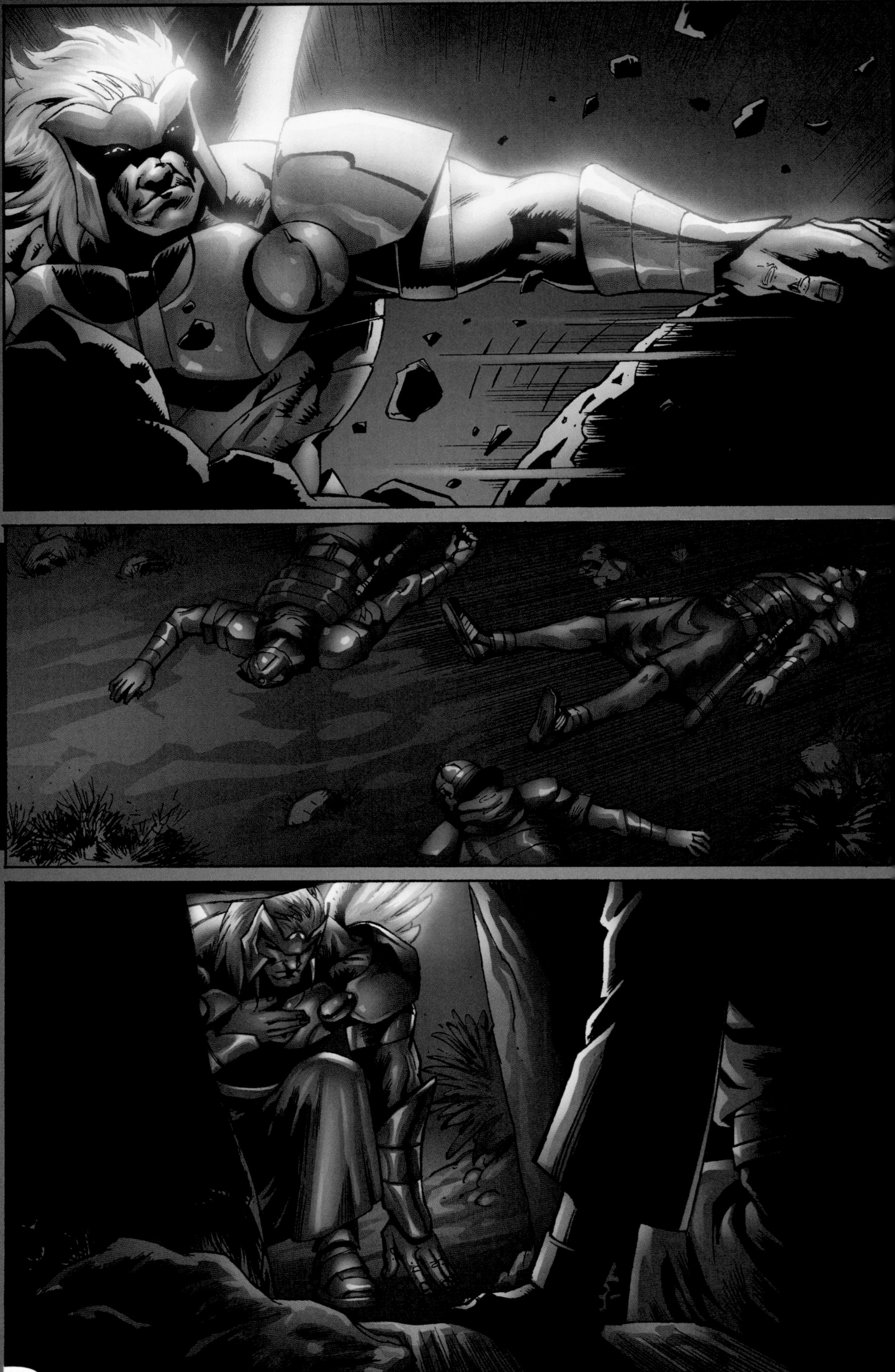

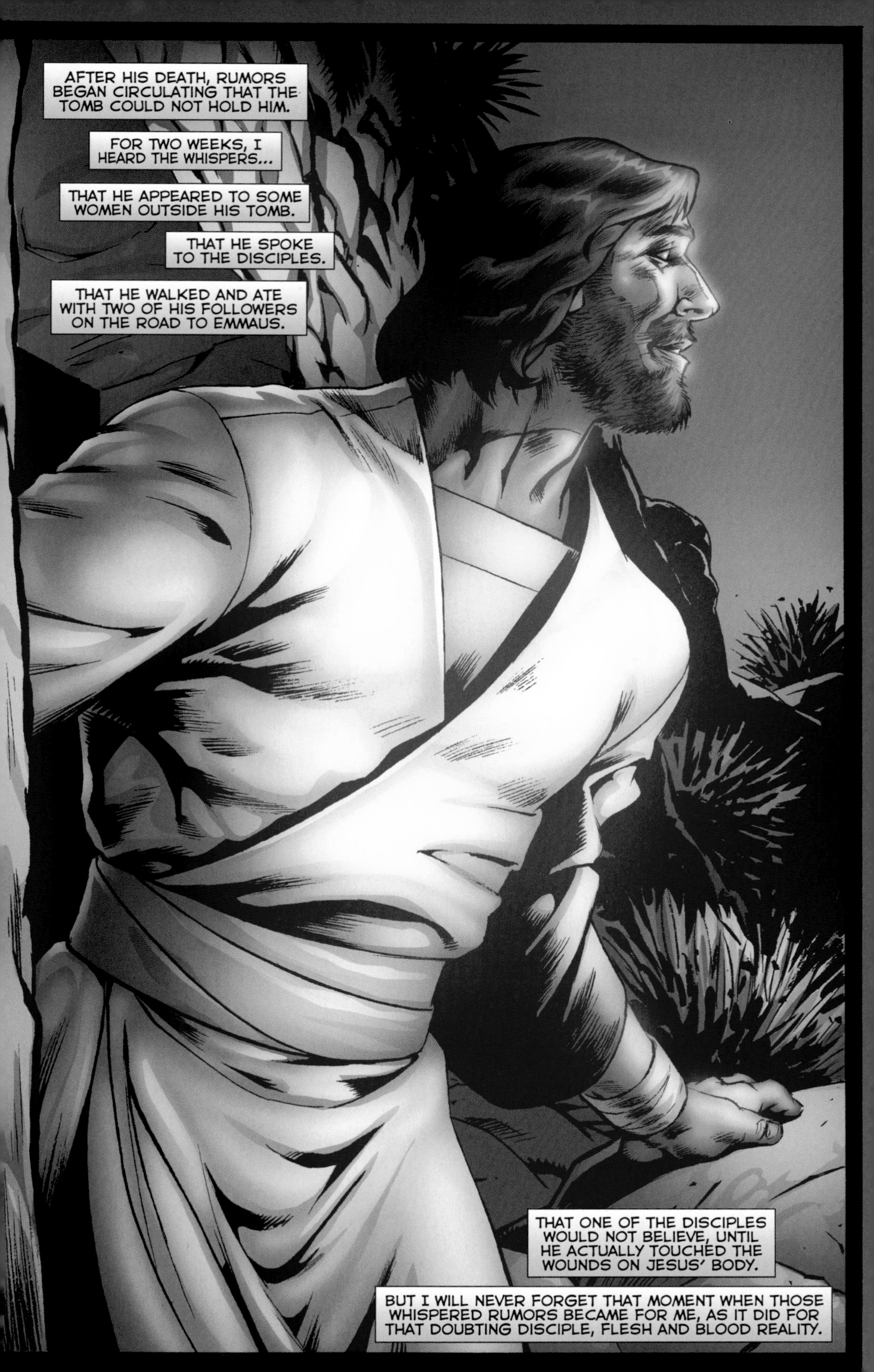
AFTER HIS DEATH, RUMORS BEGAN CIRCULATING THAT THE TOMB COULD NOT HOLD HIM.
FOR TWO WEEKS, I HEARD THE WHISPERS...
THAT HE APPEARED TO SOME WOMEN OUTSIDE HIS TOMB.
THAT HE SPOKE TO THE DISCIPLES.
THAT HE WALKED AND ATE WITH TWO OF HIS FOLLOWERS ON THE ROAD TO EMMAUS.
THAT ONE OF THE DISCIPLES WOULD NOT BELIEVE, UNTIL HE ACTUALLY TOUCHED THE WOUNDS ON JESUS' BODY.
BUT I WILL NEVER FORGET THAT MOMENT WHEN THOSE WHISPERED RUMORS BECAME FOR ME, AS IT DID FOR THAT DOUBTING DISCIPLE, FLESH AND BLOOD REALITY.

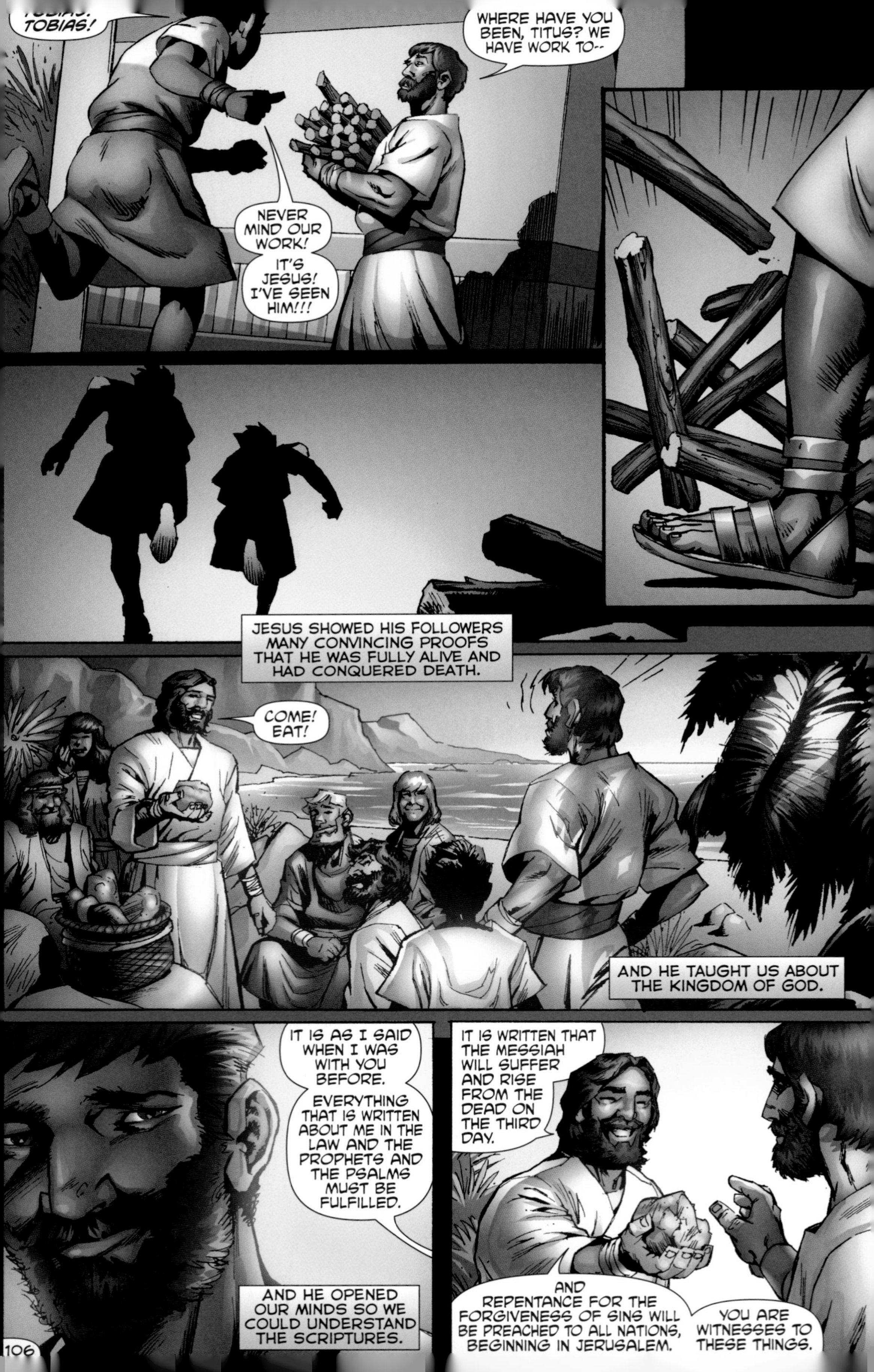
TOBIAS!
WHERE HAVE YOU BEEN, TITUS? WE HAVE WORK TO--
NEVER MIND OUR WORK!
IT'S JESUS! I'VE SEEN HIM!!!
JESUS SHOWED HIS FOLLOWERS MANY CONVINCING PROOFS THAT HE WAS FULLY ALIVE AND HAD CONQUERED DEATH.
COME! EAT!
AND HE TAUGHT US ABOUT THE KINGDOM OF GOD.
IT IS AS I SAID WHEN I WAS WITH YOU BEFORE.
EVERYTHING THAT IS WRITTEN ABOUT ME IN THE LAW AND THE PROPHETS AND THE PSALMS MUST BE FULFILLED.
AND HE OPENED OUR MINDS SO WE COULD UNDERSTAND THE SCRIPTURES.
IT IS WRITTEN THAT THE MESSIAH WILL SUFFER AND RISE FROM THE DEAD ON THE THIRD DAY.
AND REPENTANCE FOR THE FORGIVENESS OF SINS WILL BE PREACHED TO ALL NATIONS, BEGINNING IN JERUSALEM.
YOU ARE WITNESSES TO THESE THINGS.

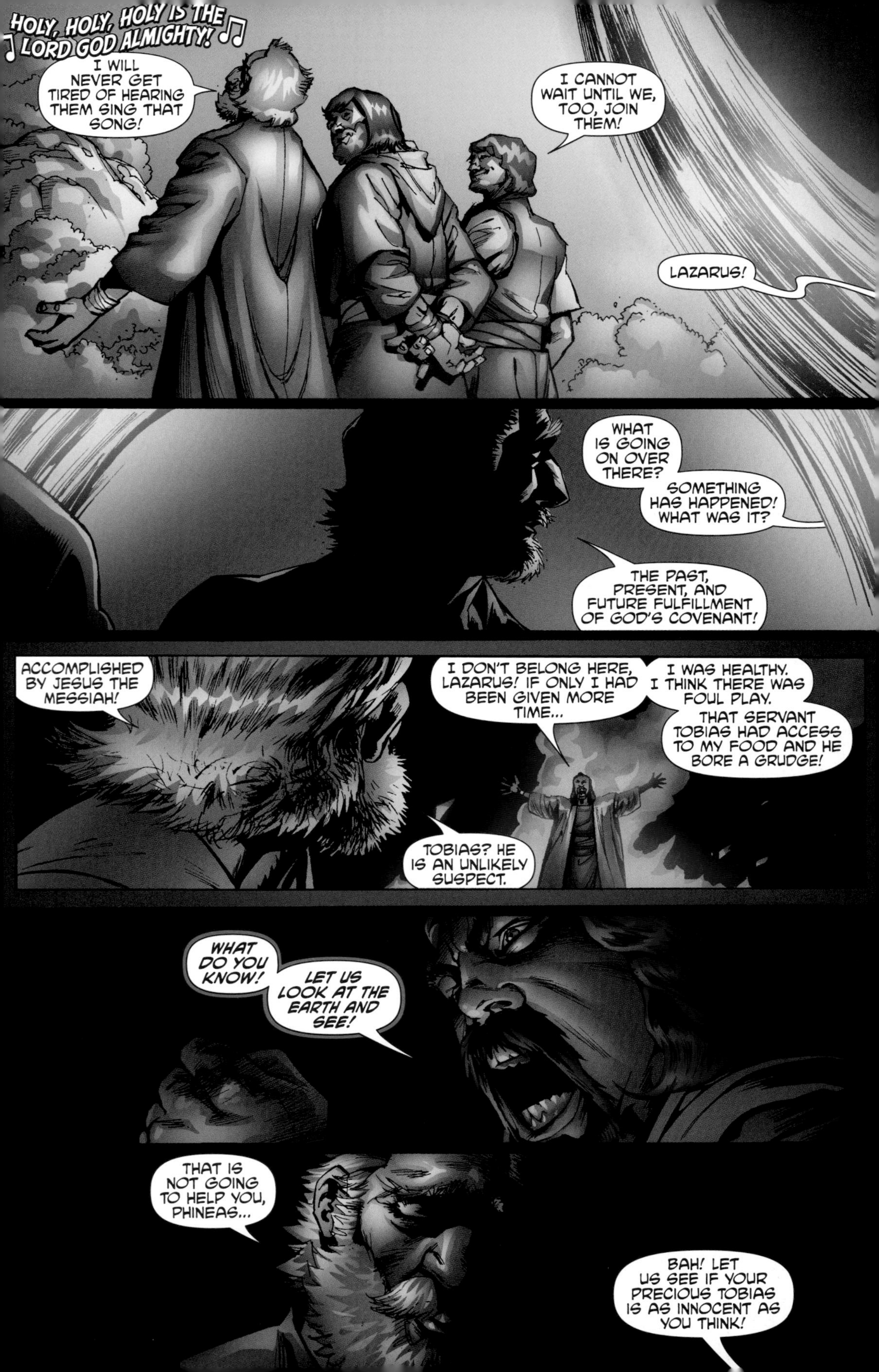
HOLY, HOLY, HOLY IS THE LORD GOD ALMIGHTY!
I WILL NEVER GET TIRED OF HEARING THEM SING THAT SONG!
I CANNOT WAIT UNTIL WE, TOO, JOIN THEM!
LAZARUS!
WHAT IS GOING ON OVER THERE?
SOMETHING HAS HAPPENED! WHAT WAS IT?
THE PAST, PRESENT, AND FUTURE FULFILLMENT OF GOD'S COVENANT!
ACCOMPLISHED BY JESUS THE MESSIAH!
I DON'T BELONG HERE, LAZARUS! IF ONLY I HAD BEEN GIVEN MORE TIME...
I WAS HEALTHY. I THINK THERE WAS FOUL PLAY.
THAT SERVANT TOBIAS HAD ACCESS TO MY FOOD AND HE BORE A GRUDGE!
TOBIAS? HE IS AN UNLIKELY SUSPECT.
WHAT DO YOU KNOW!
LET US LOOK AT THE EARTH AND SEE!
THAT IS NOT GOING TO HELP YOU, PHINEAS...
BAH! LET US SEE IF YOUR PRECIOUS TOBIAS IS AS INNOCENT AS YOU THINK!

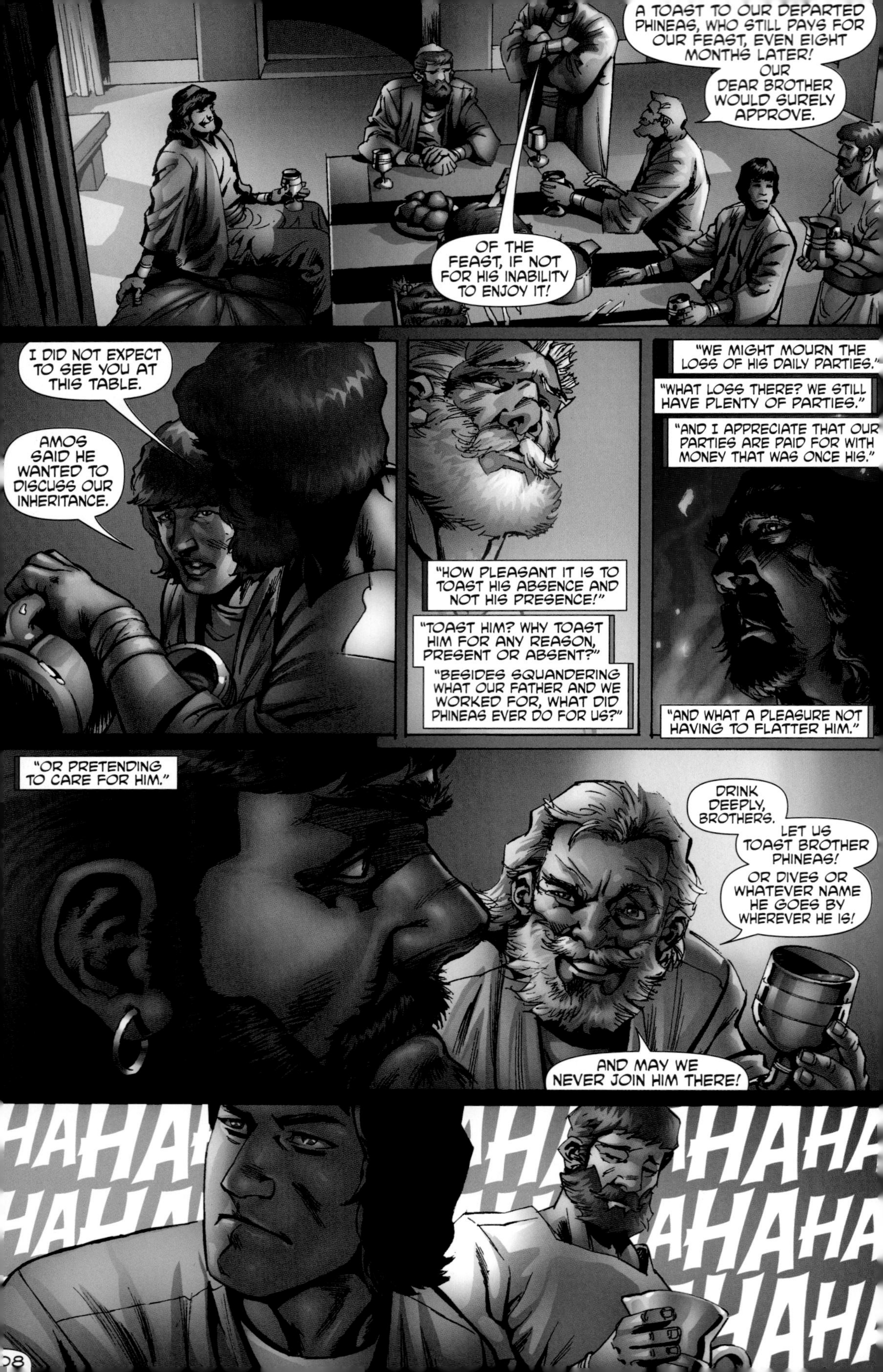

A TOAST TO OUR DEPARTED PHINEAS, WHO STILL PAYS FOR OUR FEAST, EVEN EIGHT MONTHS LATER!
OUR DEAR BROTHER WOULD SURELY APPROVE.
OF THE FEAST, IF NOT FOR HIS INABILITY TO ENJOY IT!
I DID NOT EXPECT TO SEE YOU AT THIS TABLE.
AMOS SAID HE WANTED TO DISCUSS OUR INHERITANCE.
"HOW PLEASANT IT IS TO TOAST HIS ABSENCE AND NOT HIS PRESENCE!"
"TOAST HIM? WHY TOAST HIM FOR ANY REASON, PRESENT OR ABSENT?"
"BESIDES SQUANDERING WHAT OUR FATHER AND WE WORKED FOR, WHAT DID PHINEAS EVER DO FOR US?"
"WE MIGHT MOURN THE LOSS OF HIS DAILY PARTIES."
"WHAT LOSS THERE? WE STILL HAVE PLENTY OF PARTIES."
"AND I APPRECIATE THAT OUR PARTIES ARE PAID FOR WITH MONEY THAT WAS ONCE HIS."
"AND WHAT A PLEASURE NOT HAVING TO FLATTER HIM."
"OR PRETENDING TO CARE FOR HIM."
DRINK DEEPLY, BROTHERS.
LET US TOAST BROTHER PHINEAS!
OR DIVES OR WHATEVER NAME HE GOES BY WHEREVER HE IS!
AND MAY WE NEVER JOIN HIM THERE!
HAHAHAHAHA

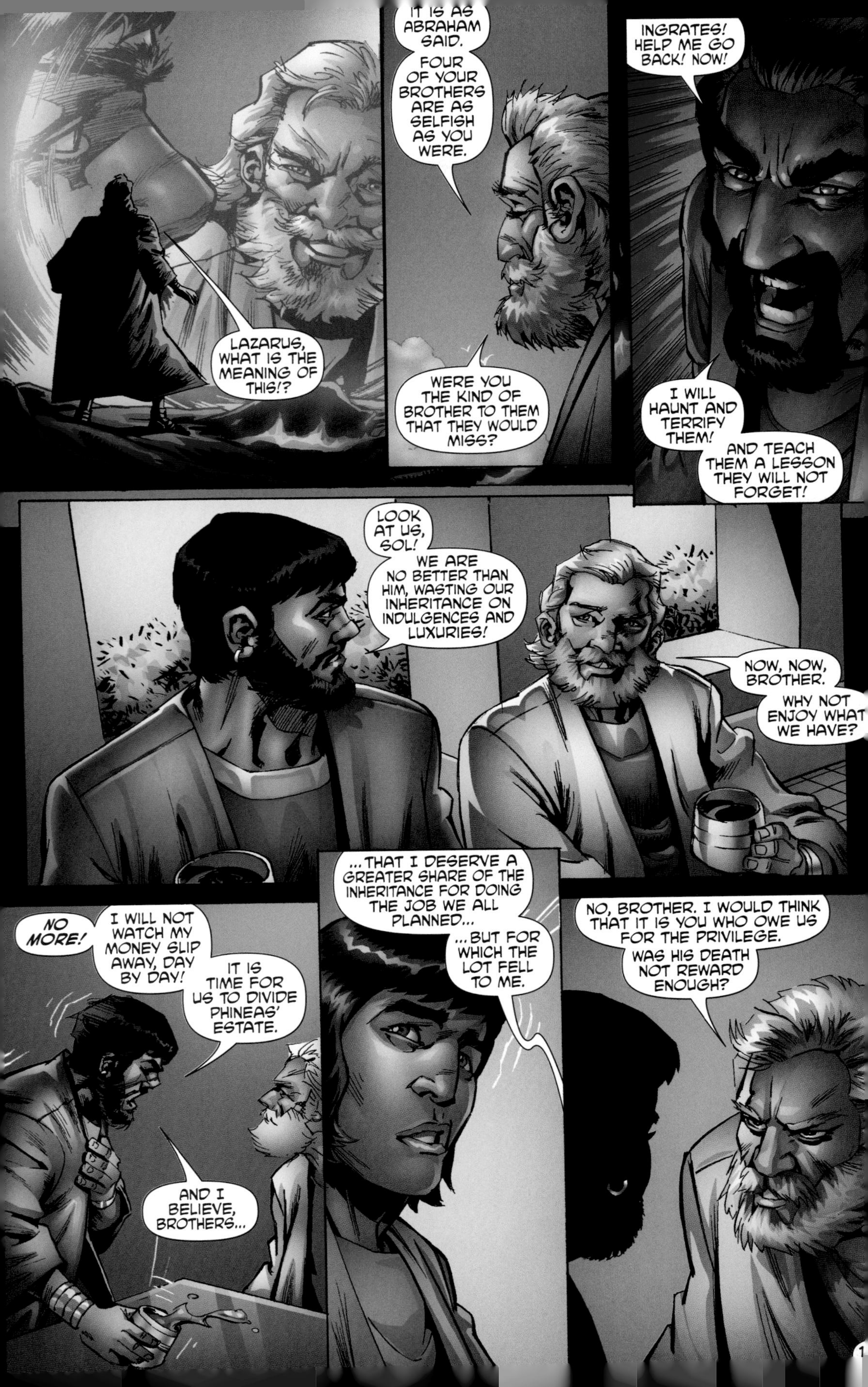

LAZARUS, WHAT IS THE MEANING OF THIS!?
IT IS AS ABRAHAM SAID.
FOUR OF YOUR BROTHERS ARE AS SELFISH AS YOU WERE.
WERE YOU THE KIND OF BROTHER TO THEM THAT THEY WOULD MISS?
INGRATES! HELP ME GO BACK! NOW!
I WILL HAUNT AND TERRIFY THEM!
AND TEACH THEM A LESSON THEY WILL NOT FORGET!
LOOK AT US, SOL!
WE ARE NO BETTER THAN HIM, WASTING OUR INHERITANCE ON INDULGENCES AND LUXURIES!
NOW, NOW, BROTHER.
WHY NOT ENJOY WHAT WE HAVE?
NO MORE!
I WILL NOT WATCH MY MONEY SLIP AWAY, DAY BY DAY!
IT IS TIME FOR US TO DIVIDE PHINEAS' ESTATE.
AND I BELIEVE, BROTHERS...
...THAT I DESERVE A GREATER SHARE OF THE INHERITANCE FOR DOING THE JOB WE ALL PLANNED...
...BUT FOR WHICH THE LOT FELL TO ME.
NO, BROTHER. I WOULD THINK THAT IT IS YOU WHO OWE US FOR THE PRIVILEGE.
WAS HIS DEATH NOT REWARD ENOUGH?

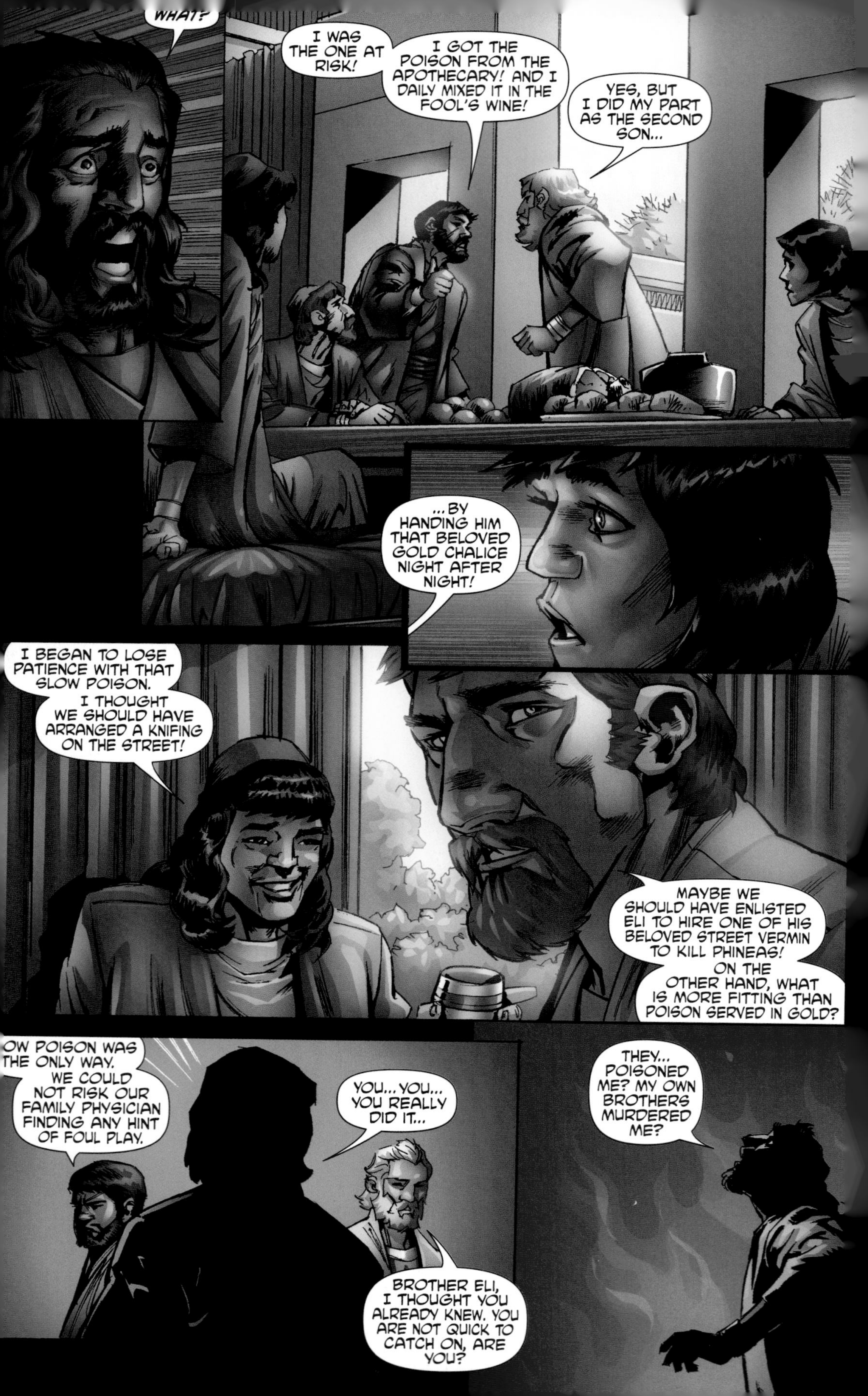
WHAT?
I WAS THE ONE AT RISK!
I GOT THE POISON FROM THE APOTHECARY! AND I DAILY MIXED IT IN THE FOOL'S WINE!
YES, BUT I DID MY PART AS THE SECOND SON...
...BY HANDING HIM THAT BELOVED GOLD CHALICE NIGHT AFTER NIGHT!
I BEGAN TO LOSE PATIENCE WITH THAT SLOW POISON.
I THOUGHT WE SHOULD HAVE ARRANGED A KNIFING ON THE STREET!
MAYBE WE SHOULD HAVE ENLISTED ELI TO HIRE ONE OF HIS BELOVED STREET VERMIN TO KILL PHINEAS!
ON THE OTHER HAND, WHAT IS MORE FITTING THAN POISON SERVED IN GOLD?
OW POISON WAS THE ONLY WAY.
WE COULD NOT RISK OUR FAMILY PHYSICIAN FINDING ANY HINT OF FOUL PLAY.
YOU... YOU... YOU REALLY DID IT...
BROTHER ELI, I THOUGHT YOU ALREADY KNEW. YOU ARE NOT QUICK TO CATCH ON, ARE YOU?
THEY... POISONED ME? MY OWN BROTHERS MURDERED ME?

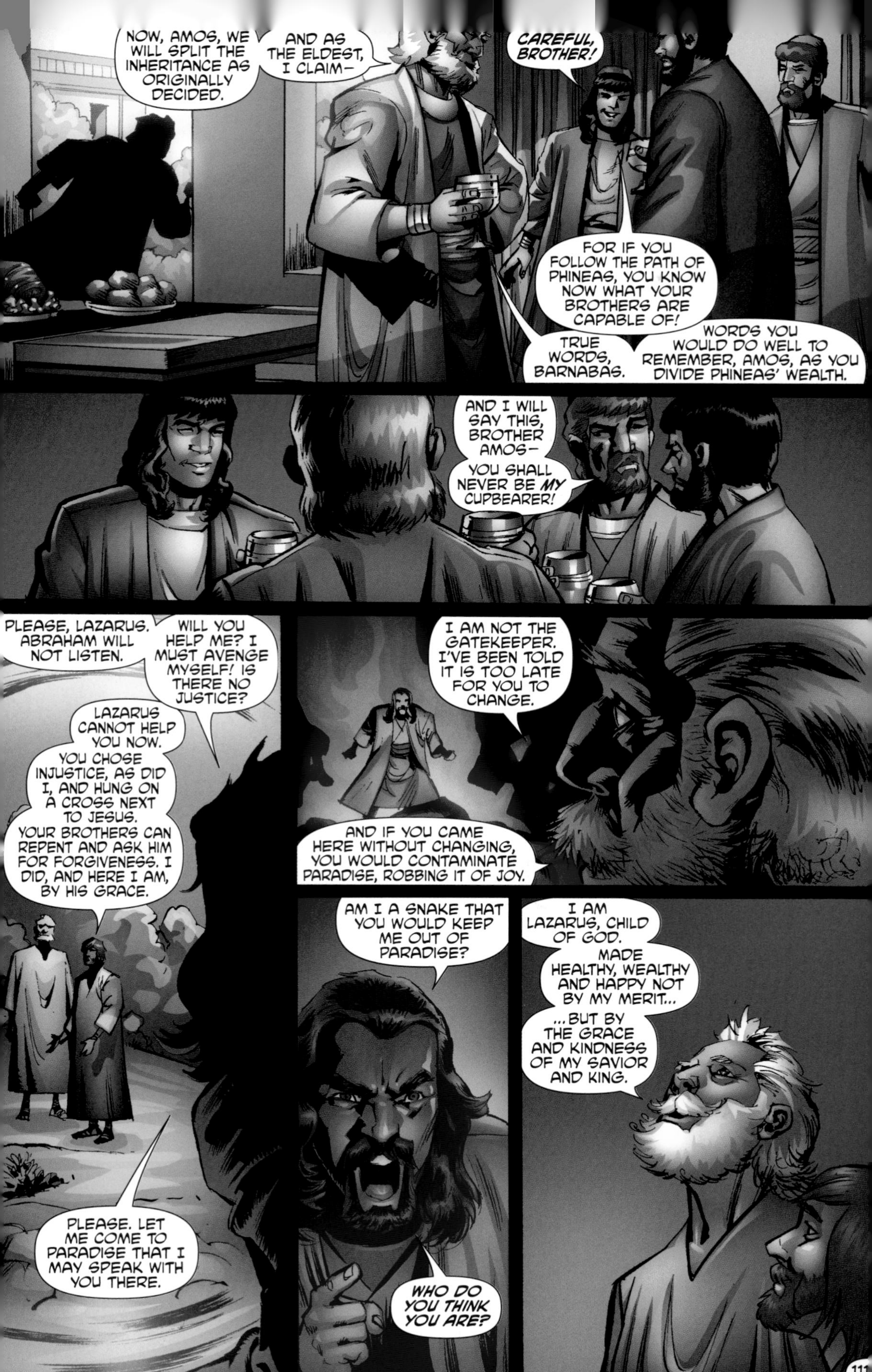
NOW, AMOS, WE WILL SPLIT THE INHERITANCE AS ORIGINALLY DECIDED.
AND AS THE ELDEST, I CLAIM—
CAREFUL, BROTHER!
FOR IF YOU FOLLOW THE PATH OF PHINEAS, YOU KNOW NOW WHAT YOUR BROTHERS ARE CAPABLE OF!
TRUE WORDS, BARNABAS.
WORDS YOU WOULD DO WELL TO REMEMBER, AMOS, AS YOU DIVIDE PHINEAS' WEALTH.
AND I WILL SAY THIS, BROTHER AMOS—
YOU SHALL NEVER BE MY CUPBEARER!
PLEASE, LAZARUS. ABRAHAM WILL NOT LISTEN.
WILL YOU HELP ME? I MUST AVENGE MYSELF! IS THERE NO JUSTICE?
LAZARUS CANNOT HELP YOU NOW.
YOU CHOSE INJUSTICE, AS DID I, AND HUNG ON A CROSS NEXT TO JESUS.
YOUR BROTHERS CAN REPENT AND ASK HIM FOR FORGIVENESS. I DID, AND HERE I AM, BY HIS GRACE.
I AM NOT THE GATEKEEPER. I'VE BEEN TOLD IT IS TOO LATE FOR YOU TO CHANGE.
AND IF YOU CAME HERE WITHOUT CHANGING, YOU WOULD CONTAMINATE PARADISE, ROBBING IT OF JOY.
PLEASE. LET ME COME TO PARADISE THAT I MAY SPEAK WITH YOU THERE.
AM I A SNAKE THAT YOU WOULD KEEP ME OUT OF PARADISE?
WHO DO YOU THINK YOU ARE?
I AM LAZARUS, CHILD OF GOD.
MADE HEALTHY, WEALTHY AND HAPPY NOT BY MY MERIT...
...BUT BY THE GRACE AND KINDNESS OF MY SAVIOR AND KING.

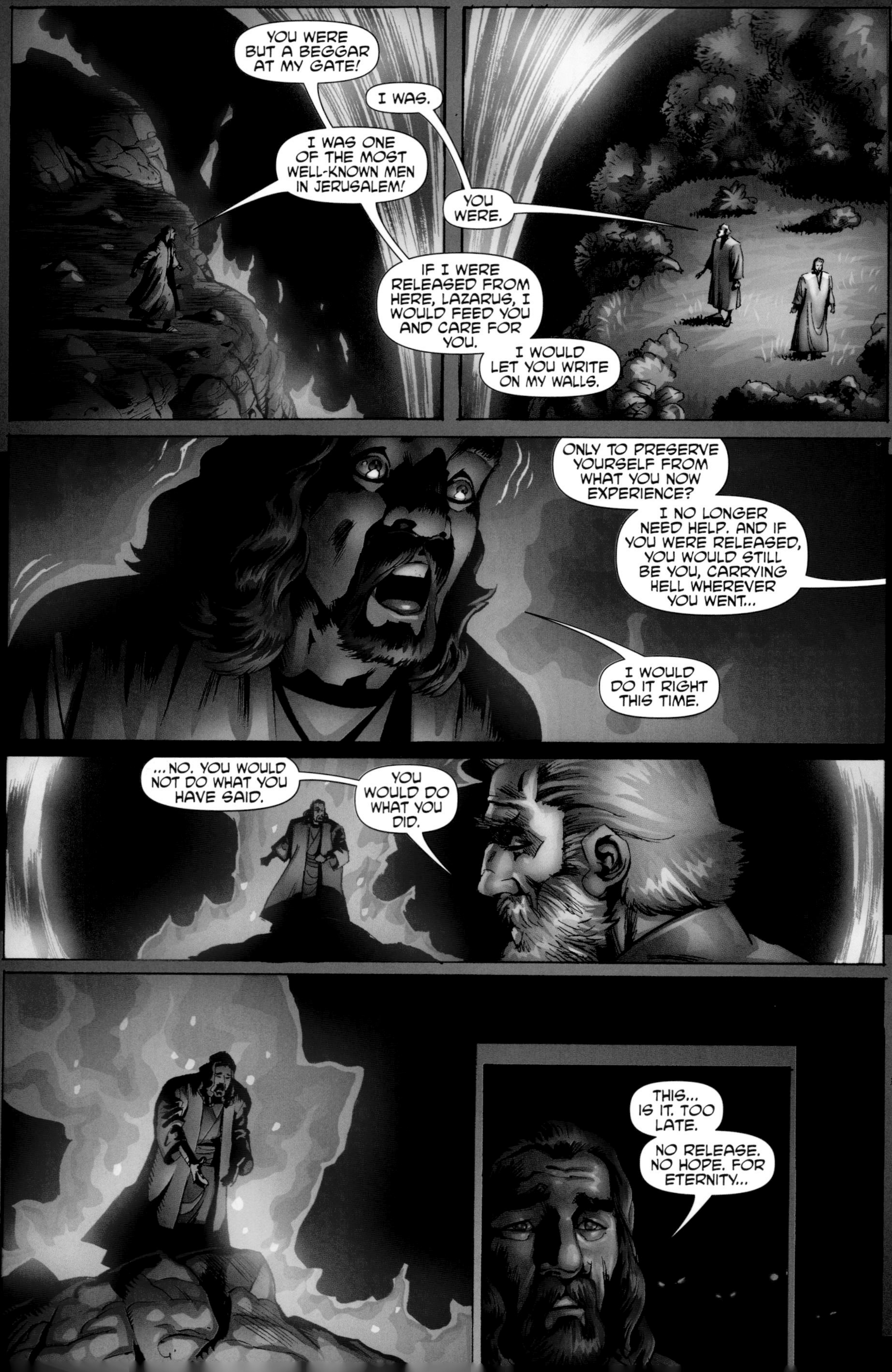
YOU WERE BUT A BEGGAR AT MY GATE!
I WAS.
I WAS ONE OF THE MOST WELL-KNOWN MEN IN JERUSALEM!
YOU WERE.
IF I WERE RELEASED FROM HERE, LAZARUS, I WOULD FEED YOU AND CARE FOR YOU.
I WOULD LET YOU WRITE ON MY WALLS.
ONLY TO PRESERVE YOURSELF FROM WHAT YOU NOW EXPERIENCE?
I NO LONGER NEED HELP. AND IF YOU WERE RELEASED, YOU WOULD STILL BE YOU, CARRYING HELL WHEREVER YOU WENT...
I WOULD DO IT RIGHT THIS TIME.
...NO. YOU WOULD NOT DO WHAT YOU HAVE SAID.
YOU WOULD DO WHAT YOU DID.
THIS... IS IT. TOO LATE.
NO RELEASE. NO HOPE. FOR ETERNITY...

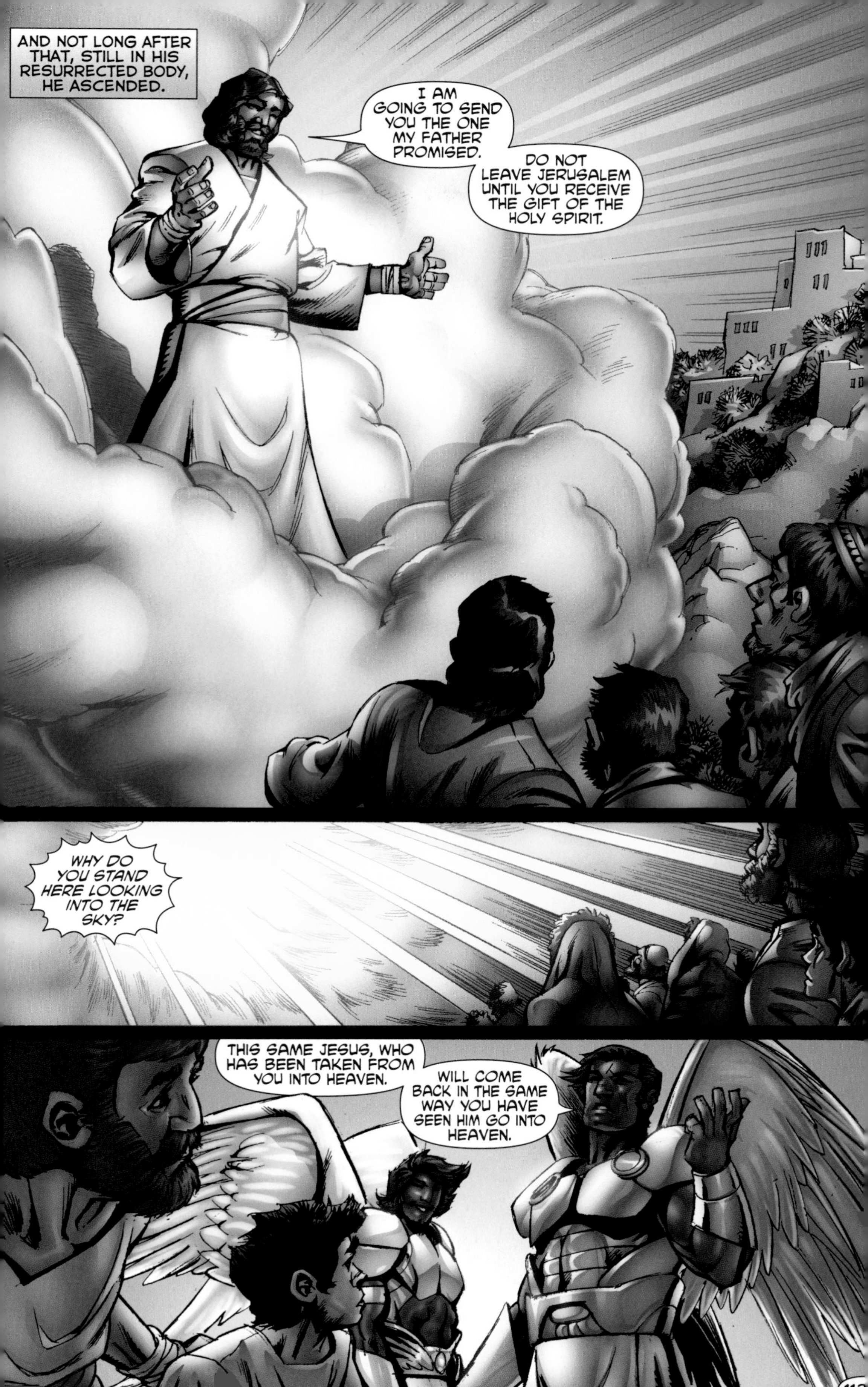
AND NOT LONG AFTER THAT, STILL IN HIS RESURRECTED BODY, HE ASCENDED.
I AM GOING TO SEND YOU THE ONE MY FATHER PROMISED.
DO NOT LEAVE JERUSALEM UNTIL YOU RECEIVE THE GIFT OF THE HOLY SPIRIT.
WHY DO YOU STAND HERE LOOKING INTO THE SKY?
THIS SAME JESUS, WHO HAS BEEN TAKEN FROM YOU INTO HEAVEN.
WILL COME BACK IN THE SAME WAY YOU HAVE SEEN HIM GO INTO HEAVEN.

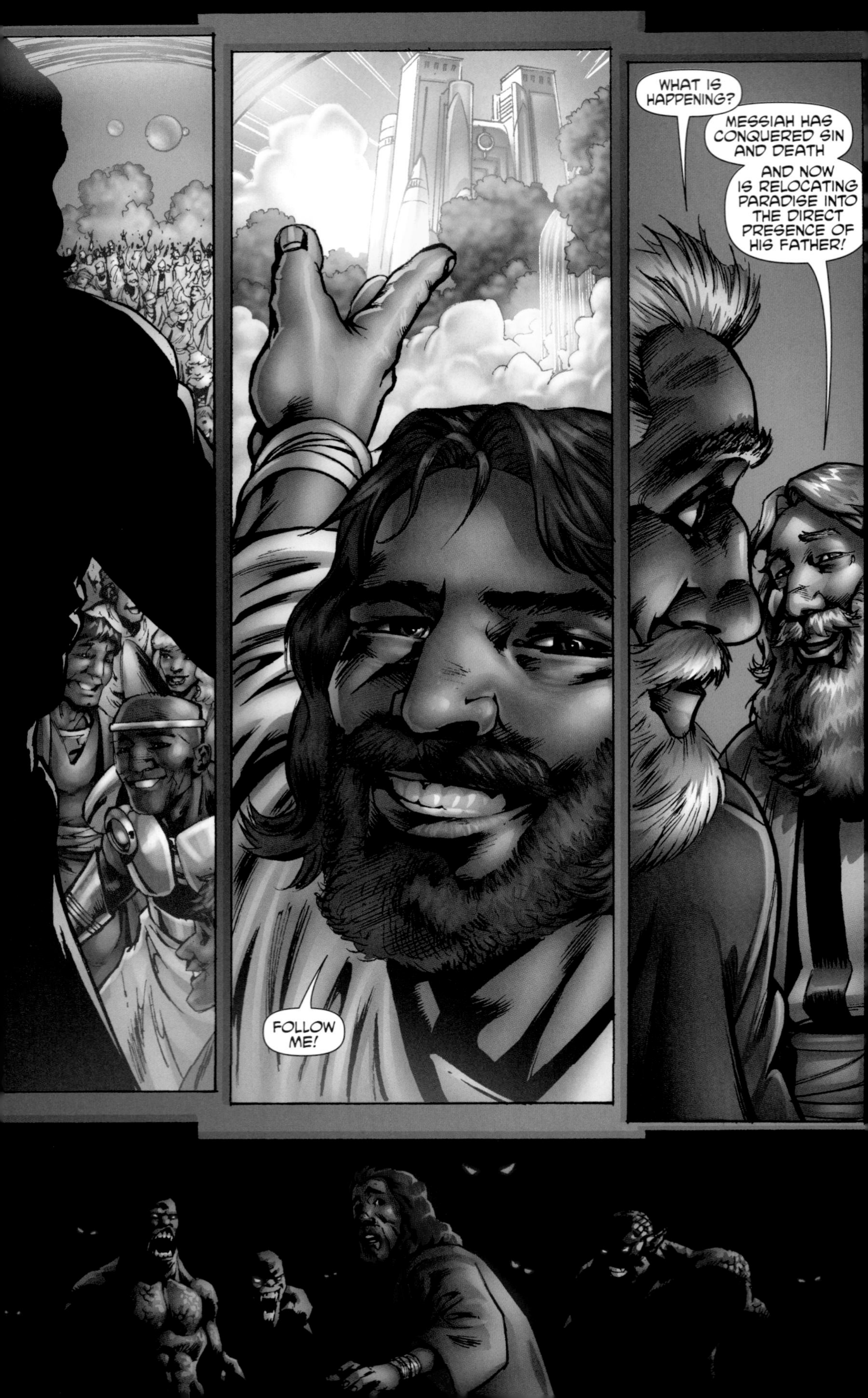
WHAT IS HAPPENING?
MESSIAH HAS CONQUERED SIN AND DEATH
AND NOW IS RELOCATING PARADISE INTO THE DIRECT PRESENCE OF HIS FATHER!
FOLLOW ME!

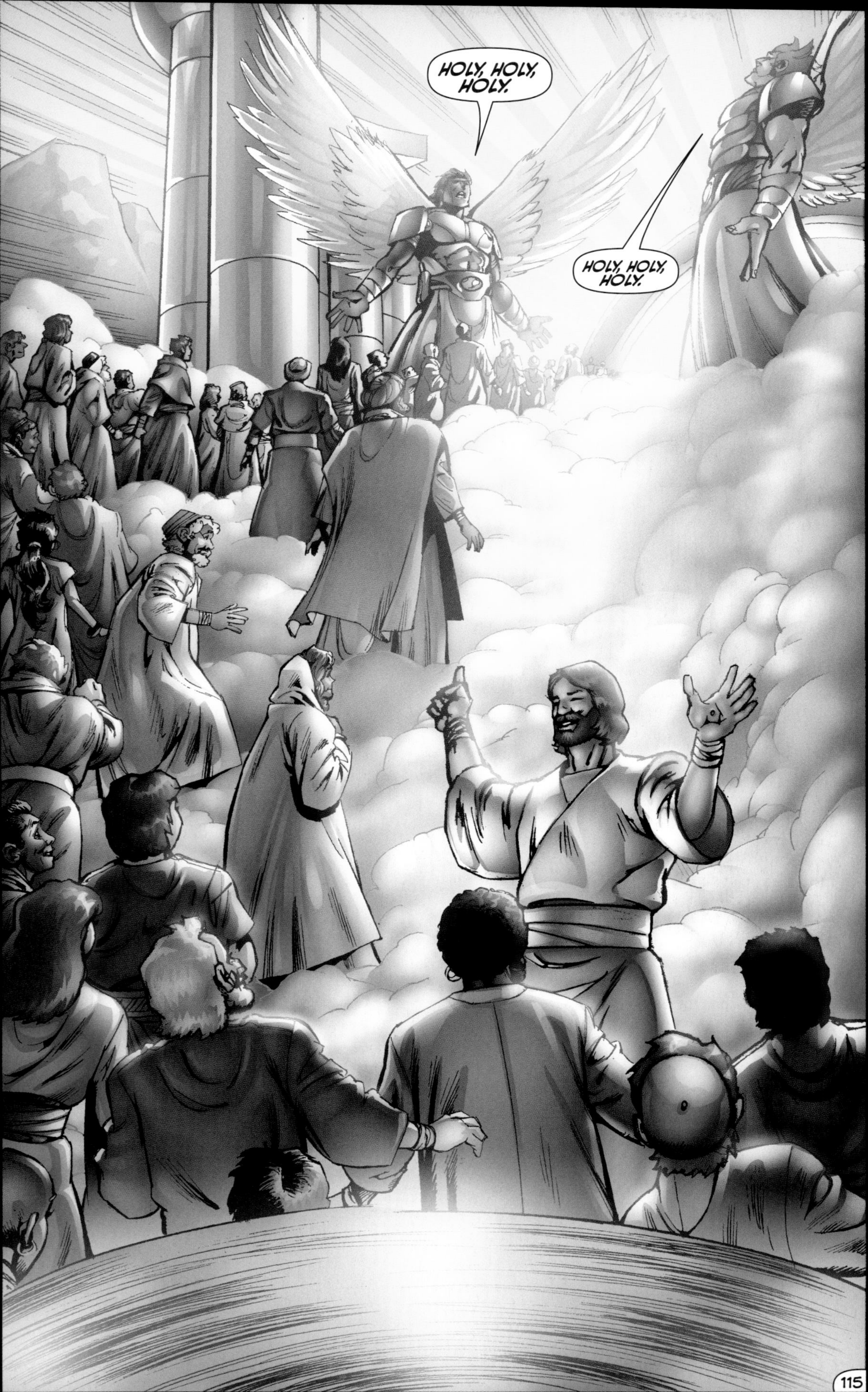
HOLY, HOLY, HOLY.
HOLY, HOLY, HOLY.

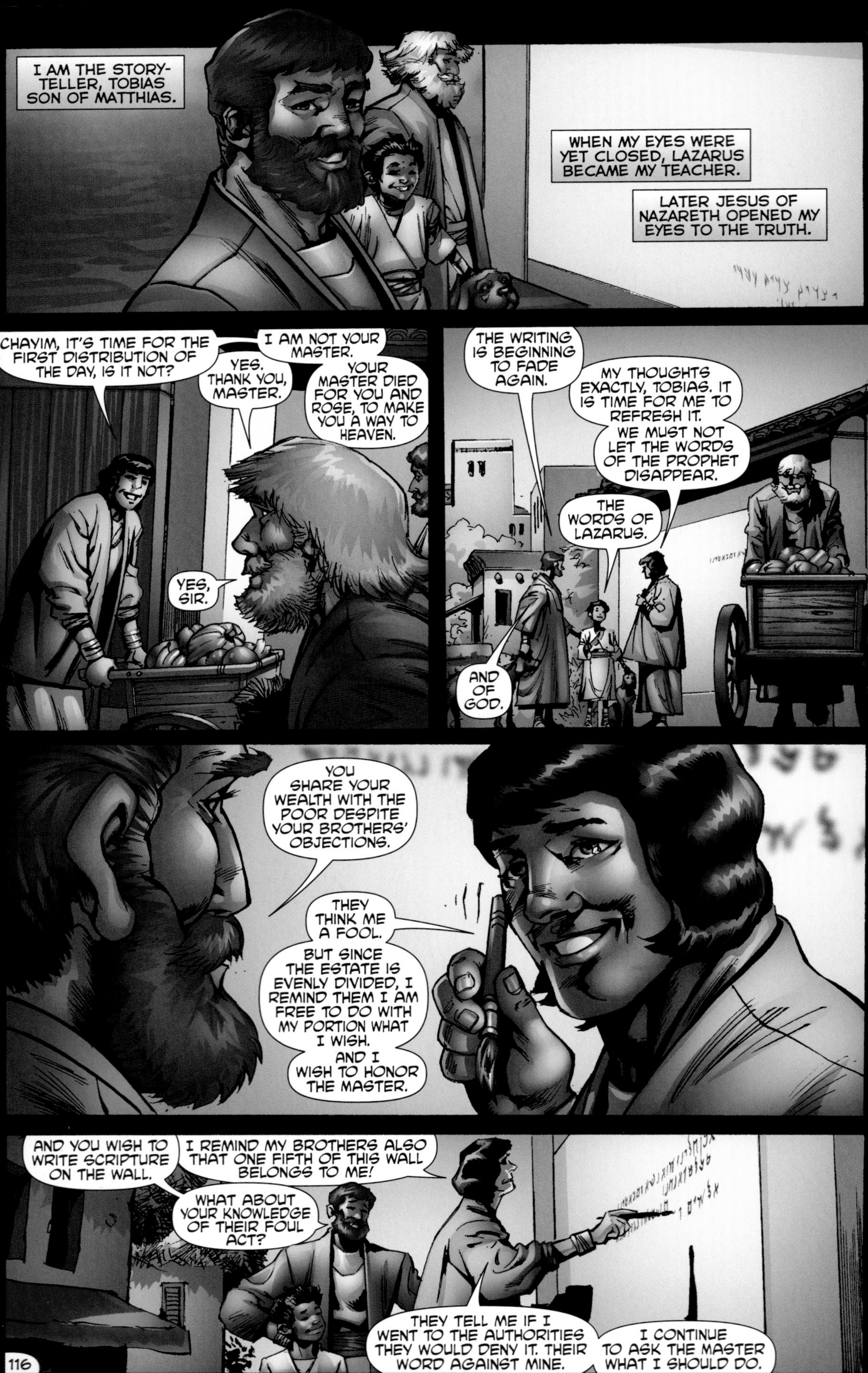
I AM THE STORY-TELLER, TOBIAS SON OF MATTHIAS.
WHEN MY EYES WERE YET CLOSED, LAZARUS BECAME MY TEACHER.
LATER JESUS OF NAZARETH OPENED MY EYES TO THE TRUTH.
CHAYIM, IT'S TIME FOR THE FIRST DISTRIBUTION OF THE DAY, IS IT NOT?
YES. THANK YOU, MASTER.
I AM NOT YOUR MASTER.
YOUR MASTER DIED FOR YOU AND ROSE, TO MAKE YOU A WAY TO HEAVEN.
YES, SIR.
THE WRITING IS BEGINNING TO FADE AGAIN.
MY THOUGHTS EXACTLY, TOBIAS. IT IS TIME FOR ME TO REFRESH IT.
WE MUST NOT LET THE WORDS OF THE PROPHET DISAPPEAR.
THE WORDS OF LAZARUS.
AND OF GOD.
YOU SHARE YOUR WEALTH WITH THE POOR DESPITE YOUR BROTHERS' OBJECTIONS.
THEY THINK ME A FOOL.
BUT SINCE THE ESTATE IS EVENLY DIVIDED, I REMIND THEM I AM FREE TO DO WITH MY PORTION WHAT I WISH.
AND I WISH TO HONOR THE MASTER.
AND YOU WISH TO WRITE SCRIPTURE ON THE WALL.
I REMIND MY BROTHERS ALSO THAT ONE FIFTH OF THIS WALL BELONGS TO ME!
WHAT ABOUT YOUR KNOWLEDGE OF THEIR FOUL ACT?
THEY TELL ME IF I WENT TO THE AUTHORITIES THEY WOULD DENY IT. THEIR WORD AGAINST MINE.
I CONTINUE TO ASK THE MASTER WHAT I SHOULD DO.

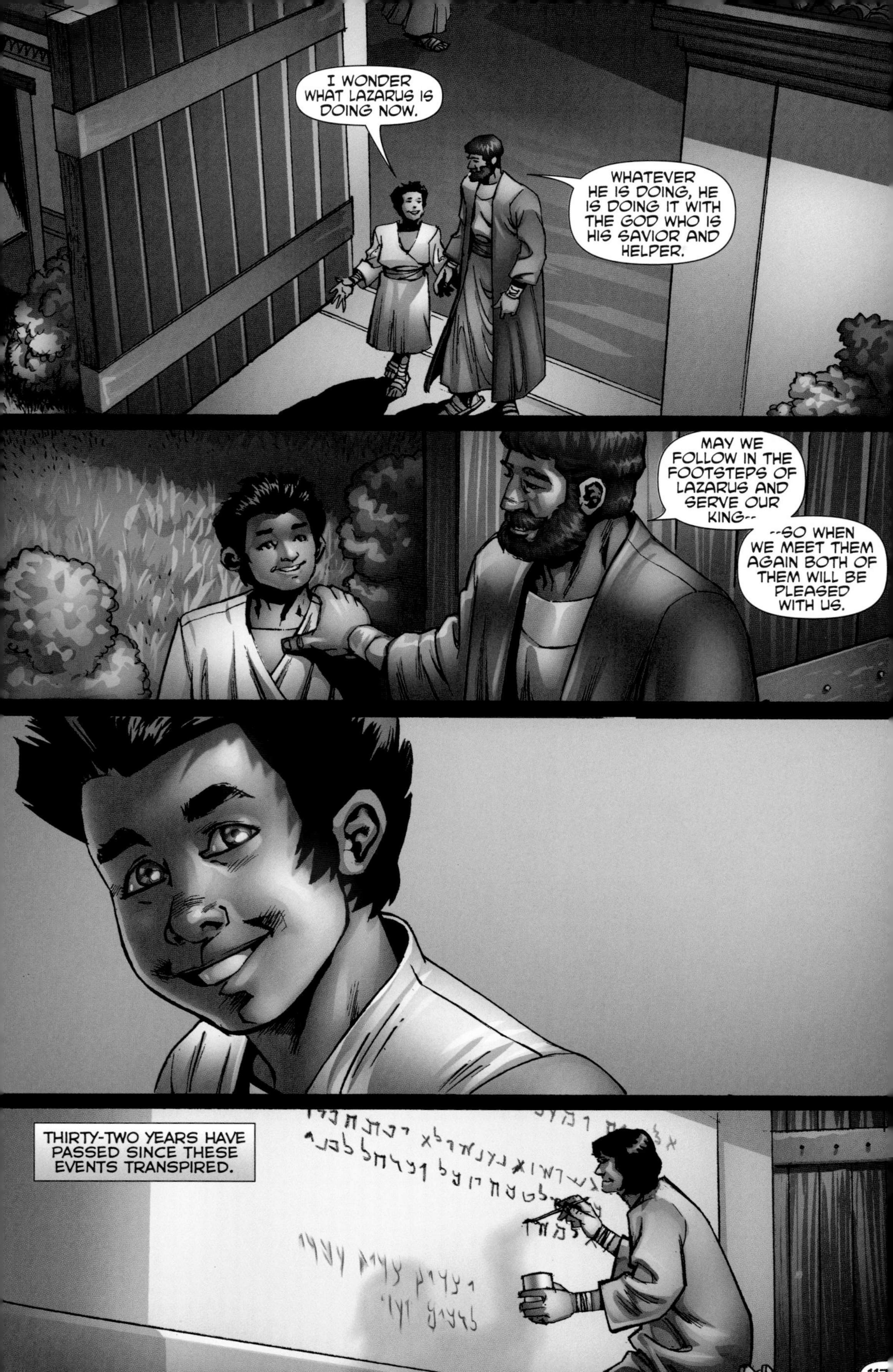
I WONDER WHAT LAZARUS IS DOING NOW.
WHATEVER HE IS DOING, HE IS DOING IT WITH THE GOD WHO IS HIS SAVIOR AND HELPER.
MAY WE FOLLOW IN THE FOOTSTEPS OF LAZARUS AND SERVE OUR KING--
--SO WHEN WE MEET THEM AGAIN BOTH OF THEM WILL BE PLEASED WITH US.
THIRTY-TWO YEARS HAVE PASSED SINCE THESE EVENTS TRANSPIRED.

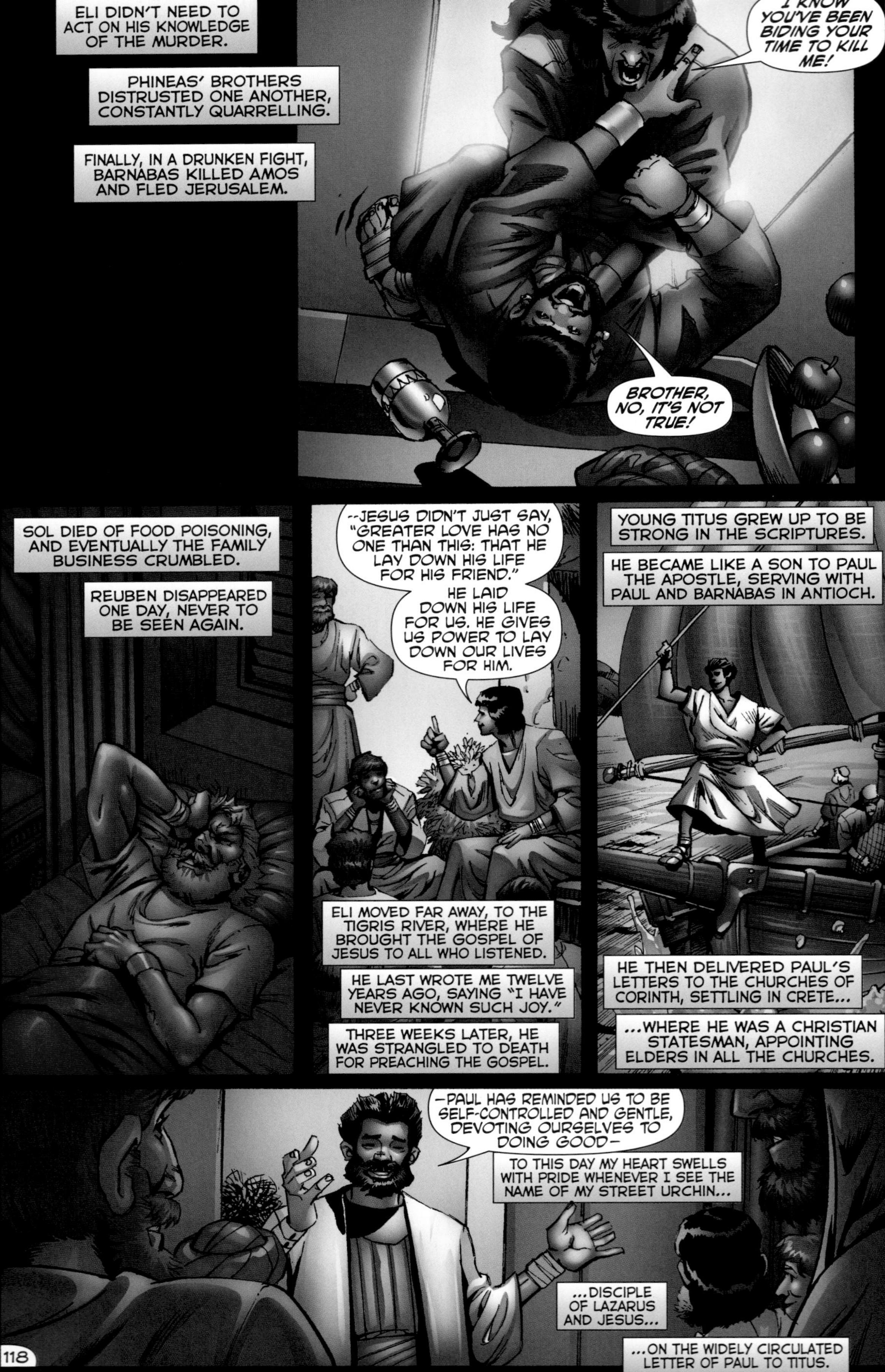
ELI DIDN'T NEED TO ACT ON HIS KNOWLEDGE OF THE MURDER.
PHINEAS' BROTHERS DISTRUSTED ONE ANOTHER, CONSTANTLY QUARRELLING.
FINALLY, IN A DRUNKEN FIGHT, BARNABAS KILLED AMOS AND FLED JERUSALEM.
I KNOW YOU'VE BEEN BIDING YOUR TIME TO KILL ME!
BROTHER, NO, IT'S NOT TRUE!
SOL DIED OF FOOD POISONING, AND EVENTUALLY THE FAMILY BUSINESS CRUMBLED.
REUBEN DISAPPEARED ONE DAY, NEVER TO BE SEEN AGAIN.
--JESUS DIDN'T JUST SAY, "GREATER LOVE HAS NO ONE THAN THIS: THAT HE LAY DOWN HIS LIFE FOR HIS FRIEND."
HE LAID DOWN HIS LIFE FOR US. HE GIVES US POWER TO LAY DOWN OUR LIVES FOR HIM.
ELI MOVED FAR AWAY, TO THE TIGRIS RIVER, WHERE HE BROUGHT THE GOSPEL OF JESUS TO ALL WHO LISTENED.
HE LAST WROTE ME TWELVE YEARS AGO, SAYING "I HAVE NEVER KNOWN SUCH JOY."
THREE WEEKS LATER, HE WAS STRANGLED TO DEATH FOR PREACHING THE GOSPEL.
YOUNG TITUS GREW UP TO BE STRONG IN THE SCRIPTURES.
HE BECAME LIKE A SON TO PAUL THE APOSTLE, SERVING WITH PAUL AND BARNABAS IN ANTIOCH.
HE THEN DELIVERED PAUL'S LETTERS TO THE CHURCHES OF CORINTH, SETTLING IN CRETE...
...WHERE HE WAS A CHRISTIAN STATESMAN, APPOINTING ELDERS IN ALL THE CHURCHES.
–PAUL HAS REMINDED US TO BE SELF-CONTROLLED AND GENTLE, DEVOTING OURSELVES TO DOING GOOD–
TO THIS DAY MY HEART SWELLS WITH PRIDE WHENEVER I SEE THE NAME OF MY STREET URCHIN...
...DISCIPLE OF LAZARUS AND JESUS...
...ON THE WIDELY CIRCULATED LETTER OF PAUL TO TITUS.

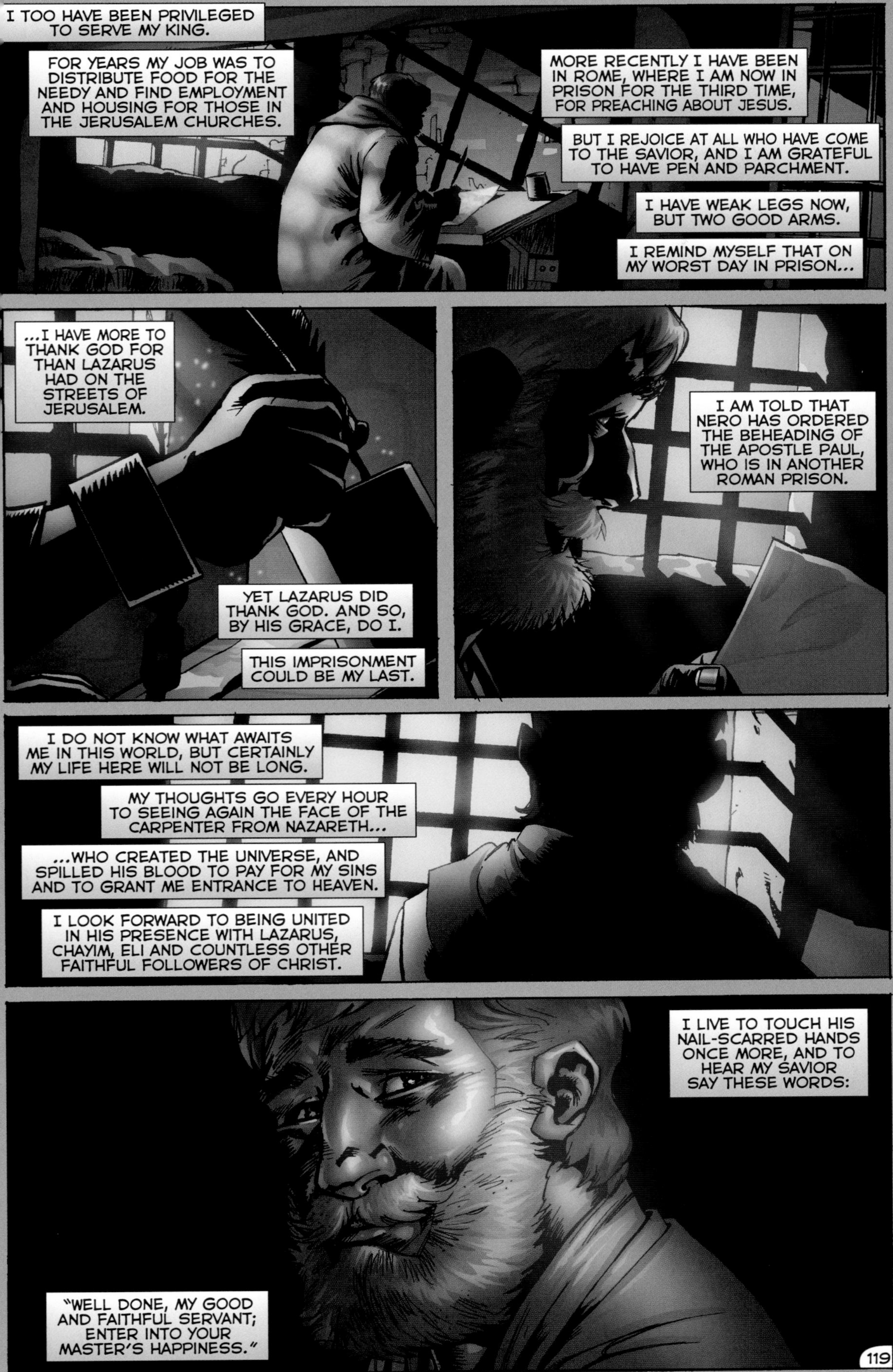
I TOO HAVE BEEN PRIVILEGED TO SERVE MY KING.
FOR YEARS MY JOB WAS TO DISTRIBUTE FOOD FOR THE NEEDY AND FIND EMPLOYMENT AND HOUSING FOR THOSE IN THE JERUSALEM CHURCHES.
MORE RECENTLY I HAVE BEEN IN ROME, WHERE I AM NOW IN PRISON FOR THE THIRD TIME, FOR PREACHING ABOUT JESUS.
BUT I REJOICE AT ALL WHO HAVE COME TO THE SAVIOR, AND I AM GRATEFUL TO HAVE PEN AND PARCHMENT.
I HAVE WEAK LEGS NOW, BUT TWO GOOD ARMS.
I REMIND MYSELF THAT ON MY WORST DAY IN PRISON...
...I HAVE MORE TO THANK GOD FOR THAN LAZARUS HAD ON THE STREETS OF JERUSALEM.
YET LAZARUS DID THANK GOD. AND SO, BY HIS GRACE, DO I.
THIS IMPRISONMENT COULD BE MY LAST.
I AM TOLD THAT NERO HAS ORDERED THE BEHEADING OF THE APOSTLE PAUL, WHO IS IN ANOTHER ROMAN PRISON.
I DO NOT KNOW WHAT AWAITS ME IN THIS WORLD, BUT CERTAINLY MY LIFE HERE WILL NOT BE LONG.
MY THOUGHTS GO EVERY HOUR TO SEEING AGAIN THE FACE OF THE CARPENTER FROM NAZARETH...
...WHO CREATED THE UNIVERSE, AND SPILLED HIS BLOOD TO PAY FOR MY SINS AND TO GRANT ME ENTRANCE TO HEAVEN.
I LOOK FORWARD TO BEING UNITED IN HIS PRESENCE WITH LAZARUS, CHAYIM, ELI AND COUNTLESS OTHER FAITHFUL FOLLOWERS OF CHRIST.
I LIVE TO TOUCH HIS NAIL-SCARRED HANDS ONCE MORE, AND TO HEAR MY SAVIOR SAY THESE WORDS:
"WELL DONE, MY GOOD AND FAITHFUL SERVANT; ENTER INTO YOUR MASTER'S HAPPINESS."

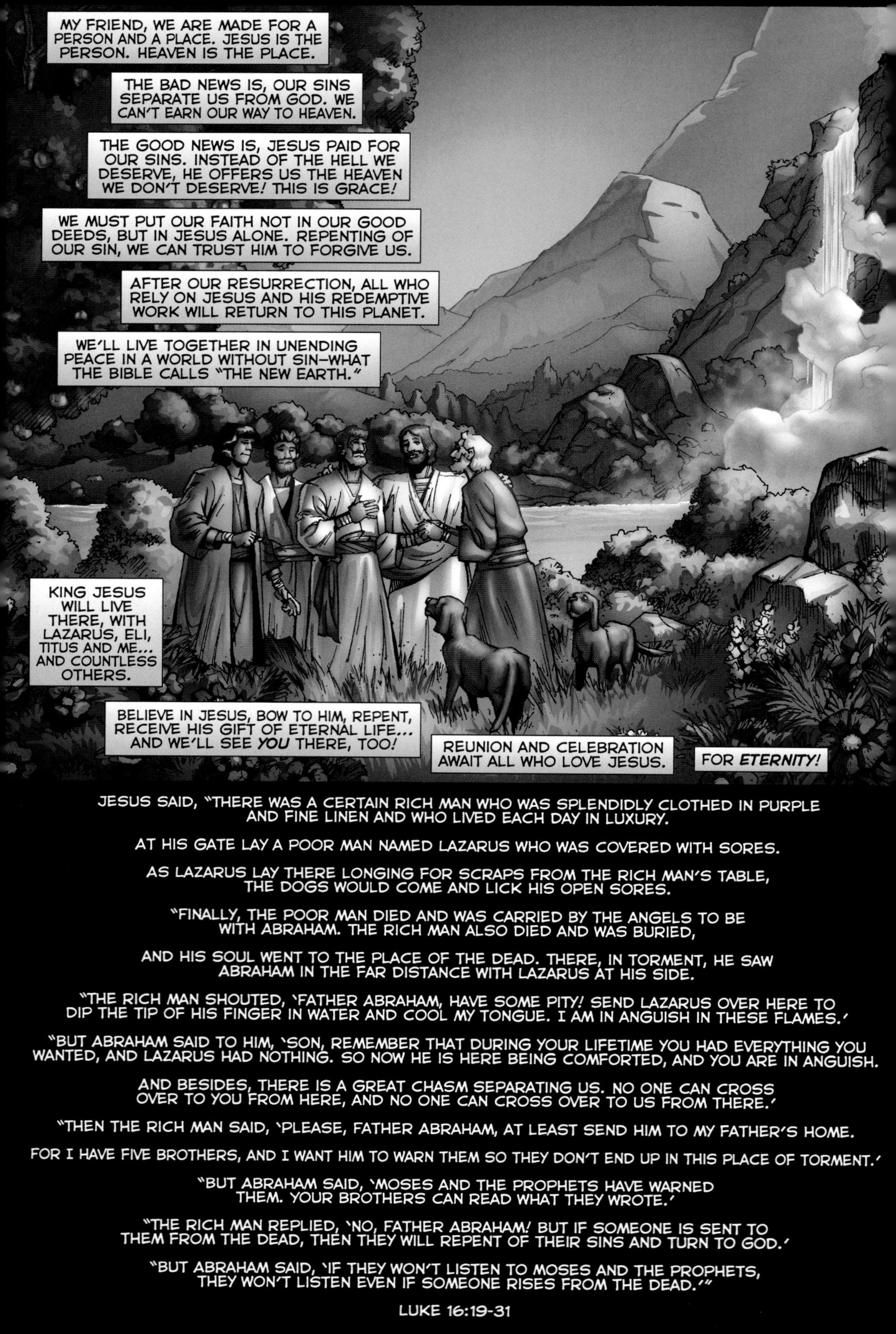
MY FRIEND, WE ARE MADE FOR A PERSON AND A PLACE. JESUS IS THE PERSON. HEAVEN IS THE PLACE.
THE BAD NEWS IS, OUR SINS SEPARATE US FROM GOD. WE CAN'T EARN OUR WAY TO HEAVEN.
THE GOOD NEWS IS, JESUS PAID FOR OUR SINS. INSTEAD OF THE HELL WE DESERVE, HE OFFERS US THE HEAVEN WE DON'T DESERVE! THIS IS GRACE!
WE MUST PUT OUR FAITH NOT IN OUR GOOD DEEDS, BUT IN JESUS ALONE. REPENTING OF OUR SIN, WE CAN TRUST HIM TO FORGIVE US.
AFTER OUR RESURRECTION, ALL WHO RELY ON JESUS AND HIS REDEMPTIVE WORK WILL RETURN TO THIS PLANET.
WE'LL LIVE TOGETHER IN UNENDING PEACE IN A WORLD WITHOUT SIN—WHAT THE BIBLE CALLS "THE NEW EARTH."
KING JESUS WILL LIVE THERE, WITH LAZARUS, ELI, TITUS AND ME... AND COUNTLESS OTHERS.
BELIEVE IN JESUS, BOW TO HIM, REPENT, RECEIVE HIS GIFT OF ETERNAL LIFE... AND WE'LL SEE *YOU* THERE, TOO!
REUNION AND CELEBRATION AWAIT ALL WHO LOVE JESUS.
FOR *ETERNITY!*

JESUS SAID, "THERE WAS A CERTAIN RICH MAN WHO WAS SPLENDIDLY CLOTHED IN PURPLE AND FINE LINEN AND WHO LIVED EACH DAY IN LUXURY.

AT HIS GATE LAY A POOR MAN NAMED LAZARUS WHO WAS COVERED WITH SORES.

AS LAZARUS LAY THERE LONGING FOR SCRAPS FROM THE RICH MAN'S TABLE, THE DOGS WOULD COME AND LICK HIS OPEN SORES.

"FINALLY, THE POOR MAN DIED AND WAS CARRIED BY THE ANGELS TO BE WITH ABRAHAM. THE RICH MAN ALSO DIED AND WAS BURIED,

AND HIS SOUL WENT TO THE PLACE OF THE DEAD. THERE, IN TORMENT, HE SAW ABRAHAM IN THE FAR DISTANCE WITH LAZARUS AT HIS SIDE.

"THE RICH MAN SHOUTED, 'FATHER ABRAHAM, HAVE SOME PITY! SEND LAZARUS OVER HERE TO DIP THE TIP OF HIS FINGER IN WATER AND COOL MY TONGUE. I AM IN ANGUISH IN THESE FLAMES.'

"BUT ABRAHAM SAID TO HIM, 'SON, REMEMBER THAT DURING YOUR LIFETIME YOU HAD EVERYTHING YOU WANTED, AND LAZARUS HAD NOTHING. SO NOW HE IS HERE BEING COMFORTED, AND YOU ARE IN ANGUISH.

AND BESIDES, THERE IS A GREAT CHASM SEPARATING US. NO ONE CAN CROSS OVER TO YOU FROM HERE, AND NO ONE CAN CROSS OVER TO US FROM THERE.'

"THEN THE RICH MAN SAID, 'PLEASE, FATHER ABRAHAM, AT LEAST SEND HIM TO MY FATHER'S HOME.

FOR I HAVE FIVE BROTHERS, AND I WANT HIM TO WARN THEM SO THEY DON'T END UP IN THIS PLACE OF TORMENT.'

"BUT ABRAHAM SAID, 'MOSES AND THE PROPHETS HAVE WARNED THEM. YOUR BROTHERS CAN READ WHAT THEY WROTE.'

"THE RICH MAN REPLIED, 'NO, FATHER ABRAHAM! BUT IF SOMEONE IS SENT TO THEM FROM THE DEAD, THEN THEY WILL REPENT OF THEIR SINS AND TURN TO GOD.'

"BUT ABRAHAM SAID, 'IF THEY WON'T LISTEN TO MOSES AND THE PROPHETS, THEY WON'T LISTEN EVEN IF SOMEONE RISES FROM THE DEAD.'"

LUKE 16:19-31

KINGSTONE
COMICS

KINGSTONECOMICS.COM

HEAVEN AND HELL IN THE BIBLE

Readers of *Eternity* may wonder why I portray Paradise as lush and beautiful. It
because "Paradise" means an Eden-like garden of delights. Scripture uses this
vivid physical term for the present Heaven where God's people go when they c
(Luke 23:43; 2 Corinthians 12:3).

Why do I depict the rich man and Lazarus physically even though the
resurrection is a future event? *Because Jesus does.* In Luke 16:19-31, the rich ma
in Hades speaks of fire, his tongue, thirst and "this place of torment." He sees
Lazarus in Paradise with water and a finger to dip in it.

Some believe this suggests an afterlife where people have transitional physica
forms until the resurrection when they'll be reunited with their bodies. But eve
if the passage is figurative, Jesus wouldn't paint such detailed word pictures
without expecting us to visualize them.

I've included everything in Christ's story, while adding fictional details and
dialogue that don't contradict it. I've incorporated gospel truths from other
biblical passages. Though fictional, the added elements are true to Scripture.

Some think we shouldn't base any theology on Christ's description of the
afterlife. They believe Jesus was only teaching in Luke 16 that God will hold
people accountable for how they treat the poor. Yet this is the only parable
where Jesus names a character, suggesting that Lazarus was an actual person.

We don't have to take every word literally to believe that Jesus intended us to
picture real people, who maintain their identity and memories from Earth, in a
real afterlife.

Most of this parable's components are supported by other scriptures. The
apostle Paul said when believers die they go to God's presence (2 Corinthians
5:8). The martyrs in Heaven, remembering they've been killed, ask God to bring
justice on Earth (Revelation 6:9-11). On the cross, Jesus said to the repentant
thief, "Today you will be with me in paradise" (Luke 23:43).

Upon dying, Lazarus and the rich man went to the present Heaven and Hell to
await the resurrection to eternal life or death (John 5:28-29). Those currently in
Hell exist in isolated misery, while those in Heaven enjoy comfort and a rich
relationship with God and others.

In the Bible's first two chapters, God planted a garden on Earth; in the last two
chapters he brings down to the New Earth the New Jerusalem, a garden paradi
at its center. Even now Eden's tree of life exists "in the paradise of God"
(Revelation 2:7). God preserved Paradise as a place Christ's followers will
eventually occupy on that New Earth (Revelation 22:2).

In Eden, there was no sin, death, or Curse; on the New Earth, there will be no more sin, death or Curse (Revelation 21:4; 22:3). In Genesis, the Redeemer is promised; in Revelation, the Redeemer returns. Genesis tells of paradise lost; Revelation of paradise regained.

Peter said Christ "must remain in Heaven until the time comes for God to restore everything" (Acts 3:21). God will restore mankind to our original design: embodied righteous beings ruling Earth to his glory.

No one desires a disembodied inhuman existence. We long for a totally happy, never-ending resurrected life on Earth. That's exactly what God promises his children!

"If anyone is in Christ, he is a new creation" (2 Corinthians 5:17). When I trusted Jesus as a teenager, I became a new person—the same person made new, by God's grace (Ephesians 2:8-9). At death I will undergo another change, and still another at the resurrection. But through it all *I will still be who I was*. Like Job, "In my flesh I will see God; *I myself* will see him *with my own eyes—I, and not another*" (Job 19:26-27).

We live now in the in-between world, hearing Eden's echoes and the New Earth's approaching footfalls. We're never fully at home on this sin-cursed planet. We long for the world to come.

God's presence and throne will one day be on the New Earth (Revelation 21:1-3; 22:1). Christ's redeemed people will live forever in Heaven on Earth. Those who reject his sacrifice on the cross will remain in their sins and experience eternal Hell.

The Bible says,

> For God so loved the world that he gave his one and only Son, that whoever believes in him shall not perish but have eternal life. For God did not send his Son into the world to condemn the world, but to save the world through him. ...Whoever believes in him is not condemened, but whoeever does not believe stands condemned already because they have not believed in the name of God's one and only Son.
> (John 3:16-18)

Will you repent of your sins and trust Jesus to give you eternal life? Will you put your faith in him to deliver you from the Hell we all deserve to the Heaven none of us deserves?

A good church will teach you God's Word and provide love and support. If you have questions about Jesus or Heaven, you can find answers there. (If you're looking for such a church nearby but can't find one, contact us at info@epm.org, and we'll gladly help you.)

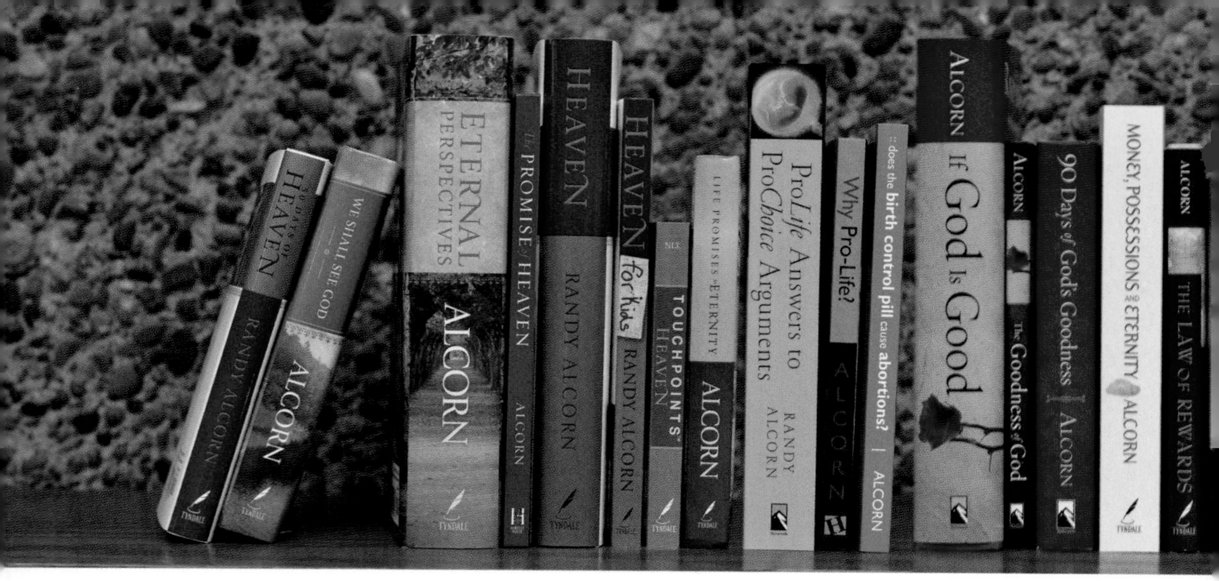
HEAVEN
WE SHALL SEE GOD
ALCORN
ETERNAL PERSPECTIVES
ALCORN
PROMISE HEAVEN
HEAVEN
RANDY ALCORN
HEAVEN for Kids
RANDY ALCORN
TOUCHPOINTS HEAVEN
ALCORN
ProLife Answers to ProChoice Arguments
RANDY ALCORN
Why Pro-Life?
does the birth control pill cause abortions?
ALCORN
If God Is Good
The Goodness of God
90 Days of God's Goodness
ALCORN
MONEY, POSSESSIONS AND ETERNITY
ALCORN
THE LAW OF REWARDS

featured nonfiction books by Randy Alcorn

90 Days of God's Goodness

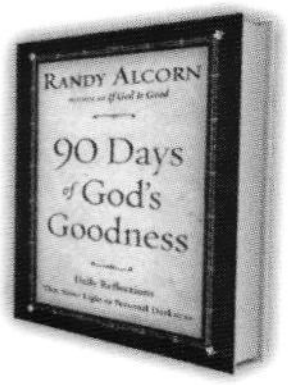
RANDY ALCORN
90 Days of God's Goodness

Here are 90 daily reflections dealing with the single biggest question that blocks people's faith in God: If God is good, why is there so much evil and suffering?

The Grace and Truth Paradox

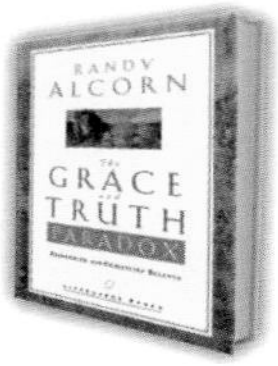
RANDY ALCORN
GRACE TRUTH PARADOX

John 1:14 boils down for us what it means to be Christlike. It means to be full of only two things: Grace and Truth. It's a two-point checklist of Christlikeness.

Heaven

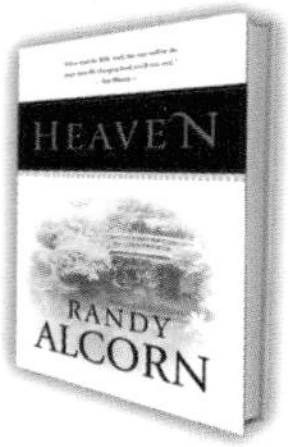
HEAVEN
RANDY ALCORN

In the most comprehensive and definitive book on Heaven to date, Randy invites you to picture Heaven the way Scripture describes it—a bright, vibrant, and physical New Earth, brimming with Christ's presence.

Managing God's Money

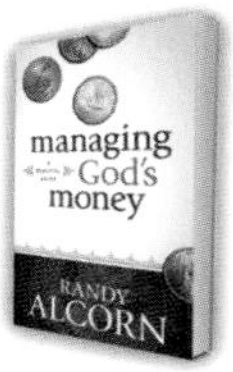
managing God's money
RANDY ALCORN

Randy breaks down what the Bible has to say about how we are to handle our money and possessions in a format that is simple and easy to follow. Readers will gain a solid biblical understanding of money, possessions, and eternity.

The Purity Principle

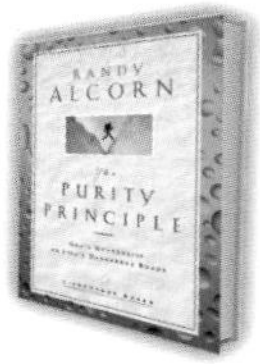
RANDY ALCORN
PURITY PRINCIPLE

Randy Alcorn shows us why, in this culture of impurity, the stakes are so high—and what we can do to experience the freedom of purity.

Why Pro-Life?

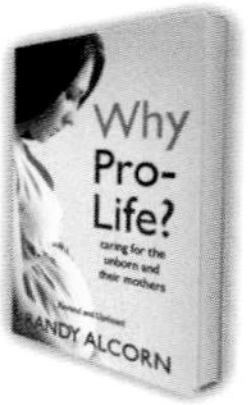
Why Pro-Life?
RANDY ALCORN

Infused with grace and compassion, and grounded in medical science and psychological studies, Randy Alcorn presents a solid case for defending both unborn children and their mothers.

connect with Randy Alcorn and Eternal Perspective Ministries

www.epm.org
Find resources and purchase books.

www.epm.org/blog
Read Randy's latest blog posts.

www.facebook.com/randyalcorn
Connect with Randy.

www.facebook.com EPMinistries
Follow EPM for news and promotions.

www.twitter.com/randyalcorn
Read short daily thoughts from Randy.

www.twitter.com/epmorg
Get links to our latest online resources.

DEADLINE ALCORN
DOMINION RANDY ALCORN
DECEPTION ALCORN
SAFELY HOME ALCORN
EDGE of ETERNITY ALCORN
LORD FOULGRIN'S LETTERS RANDY ALCORN
THE ISHBANE CONSPIRACY ALCORN
COURAGEOUS RANDY ALCORN
CHASM ALCORN
Tell Me About Heaven
WAIT UNTIL THEN ALCORN
THE TREASURE PRINCIPLE RANDY ALCORN

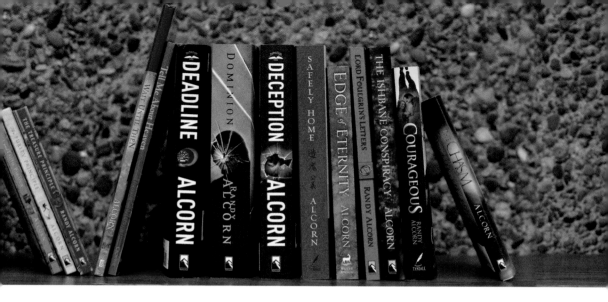

featured fiction and children's books by Randy Alcorn

Deception — fiction

RANDY ALCORN
DECEPTION

Ollie Chandler is a brilliant, quick-witted homicide detective with exceptional deductive skills and street smarts who's called to investigate the murder of a Portland State University professor.

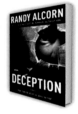

Heaven for Kids — children's nonfiction

HEAVEN for Kids
RANDY ALCORN

In a language that kids can understand, Randy explores Biblical answers to the questions kids often have about Heaven. Intended for kids age 8-12, it is an excellent resource for families.

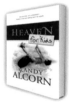

The Ishbane Conspiracy — fiction

ANGELA, KARINA & RANDY ALCORN
The Ishbane Conspiracy

By Angela (Alcorn) Stump, Karina (Alcorn) Franklin and Randy Alcorn. During one unforgettable year, four college students find themselves in a series of battles between light and darkness.

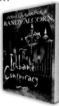

Lord Foulgrin's Letters — fiction

LORD FOULGRIN'S LETTERS
RANDY ALCORN

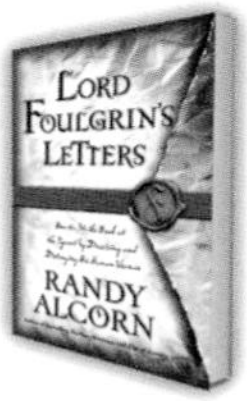

Correspondence has fallen into our hands that we were not intended to see. The demon Foulgrin instructs his subordinate how to deceive and destroy Jordan Fletcher and his family.

Safely Home — fiction

SAFELY HOME
RANDY ALCORN

American business executive Ben Fielding has no idea what his old college roommate is facing in China. In an hour of encroaching darkness, both must make choices that will determine their destinies.

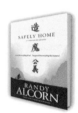

Tell Me About Heaven — children's fiction

Tell Me About Heaven
Randy Alcorn
Ron DiCianni

When Jake asks his grandfather, "What's it like where Grammy is?", children are ushered into a warm story with beautiful paintings that answers questions about Heaven.

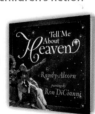

explore more books

Go to **www.epm.org/books** to browse Randy's 40+ titles, also available for purchase from Eternal Perspective Ministries.

EPM **Eternal Perspective** Ministries

info@epm.org | 503.668.5200 | toll-free order line 1.877.376.4567
39085 Pioneer Blvd., Suite 206, Sandy, OR 97055

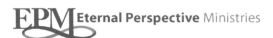

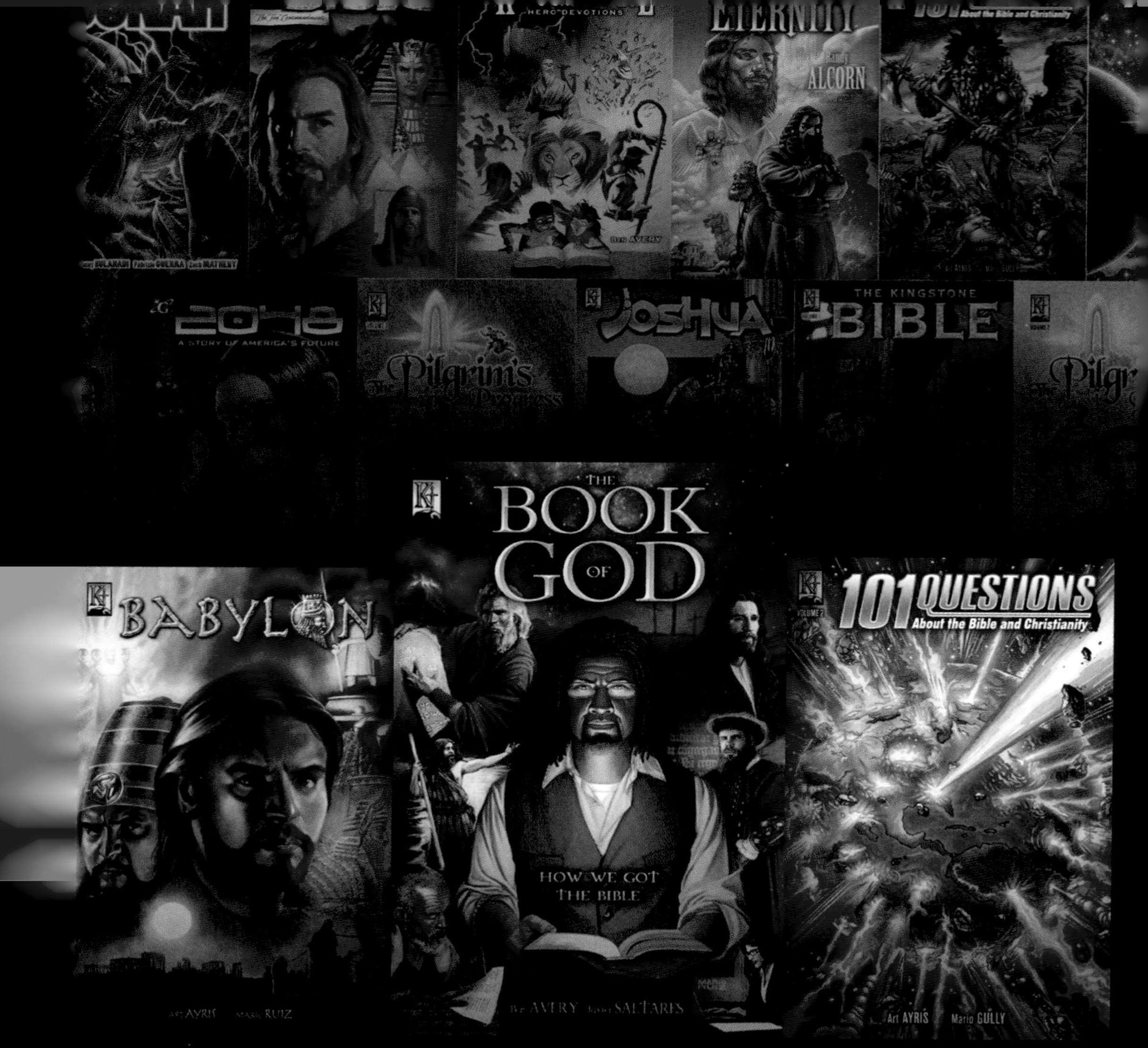
HERO DEVOTIONS
ETERNITY
Randy ALCORN
2048
A STORY OF AMERICA'S FUTURE
The Pilgrim's Progress
JOSHUA
THE KINGSTONE BIBLE
THE BOOK OF GOD
HOW WE GOT THE BIBLE
BABYLON
101 QUESTIONS
About the Bible and Christianity